Basic Bridge
A Guide to Good Acol Bidding and Play

Starting from the assumption that the reader knows nothing whatever about the game, Klinger explains, in a course of eight lessons, the basic principles of sound bidding and play. The liberal use of exercises helps the student to consolidate the knowledge he has gained in each section. This is a versatile book, designed not only for use as a self-teacher by the lone student but also as an aid to the bridge teacher in planning his classes. The teacher will particularly appreciate the four playing hands at the end of each lesson. Every hand illustrates an important principle of play, and the author explains in depth why one line of play is right and others wrong.

Ron Klinger will be known to many as an international player of distinction and to many as an author of outstanding bridge books, including the best-selling *ACOL BRIDGE FLIPPER*. His main business is teaching bridge and he is recognised as one of the world's foremost bridge teachers.

by RON KLINGER

in the Master Bridge Series

Ron Klinger

Basic Bridge

A Guide to Good Acol Bidding and Play

LONDON
VICTOR GOLLANCZ LTD
in association with
PETER CRAWLEY
1991

First published in 1978 by Ward Lock Limited
First paperback edition published
in association with Peter Crawley 1979
by Victor Gollancz Ltd,
14 Henrietta Street, London WC2E 8QJ
Second impression November 1983
Third impression June 1985
Fourth impression March 1989
Fifth impression May 1990
Sixth impression June 1991

ISBN 0 575 02637 5

Printed and bound in Great Britain by
Dotesios Ltd, Trowbridge

Contents

To Rosa

Introduction

Bridge is fun to play, but the better you play, the more fun it is. As your game improves, you will be fascinated at discovering how much there is to the game. Despite popular opinion to the contrary, bridge is not difficult to learn. At all my classes for absolute beginners they are playing the game by the end of the first lesson.

This book is the product of many classes given to beginners, intermediate and advanced players. It is intended for two classes of readers—those who have never played the game before and those who know how to play but wish to make a serious attempt to improve their game. The book is set out as an eight-lesson course in bridge, each lesson being divided into two parts. It can be used as a self-teacher or in conjunction with bridge classes.

The absolute beginner should work through the book at his own pace. Particular attention should be given to the exercises, for these cover every part of the instruction given. Do not rush on to the next lesson until you have satisfactorily completed the exercises. If you score less than 75% on the exercises, you should re-read the relevant part of the lesson and then repeat the exercises until you have a clear understanding of the area.

At your first attempt do not try and remember everything in the text but pay close attention to the charts for each lesson. They set out the vital points and principles. The commentary expands and explains the principles, but the charts themselves are sufficient to play a good game of bridge. Some of the lessons are harder than others—you can leave aside Lesson 5, Part B and also the Appendices until you have more experience.

For the reader who can play but wants to improve, skip over Lesson 1 dealing with elementary no trump bidding. But if you wish to check on yourself, try the exercises for Part B. In the other lessons you will find parts that you already know and parts that are new to you. Again, the exercises and quizzes are essential for they embed the knowledge you have gained. It is not enough to know the rules; it is their application at the table which counts. The exercises simulate countless ordinary bidding situations, and by scoring well on the exercises you will build up confidence and also score well at the table when the everyday problems occur.

This book is not for the expert and will not make you an expert bridge player. It does not deal with expert bidding, expert play or expert defence. But it does cover the ordinary standard situations, the basics that make up 95% of the game and in which most ordinary players go wrong. If you follow the exercises here recommended, you will eliminate fundamental flaws from your game and pass from a novice to a competent, proficient bridge player. If you master the principles and advice in this book, you will more than hold your own even in good company.

Although each lesson covers a basic bidding area, you should not ignore the four playing hands that accompany each lesson. It will repay you to play over the hands, setting out the cards yourself. The hands feature bidding situations appropriate to the particular lesson and cover the basics of opening leads, declarer play and defence. To play and defend well is very important, and *Basic Bridge* is designed not only to make you bid better but also to play better.

To improve you should try to play as often as possible, for the more you play, the quicker you will improve. It is all very well to take lessons and read books, but much of bridge competence is based on experience. The more often you encounter a basic situation, the more readily you will be able to deal with it in future.

Above all remember that bridge is a game to be enjoyed. It can be and should be a lot of fun, and that is how you should approach it. I hope that you derive as much enjoyment and satisfaction from it as I have.

For absolute beginners - how the game is played

There are two basic families of card games. In one the aim is to form combinations of cards, for example, gin rummy, canasta. Contract bridge belongs to the other in which the aim is to win *tricks*.

Bridge is played by four people, two playing as partners against the other two. Partners sit opposite each other. You will need a card table, four chairs, preferably two packs of cards (though you can manage with one pack), score pads and pencils.

The Pack

A pack (or deck) of fifty-two cards is used. There is no joker. There are four suits: spades ♠, hearts ♡, diamonds ◇ and clubs ♣. Each suit has thirteen cards, the highest being the ace, followed by the king, queen, jack, 10, 9, 8, 7, 6, 5, 4, 3, down to the 2 which is the lowest. The top five cards in each suit, the ace, king, queen, jack and ten are called the honour cards or honours. How many honour cards are there in the whole pack?[1]

Choosing Partners

You may agree to play in certain partnerships, for example, husband and wife against the other couple,[2] but unless there is some other arrangement, it is usual to draw for partners. This is done by spreading out the pack, face down, and each player picking a card. The two who draw the higher cards play as partners against the other two, normally for one or two 'rubbers'. Then cards are drawn again to form two new partnerships. If in drawing for partners two or more cards of the same rank are turned up, then the tie is split according to suit, the suits ranking from the highest, spades, through hearts and diamonds to the lowest, clubs.

For example, A, B, C and D are drawing for partners. The cards turned up are A: 8 ◇, B: J ♠, C: 5 ♠, D: 8 ♡. Who play together?[3]

Dealing

The person who drew the highest card has the right to choose seats (the most comfortable one, out of the draft), which pack of cards his side will deal with (for the superstitiously inclined, who might think the blue pack is luckier), and he becomes the dealer on the first hand. Each player has a turn in dealing, and the next dealer will be the person on his left and so on in clockwise direction.

The cards are shuffled by the person on the dealer's left who passes them across the table to the person on the dealer's right to 'cut' them. The dealer then 'deals' the cards, one at a time, face down, in clockwise direction, starting with the player on his left, until all fifty-two cards are dealt. How many cards will each player have? Who receives the last card?[4]

---

[1] Twenty.
[2] Probably the worst possible arrangement!
[3] B–D and A–C.
[4] Thirteen; dealer.

It is customary etiquette not to pick up your cards until the dealer has finished dealing. This allows the dealer the same time to study his cards as everyone else has. While the dealer is dealing, his partner is shuffling the other pack in preparation for the next deal (that is why two packs are used), in order to speed up the game. After he has finished shuffling, he puts the cards down on his right, ready for the the next dealer to pick up.

The Start of Play

When you pick up your thirteen cards, you sort them into suits. It is usual to separate the red suits and black suits and also to put your cards in order of rank in each suit. The bidding starts with the dealer, but we will have more to say about the bidding shortly.

After the bidding period is over, the side that has bid highest wins the right to play the hand. One member of this side, called 'the declarer', *plays* the hand while the opposition *defend* the hand. The person on the left of the declarer makes 'the opening lead', that is, he selects a card from his hand and puts it face up on the table. The partner of the declarer, called 'the dummy', now puts all his thirteen cards face up on the table arranged in suits. The dummy takes no further part in the play, declarer playing both his own hand and dummy's hand. Each player sees twenty-six cards, his own thirteen plus the dummy.

Declarer puts one of dummy's cards in the middle of the table next to the opening lead. The partner of the leader ('third hand') now also puts one card in the middle and so does the declarer. The four cards now face up in the middle of the table are called a *trick*. A trick always consists of exactly four cards played in clockwise sequence, one from each hand.

Each deal in bridge is a battle over thirteen tricks, declarer trying to win as many as his side has in the bidding undertaken to win, while the defenders try to win enough tricks to defeat declarer. A trick is won by the highest card played. The player who wins the trick gathers the four cards together and puts them face down in front of him. He then leads to the next trick, and so on until all thirteen tricks have been played.

Suppose the declarer has won a trick in his own hand; who leads to the next trick? Declarer. And what if he had won the trick with one of dummy's cards? Who leads to the next trick? Dummy, i.e., declarer must next play a card from the dummy hand.

Following Suit

The player who plays the highest ranking card *of the suit led* wins the trick. If two or more cards of the same rank are played to the one trick, who wins? The basic rule of play is: *you must follow suit*, i.e., you must play a card of the same suit as the suit led. If hearts are led, then you must play a heart if you have one, and the trick is won by the highest heart played. So that if the two of hearts is led and the other cards on the trick are the ten of hearts, the jack of spades and the ace of clubs, the trick is won by the ten of hearts. If you are unable to follow suit, you may play any other card at all, but remember it is the highest card of the first led suit which wins; if the king of spades is led, it will do you no good to play the ace of clubs, since only the ace of spades beats the king of spades.

Trumps

There is one exception to this. Where one of the four suits is made the *trump* suit in the bidding, then any card in the trump suit is higher than even an ace in one of the other suits. So if hearts are trumps, the two of hearts would beat the ace of clubs even when clubs are led. But, first and foremost, you must follow suit. Only when you are out of a suit can you beat a high card of another suit with a trump.

A trick that does not contain a trump is won by the highest card in the suit led. A trick that contains a trump is won by the highest trump in the trick.

The Bidding

The play is preceded by the bidding, also called 'the auction'. Just as in an auction an item goes to the highest bidder, so in the bridge auction each side tries to outbid the other for the right to play the hand.

The dealer makes the first bid, then the player on his left, and so on in clockwise rotation. Each player may pass (say 'no bid') or make a bid. Even though a player has passed, he may still make a bid later in the auction. A bid consists of a number (one, two, three, four, five, six or seven) and a suit or no trumps, for example, three hearts, two spades, four no trumps, seven diamonds. 'No trumps' means that there is to be no trump suit on the deal. Whenever a bid is made, the bidder says he will take more tricks than the opponents. The minimum number of tricks that you may contract for is seven. A bid of 'one club' contracts to make seven tricks with clubs as trumps. The number in the bid is the number of tricks to be won *over and above six tricks*.

How many tricks do each of the following bids contract to make? Which suit is to be trumps?

a) Three diamonds. b) Four spades. c) Six no trumps. d) Two hearts.[1]

If all players pass without making a bid, the hand is thrown in and the next dealer deals a new hand. When a player makes a bid, the auction has started and will be won by the side that bids higher. The auction is over once a bid is followed by three passes. The side that bids higher sets the trump suit (or no trumps) and the number of tricks it has to win the play; this is set by the final bid, and the member of the side who first bid the trump suit (or no trumps) becomes the declarer.

After a bid any player at his turn may make a *higher* bid. A bid is higher than a previous bid if it is a larger number than the previous bid (three clubs is higher than two hearts) or if it is the same number but in a higher-ranking denomination. The order of ranking is:

NO TRUMPS
♠ SPADES
♡ HEARTS
♢ DIAMONDS
♣ CLUBS

A bid of one heart is higher than a bid of one club. If you want to bid spades and the last bid was two no trumps, you would have to bid three spades because two spades would not be higher than two no trumps.

a) What is the highest bid possible?
b) How many tricks does it undertake to make?
c) What is the lowest bid possible?
d) If the previous bid was one spade and you want to bid diamonds, what is the lowest bid in diamonds you can make?

[1] a) Nine, diamonds. b) Ten, spades. c) Twelve, none. d) Eight, hearts.

e) The previous bid was one spade. Would a bid of one heart be legal? What about two no trumps?[1]

Game and Rubber

The unit of play is a *rubber*. The rubber is won by the first side to win two games. You win a game by scoring 100 or more points below the line on the score-sheet which looks like this:

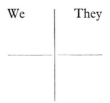

It is vital to understand how the game is scored, for this affects both the bidding and the play. Your aim is to score more points than the opposition. You may score points: (1) by bidding and making a contract; (2) by defeating the opponents at their contract; (3) by earning bonus points.

Some points are written above the line, some below the line on the score-sheet. When adding up the totals, all points count equally, but until the rubber is finished points below the line are especially valuable, since these are the only points that count towards game. *You score points below the line by bidding and making a contract,* according to this table.

(NT) NO TRUMPS	40 points for the first trick (over six), 30 for each subsequent trick.
♠ SPADES	30 points for each trick (over six).
♡ HEARTS	30 points for each trick (over six).
◇ DIAMONDS	20 points for each trick (over six).
♣ CLUBS	20 points for each trick (over six).

Since game is 100 points or more, it takes a bid of five clubs or five diamonds or more to make game in the minors. Spades and hearts are known as 'the major suits', while diamonds and clubs are known as 'the minor suits' because of the difference in scoring.

a) How high do you have to bid in spades to make game? How high in hearts?
b) How many tricks do each of these contracts undertake to make?
c) How high do you have to bid in no trumps to make game?
d) How many tricks does it take to fulfil this contract?[2]

The declaring side gets credit not for the tricks taken, *but only for the tricks bid and then taken.* So, if four hearts are bid and declarer makes nine tricks, he does not get credit for nine tricks; he suffers a penalty for failing, by one trick, to make his contract. Thus, accuracy in bidding distinguishes contract bridge from auction bridge and becomes the single most important element in the game.

On the other hand, if declarer makes more tricks than the contract calls for, the extra trick ('overtricks') are not lost, but are scored *above the line* and do not count towards game.

---

[1] a) Seven no trumps. b) Thirteen. c) One club. d) Two diamonds. e) No; yes.
[2] a) Four spades; four hearts. b) Ten. c) Three no trumps. d) Nine.

REMEMBER:

Only points scored by winning the actual number of tricks contracted for are written below the line, and only points below the line count towards winning games and rubbers.

A score below the line of less than 100 is called *a part-score*. You may combine two or more part-scores to score the 100 points for game. You cannot carry forward any points over and above 100 to the next game. After one side scores a game, both sides start again from zero towards the next game. So, if you have a part-score but the enemy score a game before you have been able to convert your part-score into a game, you have to start again from zero for the next game.

Doubles and redoubles

In the bidding any player may at his turn 'double' a bid made by an opponent. If there is no further bidding, the double increases the rewards for success and the penalties for failure. After one side makes a double, the other side may 'redouble', which increases the rewards and penalties further.

Any double or redouble is cancelled by a bid, but there may be further doubles and redoubles of later bids.

One spade making seven tricks scores 30 below the line, but one spade doubled and redoubled making seven tricks scores 120 below the line (and game!), plus a bonus of 50 points above the line for making a doubled contract ('for the insult').

Scoring

It is important to get to know the scoring, but since there is a lot of it, you need not learn it all at once. There is a complete scoring table on page 125 to which you can refer if in doubt. You should know the trick value of each suit as set out on page 12 and you should also know some of the more common scores which go above the line, but the rest you can learn gradually.

As soon as a side has scored a game they are said to be *vulnerable*: they need only one more game to complete the rubber. Penalties are more severe for failing to make a contract when vulnerable than when not vulnerable.

When one side fails to make its contract, the other side scores points above the line as follows:

The declaring side is not vulnerable: 50 points per undertrick.

The declaring side is vulnerable: 100 points per undertrick.

If the final contract is doubled or redoubled, the penalties are more severe (see the scoring table, page 125). Note that the penalties are the same no matter what the contract is: one down in two hearts is the same score as one down in seven no trumps.

Remember that all points for setting the opponents' contract are written above the line.

Bonus points, too, are written above the line.

You may score bonus points for winning the rubber. If you win the rubber, you score above the line:

700 points if the opponents are not vulnerable (2 games to 0).

500 points if the opponents are vulnerable (2 games to 1).

You also score bonus points for making overtricks in a doubled or redoubled contract (see scoring table).

A contract of six (twelve tricks) is called a small slam, and if you *bid and make* a small slam, you score above the line:

500 points if not vulnerable.

750 points if vulnerable.

A contract of seven (thirteen tricks) is called a grand slam, and if you *bid and make* a grand slam, you score above the line:

1,000 points if not vulnerable.

1,500 points if vulnerable.

A grand slam is so valuable because you undertake not to lose any trick.

You also score bonus points for being lucky enough to hold good cards. These are points for holding honours in the trump suit, honours being the ace, king, queen, jack and ten. You score above the line:

100 points for four of the five trump honours in one hand.

150 points for all five trump honours in one hand.

150 points for all four aces in one hand, but only if the contract is no trumps.

The 100 or 150 bonuses for honours are scored whether or not the contract is made. Honours may be held by declarer, dummy or either defender. In order not to tell the opposition what cards you hold honours are usually claimed after the hand has been played.

In tournament bridge ('duplicate') honours are not counted in the scoring. Each hand is scored independently with no part-scores carried forward from a previous deal. For bidding and making a part-score add 50 to the trick total.

For bidding and making a game, not vulnerable, add 300 to the trick total.

For bidding and making a game, vulnerable, add 500 to the trick total.

All other scoring in 'duplicate' bridge is the same as in rubber bridge.

The aim of the game

The aim of the game is to score more points than the opponents. The central feature is *the game*; if the partnership hands can produce game and game is not bid, a valuable score has been lost. Similarly, if the partnership hands can produce slam, but slam is not bid, again a valuable score has been lost.

It is important, therefore, to bid up to the full value of your cards, but remember that if you undertake to make more tricks than you can produce you will be penalized (cf. 'breach of contract').

A sample rubber

Let's imagine that you and I are partners. Here are six hands from a rubber. Score the six hands and then compare your score-sheet with the one given.

1) They bid two no trumps and make ten tricks.
2) We bid four hearts and make ten tricks.
3) They bid three spades and make ten tricks.
4) We bid three clubs and make ten tricks.
5) They bid one no trump and make five tricks.
6) We bid six diamonds and make twelve tricks.

Your score-sheet should look like this:

We	They
(6) 750	
(6) 700	
(5) 100	(3) 30
(4) 20	(1) 60
(2) 120	(1) 70
(4) 60	(3) 90
(6) 120	

The numbers in brackets would not, of course, appear on the score-sheet; they just refer to the hands above. Notice that the opposition did not make the most of their chances: on the first hand they failed to bid game even though they were able to make ten tricks. The same thing happened in the third deal, where they made ten tricks in spades but only bid three spades which was not enough to give them game. If they had bid and made both games, the rubber would have been won by them instead of us. However, we were able to underline their part-scores firstly by bidding game in hearts on the second hand and small slam in diamonds on the sixth hand. In this way we scored +750 for a vulnerable small slam, +700 for a 2—0 rubber, +100 on the fifth hand where the enemy went two down not vulnerable, +20 on the fourth hand for the overtrick, in addition to our scores below the line. We therefore scored a total of $+1,870$ to their score of $+250$, which means we won the rubber by 1,620 points. These figures are rounded off to the nearest 100 (50 goes down, rather than up), so that we would say we have won a rubber of 16.

The score for the rubber would be entered next to each player's name and then the next rubber started, either with the same partnerships or drawing again for new partners. Bridge may be played without stakes or with stakes. The amount of stakes will be by agreement among the players involved: it is usually stipulated at so much per hundred. The 1970 Rubber Bridge Match between Omar Sharif's Team and two top English players, Jeremy Flint and Jonathan Cansino, was for stakes of £100 per hundred, plus side wagers on the rubbers—not bad petty cash.

Quiz

1) Which is the highest-ranking suit?
2) Which counts more in scoring, clubs or diamonds?
3) How many points does it take to make game?
4) A bid of 'two spades' contracts for how many tricks?
5) Must you trump if you cannot follow suit?
6) Which suits are the majors?
7) Can you combine two or more scores to make game?
8) Can you refuse to follow suit, even if you are able to do so?
9) If you hold high cards and low cards in the suit led, must you try to win the trick?
10) You bid four diamonds and make nine tricks. Can you score +60 for the nine tricks you made?
11) You have a score of +70 below the line. On the next hand, you score +90 below the line. How much do you carry forward to the next game?
12) Although you pass constantly, your (maniac) partner all on his own bids to four hearts, is doubled and penalized 1,700 points. Since you took no part in this disaster, can you disclaim responsibility and avoid paying the penalty?
13) Both sides have bid and made a game. Are you vulnerable or not vulnerable?
14) The opponents are playing four hearts. You hold the A Q J 10 of hearts. Can you as a defender receive the bonus for honours? If so, how much for the above?
15) You are not vulnerable. You bid four spades and make twelve tricks. What slam bonus do you receive?

Lesson 1

Part A: High-card points and hand shape

High-card points (HCP): Ace = 4; King = 3; Queen = 2; Jack = 1.

TO MAKE	YOU + PARTNER NEED
3 NT (nine tricks)	25-26 points
4 ♡ or 4 ♠ (ten tricks)	26 points
5 ♣ or 5 ♢ (eleven tricks)	29 points
small slam (twelve tricks)	33 points
grand slam (thirteen tricks)	37 points

Shape

BALANCED	SEMI-BALANCED	UNBALANCED
4-3-3-3, 4-4-3-2, 5-3-3-2	5-4-2-2, 6-3-2-2, 7-2-2-2	all others (must include
no void, no singleton,	no void, no singleton,	a void or singleton)
at most one doubleton	two or three doubletons	

COMMENTARY

The aim of bidding is for you and your partner to reach the correct contract and also to hinder the opposition from reaching their best contract. In reaching your own contract the less information you give the opposition the better, since that makes their defence more difficult. A bidding system is a system giving meanings to the bids made by each partner; each bid conveys a message to partner, telling him about the strength of your hand and where that strength is located. Some bids are very precise, others are vague. The meaning of a bid may change depending on the preceding sequence of bids; for example, a bid of one no trump has a different meaning when made by the opener as his first bid, when made by the opener as his rebid, when made by the responder (partner of the opener) or when made by the defenders.

A bidding system is a language (with very limited vocabulary). Just as there are many languages there are many bidding systems in existence. The system in this book will enable you to play with any partner, since even those who generally use some other system will be familiar with this one. The system is known as *Acol* (after the name of the street which contained the bridge club in which the system was born) and it is the most *natural* of all bidding systems.

HAND VALUATION

When the cards have been dealt and you pick up your hand, the first thing that concerns you is 'How strong is my hand?'. We know that aces and kings are jolly good things, but how can we measure the strength of different hands? Tricks are won with: (a) high cards; (b) long cards (length in a suit); (c) trumps. Each of these three aspects is measured by the *point count method* in which points are counted for various features of your hand, and the more points, the stronger the hand. These points represent the trick-taking power of the hand, and, roughly, 3 points equal one trick. Since different bids show different values, it is important for you to be able to value your hand so that you can describe it accurately with the correct bids. This lesson is concerned only with high-card points, the other aspects are taken up in later lessons.

Counting high-card points is very simple (A=4, K=3, Q=2, J=1). How many high-card points are there in each suit? In the whole pack? How many high-card points do you hope to hold each deal on the average? What is the greatest number of high card points possible to hold in one hand?[1]

Points measure the strength of a hand. Also important in the assessment of a hand is its *shape*. Balanced hands (those with no void, no singleton and at most one doubleton) are ideal for no trumps, while unbalanced hands (singleton or void) generally play better in a trump suit. The semi-balanced hands (no void, no singleton, two or three doubletons) fall on the border.

BIDDING TO GAME OR SLAM

To say that you need 26 points for a game in no trumps or a major, 29 points for game in a minor, 33 points for a small slam and 37 points for a grand slam does not mean that if you have the required points you will always make game or slam (after all, you—or, more probably, your partner—may play the hand badly); or that you cannot make game with fewer points (you may play the hand brilliantly or the enemy may defend badly). These points are the minimum which should give you a good chance for game. With fewer points game or slam may be made but it is unlikely, and more probably you will be defeated. The points given are for the combined hands—yours and partner's. They are solely high-card points; distribution points count also (see later lessons).

Whenever you make a bid, you say something about the range of points in your hand. Partner then takes the bottom limit and the top limit and decides whether: (a) game is impossible; (b) game is possible, but not certain; (c) game is certain. If game is impossible, stop bidding at the lowest suitable part score (40 below the line and 60 below the line are not essentially different. You do not bid three clubs rather than two clubs merely to score an extra twenty below the line, because by so doing you may endanger the contract, since it is harder to make nine tricks than eight). If game is possible, invite partner to proceed to game if he holds maximum values but to stop in a part-score if he holds minimum values. If game is certain, make sure that game is reached. Similarly, the partners can see from the bidding whether slam is impossible (stop in game), possible (invite slam), or certain (bid slam). Incidentally, if slam is impossible, you should not push past game; four spades making eleven tricks score exactly the same as five spades making eleven tricks, and it is particularly annoying to be in five spades one down when you would have scored game if you had stayed in four spades. Remember ten tricks are easier than eleven.

[1] 10, 40, 10, 37.

EXERCISES

1) What are each of the following combinations worth in high-card points (x=any low card)?

a) KJx   f) Kxx   k) AQx
b) AQJ   g) AKx   l) Qxx
c) AJx   h) QJx   m) Axx
d) KQJ   i) AKQJ   n) AKJ
e) AKQ   j) KQx   o) Jxx

2) What is the shape of each of the following hands, balanced, semi-balanced or unbalanced?

a) xxxx   b) xxxx   c) xxx   d) xx
    xx   xxxxx   xxxxx   xxxx
    xxx   xxxx   xx   xx
    xxxx   —   xxx   xxxxx

e) xxx   f) xx   g) xxx   h) xxxx
    xxxx   xxx   x   xxxx
    xxx   xxxxxx   xxxx   x
    xxx   xx   xxxxx   xxxx

3) How many high-card points does each of the following hands contain? Which hands are balanced?

a) ♠ AJ10   b) ♠ AQ63   c) ♠ AJ7   d) ♠ KJ7   e) ♠ QJ73
    ♡ Q52   ♡ 7642   ♡ 83   ♡ AQ3   ♡ A6
    ◇ KQ74   ◇ AQ   ◇ KQJ6   ◇ A107   ◇ KQ543
    ♣ AJ3   ♣ KQ4   ♣ KQ102   ♣ J543   ♣ A5

f) ♠ A72   g) ♠ AQ42 h) ♠ A4   i) ♠ AJ983 j) ♠ AQJ3
    ♡ Q943   ♡ AJ53   ♡ KQ3   ♡ QJ7   ♡ A4
    ◇ AK7   ◇ 7   ◇ QJ7   ◇ KQ3   ◇ Q107
    ♣ AQ5   ♣ KQJ4   ♣ AJ983 ♣ A4   ♣ KQ72

Part B: Opening with a bid of no trumps

WHAT DO YOU NEED TO OPEN
WITH A NO TRUMP BID?

RESPONDING WITH A BALANCED HAND

1 NT, The weak no trump:
12—14 HCP
+ A balanced hand

0—10	HCP: PASS
11—12	HCP: 2 NT (invite game)
13—18	HCP: 3 NT (sign-off, the end)
19—20	HCP: 4 NT (invite slam)
21—up	HCP: 6 NT (sign-off, the end)
25—up	HCP: 7 NT (sign-off, the end)

1 NT, The strong no-trump:
15—17 HCP
+ A balanced hand

0—7	HCP: PASS
8—9	HCP: 2 NT (invite game)
10—15	HCP: 3 NT (sign-off, the end)
16—17	HCP: 4 NT (invite slam)
18—up	HCP: 6 NT (sign-off, the end)
22—up	HCP: 7 NT (sign-off, the end)

2 NT: 20—22 HCP
+ A balanced hand

0—4	HCP: PASS
5—10	HCP: 3 NT (sign-off, the end)
11—12	HCP: 4 NT (invite slam)
13—up	HCP: 6 NT (sign-off, the end)
17—up	HCP: 7 NT (sign-off, the end)

3 NT: A solid six-card or
longer minor suit with
no more than a king or
a queen outside

This is a gambling, shut-out opening
bid and will be covered in Lesson 6
which deals with such openings.

HOW TO HANDLE BALANCED HANDS AS OPENER

0—11 Points:	Pass
12—14 Points:	Using the weak no trump, open 1 NT.
	Using the strong no trump, open with one of a suit; rebid 1 NT (e.g., 1 ◇ : 1 ♠, 1 NT).
15—17 Points:	Using the weak no trump, open with one of a suit; rebid 1 NT (e.g., 1 ♣ : 1 ♡, 1 NT).
	Using the strong no trump, open 1 NT.
18—19 Points:	Open with one of a suit; jump rebid no trump (e.g., 1 ♣ : 1 ◇, 2 NT).
20—22 Points:	Open 2 NT.
23—24 Points:	Open 2 ♣; rebid 2 NT (see Lesson 5).
25—27 Points:	Open 2 ♣; rebid 3 NT (see Lesson 5).

COMMENTARY

Both the weak no trump (12—14 points) and the strong no trump (15—17 points) are in common use. The one to be used will be a matter of partnership agreement. A very common and sensible agreement is to vary the range according to vulnerability, using the weak no trump when not vulnerable and the strong no trump when vulnerable. This combines the desirable bridge traits of aggression and discretion.

One of the aims behind the 12—14 one no trump is to make it as hard as possible for the opponents to enter the bidding. Over one no trump they are unable to bid one spade, one heart, one diamond or one club. However, when you are vulnerable, the penalties for failing in a contract are much more severe than when you are not vulnerable; the risk of a severe penalty outweighs the advantage of shutting out the opposition, and so when vulnerable a safer range of 15—17 points is recommended.

Dare-devils use the 12—14 one no trump at any vulnerability ('weak throughout'), while a conservative approach uses only the 15—17 point range ('strong throughout').

When you become experienced at hand valuation, you will be able to tell when a hand is suitable for a suit opening even though it appears to fall in a no trump range. Hands with packing tens and nines should be upgraded; hands with a good five-card minor should be upgraded; hands with all the points packed into two suits in a 4—4—3—2 hand may be better described by bidding the two suits than by simply blasting into no trumps. In general, however, you will not go far wrong by bidding no trumps with a balanced hand in the given ranges.

The balanced shapes are the 4—3—3—3, the 4—4—3—2 and the 5—3—3—2. With a 5—3—3—2 shape and the five-card suit a major prefer to open with a bid of one heart or one spade as the case may be. Since game in no trumps and game in a major both require about 26 points, you can try for both the major and later for no trumps, if partner does not support your suit. With a five-card minor and one no trump strength prefer to open one no trump, since three no trumps require only 25—26 points (and nine tricks) rather than five clubs or five diamonds which require 29 points (and eleven tricks).

You will notice from the charts above that the only significant difference in using the weak no trump or the strong no trump is in your choice of opening bid on the 12—14 and 15—17 point hands and in the action taken by the responder in the quest for game or slam.

When partner opens one no trump and you hold a balanced hand, your bidding is straightforward—you add your points to those shown by partner and make the appropriate bid, indicating whether game is impossible, possible or certain. Facing a 12—14 one no trump you should pass on a balanced 0—10 points, for there is no way your side can have enough points for game, even if partner has a maximum of 14. Remember also that partner is more likely to be minimum than maximum. Similarly, opposite a 15—17 one no trump you should pass on a balanced 0—7 points.

If you hold 11—12 points opposite a 12—14 one no trump, you calculate that if partner is maximum you have enough points for game but not if he is minimum. So what should you bid? Two no trumps, inviting game. The bid of two no trumps says, 'Partner, I have 11—12 points. Please bid three no trumps if you are maximum, pass if you are minimum.' The opener of one no trump will pass on 12 points and will bid three no trumps on 14 points. What should he do with 13 points? As you gain experience you will be able to distinguish 'good 13s' and 'bad 13s', but as a general rule with 13 points you should prefer to bid three no trumps rather than pass two no trumps. The reason is that the rewards for making game are very high, and if sometimes you reach game on 24 points (for example, $13 + 11 = 24$), that is no great disaster as you will frequently still make it. It is reaching game on, say, 20 points which has no chance and, even worse, failing to reach game when you have 26 points or more that are the disasters of bridge. In general it pays to bid boldly but not recklessly.

Opposite a 15—17 opening of one no trump the *invitational* range when game is a 'maybe' is 8—9 points. Maybe you have 25 points, maybe not. The response of two no trumps invites the opener to bid three no trumps if he is maximum (16—17), pass if he is minimum (15).

Facing a 12—14 one no trump suppose you hold 13—18 points. You know that you have at least 25 points, even if partner has a minimum one no trump, so what should you bid? Three no trumps, of course. When you see enough points for game, do not merely invite game, insist on game. Note also that with 13—18 points you know that there is not enough for slam even if partner is maximum. When you respond three no trumps, opener must, of course, pass. The corresponding range for responder opposite a 15—17 one no trump is 10—15 points, enough to be sure of at least 25 together, but no possibility of a combined count of 33.

Opposite a 12—14 one no trump suppose you are lucky enough to hold 19—20 points. You know that game is certain, but it may be that a slam is possible, and the slam bonuses are highly attractive. With 19—20 points (16—17 opposite a 15—17 one no trump) you should bid four no trumps, inviting a slam. The response of four no trumps, being more than necessary for game, should alert partner that you have a slam in mind. The bid of four no trumps says, 'Partner, please bid six no trumps if you are maximum, pass if you are minimum.'

With 21 points opposite a 12—14 one no trump or 18 points opposite a 15—17 one no trump (both occur rarely) you can bid six no trumps direct. Bid seven no trumps when you have 25 points or more opposite 12—14, or 22 points or more opposite 15—17, since you can see that there are at least 37 points in the combined hands.

Similar principles apply after an opening of two no trumps (20—22 points). Note that all the above comments refer to the situation where the opening bid is one no trump and responder holds a balanced hand. What to do with an unbalanced hand will be seen in the next lesson.

EXERCISES

1) What is your opening bid on each of these hands: (i) using the weak no trump? (ii) using the strong no trump?

	a)	b)	c)	d)	e)
♠	A108	AQ	AJ9	874	AQ3
♡	K107	J98	KQ3	AQJ	KQ96
◇	QJ6	KQ843	AJ84	K98	KJ97
♣	K986	K86	K97	KJ64	AQ

2) Partner opens the bidding with one no-trump. What do you respond if: (i) you are using the weak no trump? (ii) you are using the strong no trump?

	a)	b)	c)	d)	e)
♠	832	432	AQ5	J872	AQ7
♡	Q54	76	K432	754	K83
◇	765	AQ5	A76	A5	KJ7
♣	Q832	Q10764	974	Q543	KQ54

	f)	g)	h)	i)	j)
♠	KQ4	AQ7	32	A6	KQ84
♡	865	86	54	J32	J65
◇	J84	K864	AK7432	J86	AJ10
♣	KJ97	9832	K62	98432	AQ4

3) What would you respond on each of these hands if partner opened two no trumps?

	a)	b)	c)	d)	e)
♠	7643	AJ9	962	AK8	Q98
♡	83	8764	83	K7	432
◇	8542	Q43	AJ743	QJ43	K86
♣	964	987	972	10987	AJ107

4) Each of the following auctions contains at least one error. Which calls are wrong and why? You are using a weak no trump.

a) Opener	Responder	b) Opener	Responder	c) Opener	Responder
♠ AQ	♠ K93	♠ AK7	♠ QJ3	♠ KQJ6	♠ A98
♡ K984	♡ AJ7	♡ 964	♡ A87	♡ A4	♡ K75
◇ KJ43	◇ AQ6	◇ K984	◇ QJ76	◇ QJ8	◇ 632
♣ 743	♣ J1085	♣ Q104	♣ 952	♣ Q973	♣ KJ102
1 NT	3 NT	1 NT	2 NT	1 NT	No bid
6 NT	No bid	3 NT	No bid		

PLAYING HANDS

Both partnerships use the weak no trump when not vulnerable, the strong no trump when vulnerable.

Hand 1: Winning tricks with high cards—don't block that suit

Dealer North
Nil vulnerable

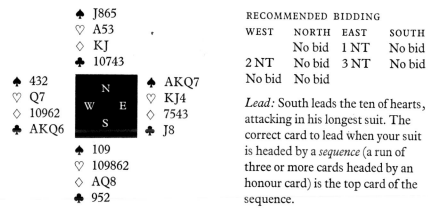

♠ J865
♡ A53
◇ KJ
♣ 10743

♠ 432
♡ Q7
◇ 10962
♣ AKQ6

♠ AKQ7
♡ KJ4
◇ 7543
♣ J8

♠ 109
♡ 109862
◇ AQ8
♣ 952

RECOMMENDED BIDDING

WEST	NORTH	EAST	SOUTH
	No bid	1 NT	No bid
2 NT	No bid	3 NT	No bid
No bid	No bid		

Lead: South leads the ten of hearts, attacking in his longest suit. The correct card to lead when your suit is headed by a *sequence* (a run of three or more cards headed by an honour card) is the top card of the sequence.

RIGHT PLAY North wins the ace of hearts and plays back a heart. Unless you can see a better plan of attack, it is usually best to return partner's suit.

Declarer should win (with the queen in dummy or the king in his hand), play the jack of clubs (putting on dummy's six), then the eight of clubs won in dummy, then two more club tricks and then the other winners, making nine tricks.

WRONG PLAY 1) Blocking the club suit. If you play the ace, king or queen of clubs on the first round of clubs, you will have only three club tricks instead of four.

When cashing winners in a suit, usually play first the high cards from the hand which has the shorter length so that you can end in the hand with the greater length.
2) Stranding winners in dummy. If you win the first club in dummy and then win the second club with the jack, dummy has two club winners but you have no way to get to dummy to use them. The same would result if you play first the jack of clubs, then a club to dummy and then switch to another suit. Dummy has winners but *no entry* to cash them.

Hand 2: Winning tricks with high cards—overtaking to gain an entry

Dealer East
East-West vulnerable

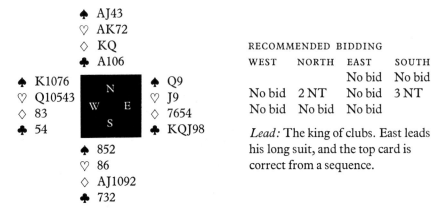

♠ AJ43
♡ AK72
◇ KQ
♣ A106

♠ K1076   ♠ Q9
♡ Q10543   ♡ J9
◇ 83   ◇ 7654
♣ 54   ♣ KQJ98

♠ 852
♡ 86
◇ AJ1092
♣ 732

RECOMMENDED BIDDING

WEST	NORTH	EAST	SOUTH
		No bid	No bid
No bid	2 NT	No bid	3 NT
No bid	No bid	No bid	

Lead: The king of clubs. East leads his long suit, and the top card is correct from a sequence.

RIGHT PLAY When North gains the lead with the ace of clubs, he should play the king of diamonds (low from dummy), then the queen of diamonds (*ace* from dummy); by *overtaking* the second round of diamonds, he gains entry to dummy to cash three more diamond tricks, making nine tricks.

There are many occasions when it is necessary to overtake high cards to gain an entry to your hand or to dummy.

WRONG PLAY 1) Failing to overtake the second round of diamonds with dummy's ace. This leaves the lead in the North hand, and dummy has three good diamonds which cannot be used because dummy has no entry.

2) Playing the ace of diamonds on the first round of diamonds. This blocks the diamond suit and means the second lead of diamonds is again won in the North hand (check it). Again there would be three diamond winners stranded in dummy.

Hand 3: Winning tricks with low cards in a suit—discarding

Dealer South
Both vulnerable

RECOMMENDED BIDDING

WEST	NORTH	EAST	SOUTH
			1 NT
No bid	No bid	No bid	

♠ 652
♡ 942
◇ 108
♣ AQ652

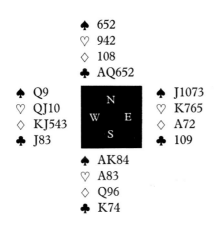

♠ Q9
♡ QJ10
◇ KJ543
♣ J83

♠ J1073
♡ K765
◇ A72
♣ 109

♠ AK84
♡ A83
◇ Q96
♣ K74

Lead: West leads the four of diamonds. Where your long suit does not contain a sequence, the correct card is the fourth from the top ('fourth highest of your long suit'). Note that the 543 in diamonds does not constitute a sequence for your opening lead—*a sequence must be headed by an honour card for you to lead the top card of the sequence.*

RIGHT PLAY East wins the ace of diamonds and returns a diamond. West takes his five diamond tricks and then switches to the queen of hearts (top of the sequence).

Declarer must make sure he does not discard any of dummy's clubs on the diamonds. He can discard either some useless hearts or useless spades. He wins the ace of hearts, leads the king of clubs and then continues clubs. After three rounds of clubs, no one has any clubs left. Declarer plays the last two clubs from dummy and then cashes his other winners, making eight tricks.

WRONG PLAY 1) If declarer discards one of dummy's clubs on the run of the diamonds, he is limited to seven tricks. If he discards two clubs, he will fail in his contract.

Do not discard winners or potential winners.

2) In playing clubs it would be an error to play ace, queen, then king. That would leave the lead in the South hand and strand two winners in dummy.

In cashing a long suit make sure you finish in the hand which has the length in the suit.

Hand 4: Establishing winners before cashing high cards

Dealer West
Both vulnerable

North-South have
a part score of 40

```
              ♠ J10982
              ♡ 865
              ◇ 8753
              ♣ 7
  ♠ AK5           N         ♠ Q43
  ♡ KQ9                     ♡ J104
  ◇ Q4        W     E       ◇ AKJ6
  ♣ Q8643        S          ♣ AK5
              ♠ 76
              ♡ A732
              ◇ 1092
              ♣ J1092
```

RECOMMENDED BIDDING

WEST	NORTH	EAST	SOUTH
1 NT	No bid	6 NT	No bid
No bid	No bid		

Bidding: West opens with 1 NT
(15—17 when vulnerable). It
would be poor to open one club. If
your hand fits a no trump opening,
prefer that to any other opening.
East knows the partnership must
have at least 33 points, maybe
more, so East bids six no trumps.
Three no trumps by East would be
very timid. Note that on the hand
six clubs would fail, while six no
trumps is unbeatable.

Lead: North leads the jack of spades, top of the sequence. (The only solid sequence
from which the top card is not led is from AKQ; here the standard lead is the king.)

RIGHT PLAY Win the lead and play hearts. If South takes the ace of hearts, you
have three spades, two hearts, four diamonds and three clubs. If South refuses the
first heart, play another heart. If South still refuses to take the ace, cash your other
winning cards.

WRONG PLAY 1) Winning the spade lead and playing two more rounds of spades.
If North held the ace of hearts, you would fail, but on the actual hand you would
still make the contract. In bridge, as in life, not every wrong is punished.
2) Playing three rounds of clubs before attacking hearts. South can cash a club
winner when he wins the ace of hearts.

Establish your necessary tricks first, cash your sure winners later.

Lesson 2

Part A: Opening bids of one in a suit

You have 12 HCP or more: open the bidding
You have less than 12 HCP: don't open the bidding
Which suit do you bid first?

1) Bid your longest suit first (length before strength).
2) With two equally long suits bid the higher ranking first.
   Long suit = five card or longer suit
3) With no five card or longer suit:
   a) 4—4—4—1: Open one of the four-card suits, preferably the one below the singleton.
   b) 4—4—3—2: Open one of the four-card suits, preferably the one below the doubleton (unless you have a no trump opening).
   c) 4—3—3—3: If too strong to open one no trump, open the four-card suit. But with a weak hand when using a strong no trump open one club.

DISTRIBUTION POINTS

For	Your side has a known eight card or better fit, *Add*	You don't know yet whether an eight card or better trump fit exists, *Add*
Void	5 points	3 points
Singleton	3 points	2 points
Doubleton	1 point	1 point

Principle: With eight card or better fit use 5—3—1 scale.
With no eight card fit yet found use 3—2—1 scale.
But don't count distribution points
a) When opening the bidding.
b) When bidding no trumps.
c) For shortage in suit bid by partner until you have found an eight card or better fit.

COMMENTARY

The opening bids of one spade, one heart, one diamond and one club are by far the most frequent opening bids. In contrast to the opening no trump bids which have a narrow three-point range opening bids of one in a suit have a wide range, from 12 points up to 20 and sometimes even more points. No trump openings describe the hand very accurately—suit openings are only a very vague description—hence, *if your hand is suitable for a no trump opening, make that opening bid and no other.*

The general rule is that you should have 12 HCP or more to open the bidding. As you gain playing experience, you will know when you may relax this rule; for example, with a very good six-card suit or two five-card suits but only 11 HCP you may open, or after two passes (i.e., in third position) you may, but don't have to, open with less than 12 HCP provided that your bid indicates a good lead to partner, should the opponents end up playing the hand. In other words, in third position you may take the opportunity of showing an excellent suit, but would not bother with a moth-eaten collection.

When you open the bidding with a major, if it is only four-cards long, it should contain 3 or more HCP. Any five-card or longer major, even with no points, may be opened.

With a minor suit opening you need not be so particular and may even occasionally open a three-card minor in the case of the 4—3—3—3 shape. The reason is that partner will be anxious to raise your major suit (hence it should be a decent suit), but he will be reluctant to raise your minor suit. When you bid any suit twice without support from partner, the suit should be rebiddable, i.e., six cards or longer, or if it is only five-cards long, it should contain 3 or more HCP. Do not rebid a four-card suit unless partner has supported it.

In general you need four cards in a suit before you can bid it. In addition to the strength of the hand (points) and its shape (balanced, semi-balanced or unbalanced) we think of hands in terms of the number of four-card or longer suits they contain. Thus hands may be *one-suiters* (no more than one suit of four or more cards), *two-suiters* (two four-card or longer suits) or *three-suiters* (three such suits, i.e., 4—4—4—1 or 5—4—4—0).

With two five-card suits the rule is to open the higher ranking. With a bare minimum opening including five spades and five clubs it is more economical to open one club.

Although the rules given at the beginning of this lesson are sufficient to stand you in good stead, if you want to improve your hand valuation technique, the following pointers will be helpful.

Special pointers for more accurate hand valuation for suit bidding:

1) For singleton king, queen or jack — deduct one point.
2) For QJ doubleton, Qx or Jx doubleton — deduct one point.
3) For 12 point or higher hand with 4—3—3—3 shape — deduct one point.
4) For 12 point or higher hand with no aces — deduct one point.
5) For 12 point or higher hand with fewer than two defensive tricks (defensive tricks: AK$=2$, AQ$=1\frac{1}{2}$, A$=1$, KQ$=1$, K$=\frac{1}{2}$; no more than two defensive tricks to be counted in any one suit) — deduct one point.
6) For a hand with all four aces — add one point.
7) For holding one or more top honours (ace, king, or queen) in a suit bid by partner. — add one point.

EXERCISES

1) What is your opening bid on each of these hands? Which hands are one-suiters, which two-suiters and which three-suiters?

a) ♠ 6
   ♡ AQ7642
   ◇ K842
   ♣ A5

b) ♠ AKQ7
   ♡ 8
   ◇ K32
   ♣ J10542

c) ♠ K8532
   ♡ KQJ76
   ◇ A5
   ♣ 3

d) ♠ A9842
   ♡ 5
   ◇ AKJ87
   ♣ K6

e) ♠ 6
   ♡ A85432
   ◇ AK7654
   ♣ —

f) ♠ K6
   ♡ A54
   ◇ KQ8642
   ♣ 73

g) ♠ AK
   ♡ 109543
   ◇ AQ
   ♣ Q865

h) ♠ —
   ♡ KQJ8
   ◇ A76532
   ♣ A94

i) ♠ AJ75
   ♡ 76
   ◇ J8
   ♣ A8632

j) ♠ AK984
   ♡ 76
   ◇ 8
   ♣ AKJ97

2) Do you agree with the opening bids given under each of the following hands: (i) using a weak no trump? (ii) using a strong no trump? If not, what would your opening bid be?

a) ♠ AQ54
   ♡ AK83
   ◇ 76
   ♣ 853
   One heart

b) ♠ K54
   ♡ AJ54
   ◇ A973
   ♣ K8
   One club

c) ♠ K986
   ♡ Q42
   ◇ K3
   ♣ AJ72
   One spade

d) ♠ AJ3
   ♡ 76
   ◇ K432
   ♣ AK95
   One no trump

e) ♠ KQJ7
   ♡ 8
   ◇ AQ62
   ♣ J987
   One spade

f) ♠ AJ74
   ♡ A643
   ◇ AKJ6
   ♣ 6
   One spade

g) ♠ J976
   ♡ K54
   ◇ AQ3
   ♣ KJ6
   One spade

h) ♠ KQ43
   ♡ J842
   ◇ A93
   ♣ J6
   One spade

i) ♠ AQ54
   ♡ K6
   ◇ Q764
   ♣ K98
   One club

j) ♠ AQ54
   ♡ K98
   ◇ Q764
   ♣ K6
   One club

Part B: Suit responses to no trump openings

ADEQUATE TRUMP SUIT—At least eight trumps in the combined hands

Over one no trump:
Suit bids at the two-level are weak.
Suit bids at the three-level force to game.
Suit bids at game-level or slam-level are sign-offs.

Over two no trumps:
Suit bids less than game are forcing to game.
Suit bids at game-level or slam-level are sign-offs.

AUCTION	MEANING OF RESPONDER'S BID	ACTION BY OPENER
1 NT : 2 ♣*	Weakness—unbalanced hand—five-card	Pass, pass, pass
1 NT : 2 ◇	or longer suit—no hope of game—	(quickly!)
1 NT : 2 ♡	rescue from hopeless no trump contract	
1 NT : 2 ♠		
1 NT : 3 ♣	Game-force—five-card suit—	Raise suit with
1 NT : 3 ◇	responder's hand unsuitable for no	three-card or longer
1 NT : 3 ♡	trumps—N.B. Do not respond three	support; with only
1 NT : 3 ♠	clubs or three diamonds unless there is	doubleton support
	a compelling reason to avoid three no	bid three no trumps.
	trumps (e.g., slam prospects). Ditto	
	over an opening of two no trumps.	
1 NT : 4 ♡	Sign-off—responder has six-card or	Pass
1 NT : 4 ♠	longer suit + enough for game (but	
1 NT : 5 ♣	not enough for slam)—hand unsuitable	
1 NT : 5 ◇	for no trumps. Ditto over an opening of	
	two no trumps.	
1 NT : 6 Anything	Sign-off—responder judges he has	Pass
1 NT : 7 Anything	enough for slam. Ditto over openings of	
	two no trumps or three no trumps.	

*For a different meaning for the response of two clubs to one no trump see the Stayman convention on the next page.

COMMENTARY

When the partnership agrees on a trump suit, they should be able to outgun the enemy in trumps. Seven trumps versus six is hardly outgunning the enemy (if declarer has to trump once, he is reduced to the same number of trumps as the enemy, which may lead to his losing control of the hand). Eight trumps versus five is the minimum superiority in trumps with which you should be satisfied.

The suit responses to no trump openings are simple and logical. For example, that 1 NT : 3 ♠ shows a five-card suit is easily worked out. Three spades is forcing to game; if responder has six spades and enough for game, he would bid four spades direct since partner's opening of one no trump promises a balanced hand and therefore at least doubleton support which would give him an adequate trump suit. By bidding three spades responder indicates he needs more than the minimum support, i.e., he needs three-card or better support; hence, his suit must be a five-card suit.

Where responder has a balanced or semi-balanced hand with a long minor suit and enough points for game, it is best tactics to try for the easier game of three no trumps (nine tricks) rather than bid your minor suit and possibly end in five clubs or five diamonds (eleven tricks).

THE STAYMAN CONVENTION

The above scheme leaves a number of problem hands. Suppose partner opens one no trump, weak, and you hold ♠: AQ86, ♡: AJ83, ◇: 7, ♣: K742. You have enough points for game, but three no trumps is unattractive with that singleton diamond. A suit bid at the two-level is not forcing. Three hearts or three spades would be forcing but would show a five-card suit, and partner would raise with three-card support. Then you would be in the *worse* position of four hearts or four spades with only seven cards in the trump suit. You would like to be in four hearts or four spades only if partner has *four*-card support for your suit.

Similarly, if you hold ♠: AQ864, ♡: KJ83, ◇: 7, ♣: K43 and partner opens a weak no trump, you could bid three spades, forcing to game and showing a five-card suit. Things will probably be all right if partner raises to four spades, but what if partner bids three no trumps with a doubleton spade? You may well have missed a contract of four hearts if partner has four cards in hearts.

The solution to these and similar problems is the Stayman convention. If your partnership is using this convention, the response of two clubs to an opening of one no trump is artificial and has nothing to do with clubs.

1 NT: 2 ♣ = 'Do you have a four-card major?'
Opener rebids: 2 ◇ = 'No, I have no four-card major.'
               2 ♡ = 'Yes, I have four hearts.'
               2 ♠ = 'Yes, I have four spades.'

Those are the only rebids available to opener. If he has four cards in hearts and in spades, opener's rebid is two hearts.

With the first hand above responder bids two clubs. If opener rebids two hearts or two spades, responder raises to four hearts or four spades, while if opener rebids two diamonds, responder tries three no trumps after all, despite the singleton diamond. With the second hand above responder bids two clubs. If opener rebids two hearts or two spades, responder raises to four hearts or four spades, while if opener rebids two diamonds, responder jumps to three spades, forcing to game and showing a five-card suit (like 1 NT: 3 ♠ immediately). This will ensure that you reach a major-suit game if you have an eight-card major fit.

The Stayman convention can also be used over two no trumps (2 NT: 3 ♣), but another popular arrangement over two no trumps is the Baron convention:
2 NT: 3 ♣ = 'Please bid your cheapest four-card suit.' Now any suits bid by the partnership at the three-level are only four-card suits, and you need four-card support before raising partner's suit.

EXERCISES

1) Partner opens one no trump. What do you bid on each of these hands: (i) using a weak no trump? (ii) using a strong no trump?

a) ♠ J43
   ♡ 943
   ◇ Q76432
   ♣ 8

b) ♠ 9876432
   ♡ 75
   ◇ 6
   ♣ 432

c) ♠ K876432
   ♡ K5
   ◇ 6
   ♣ 432

d) ♠ 5
   ♡ QJ543
   ◇ 98642
   ♣ 43

e) ♠ 43
   ♡ Q9543
   ◇ J98
   ♣ Q85

f) ♠ K54
   ♡ AQ8432
   ◇ 932
   ♣ 5

g) ♠ K64
   ♡ AQ765
   ◇ Q532
   ♣ 5

h) ♠ Q62
   ♡ 64
   ◇ AK8432
   ♣ Q3

i) ♠ KQJ743
   ♡ 6
   ◇ QJ32
   ♣ 64

j) ♠ AQJ75
   ♡ KJ954
   ◇ 83
   ♣ 5

2) Partner opens two no trumps. What do you bid on each of these hands?

a) ♠ KJ854
   ♡ J8743
   ◇ 62
   ♣ 8

b) ♠ 76
   ♡ 64
   ◇ KQ843
   ♣ 8742

c) ♠ J96543
   ♡ 6
   ◇ 5432
   ♣ 74

d) ♠ —
   ♡ A98632
   ◇ 543
   ♣ 6532

e) ♠ 9874
   ♡ 6
   ◇ J432
   ♣ 7632

3) For each of the following hands you have opened with a strong one no trump. What is your rebid on each of the auctions?

i) ♠ KJ8
   ♡ A943
   ◇ KQJ10
   ♣ Q7

  a) 1 NT : 3 ♠   b) 1 NT : 4 ♡   c) 1 NT : 2 ♠
      ?   ?   ?
  d) 1 NT : 3 ♣   e) 1 NT : 3 NT   f) 1 NT : 2 ♡
      ?   ?   ?

ii) ♠ AQ
    ♡ 843
    ◇ KQJ7
    ♣ AJ97

  a) 1 NT : 3 ♠   b) 1 NT : 2 ◇   c) 1 NT : 6 ♡
      ?   ?   ?
  d) 1 NT : 3 ♡   e) 1 NT : 4 ♠   f) 1 NT : 2 ♠
      ?   ?   ?

iii) ♠ KQ6
     ♡ A95
     ◇ K6432
     ♣ A8

  a) 1 NT : 2 ♡   b) 1 NT : 3 ◇   c) 1 NT : 3 ♣
      ?   ?   ?
  d) 1 NT : 2 ◇   e) 1 NT : 3 ♡   f) 1 NT : 3 ♠
      ?   ?   ?

4) Match each *responder's* hand below with the appropriate response. The partnership is using a strong one no trump.

i) ♠ A72
   ♡ K543
   ◇ Q43
   ♣ J76

ii) ♠ 75
    ♡ KQ853
    ◇ K93
    ♣ 874

iii) ♠ 843
     ♡ J10864
     ◇ 5
     ♣ 6432

  a) 1 NT : Pass   b) 1 NT : 2 NT

  c) 1 NT : 3 NT   d) 1 NT : 2 ♡

iv) ♠ 7
    ♡ QJ107543
    ◇ A8
    ♣ 632

v) ♠ A94
   ♡ Q7432
   ◇ 85
   ♣ 763

vi) ♠ 54
    ♡ KJ876
    ◇ A432
    ♣ J2

  e) 1 NT : 3 ♡   f) 1 NT : 4 ♡

5) You are a bridge psychiatrist. Each of your patients produces one of the problems below giving you the partnership hands and the actual bidding sequence. You are asked to advise which bids, if any, are wrong, why they are wrong, and what the correct auction should be. The partnership is using a weak no trump in each case.

34

a)	Opener	Responder	b)	Opener	Responder	c)	Opener	Responder
	♠ KJ43	♠ Q9652		♠ AQ96	♠ 7		♠ 85	♠ QJ10764
	♡ A75	♡ KQJ82		♡ J1072	♡ Q98643		♡ QJ4	♡ 86
	♦ KQJ9	♦ 63		♦ AQ	♦ K54		♦ K93	♦ Q102
	♣ J5	♣ 8		♣ 743	♣ 865		♣ AK872	♣ 54
	1 NT	3 ♠		1 NT	2 ♡		1 NT	2 ♠
	4 ♠	Pass		4 ♡	Pass		3 ♣	Pass

d)	Opener	Responder	e)	Opener	Responder	f)	Opener	Responder
	♠ 9832	♠ KQJ		♠ AQ85	♠ K43		♠ A843	♠ QJ10965
	♡ Q6	♡ A7432		♡ 962	♡ KJ10843		♡ AK5	♡ 8432
	♦ AK94	♦ 7		♦ A5	♦ 7		♦ 9842	♦ AK5
	♣ AJ5	♣ Q1063		♣ QJ32	♣ K96		♣ K10	♣ —
	1 NT	3 ♡		1 NT	2 ♡		1 NT	4 ♠
	Pass			Pass			6 ♠	Pass

6) You have opened one no trump, weak, and partner responds two clubs Stayman. What is your rebid?

a)	♠ K84	b)	♠ 764	c)	♠ AQ43	d)	♠ KJ42	e)	♠ AQ
	♡ J762		♡ A93		♡ K762		♡ A7		♡ 9843
	♦ AK		♦ K7		♦ A8		♦ QJ8		♦ KJ10
	♣ Q864		♣ KQ932		♣ J43		♣ J1076		♣ K1076

7) Partner opened one no trump, weak. You responded two clubs Stayman. What is your next bid if partner's rebid is: (i) two hearts? (ii) two spades? (iii) two diamonds?

a)	♠ K864	b)	♠ K8653	c)	♠ 9864	d)	♠ AQ76	e)	♠ KJ102
	♡ 7		♡ Q983		♡ 7652		♡ KJ103		♡ AQ1043
	♦ 43		♦ —		♦ J10764		♦ 76		♦ Q83
	♣ Q98742		♣ 6432		♣ —		♣ J86		♣ 6

PLAYING HANDS

Hand 1: Removing one no trump on a weak hand with a long suit—drawing trumps

Dealer North
Nil vulnerable

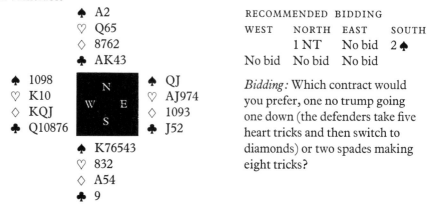

♠ A2
♥ Q65
♦ 8762
♣ AK43

♠ 1098
♥ K10
♦ KQJ
♣ Q10876

♠ QJ
♥ AJ974
♦ 1093
♣ J52

♠ K76543
♥ 832
♦ A54
♣ 9

RECOMMENDED BIDDING

WEST	NORTH	EAST	SOUTH
	1 NT	No bid	2 ♠
No bid	No bid	No bid	

Bidding: Which contract would you prefer, one no trump going one down (the defenders take five heart tricks and then switch to diamonds) or two spades making eight tricks?

Lead: The king of diamonds, top of a sequence. The diamond lead sets up diamond winners for the defence, while the club lead is unlikely to help. Against a suit contract prefer to lead a strong sequence rather than your long suit.

RIGHT PLAY Win the ace of diamonds and play the ace and king of spades. Then play the two top clubs, discarding a losing diamond.

Note that East on the diamond lead should play the three of diamonds, his lowest, signalling that he does *not* like diamonds and asking West to try another suit. Since West can see the strong clubs in dummy, obviously East must want a switch to hearts. Bridge reasoning is easy.

WRONG PLAY 1) Winning the ace of diamonds and failing to play trumps. If you play the other suits, you will in fact go down, losing three hearts, two diamonds and one spade.

2) Winning the ace of diamonds and playing three rounds of trumps instead of just two. West will win the third round of trumps, and now the enemy can win one spade, two diamonds and three hearts, holding you to seven tricks. The enemy's last trump will always make a trick. To remove it from them is unnecessary and costs you time.

Under normal circumstances draw trumps as soon as possible. In signalling by the defenders high-low encourages, low-high discourages.

Hand 2: Raising no trumps rather than bidding a minor—'ducking' to preserve an entry to dummy.

Dealer East
Nil vulnerable

North-South have a part-score of 60.

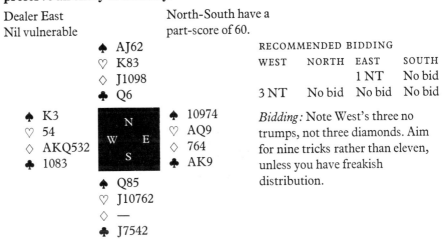

```
              ♠ AJ62
              ♡ K83
              ◇ J1098
              ♣ Q6
  ♠ K3                      ♠ 10974
  ♡ 54          N          ♡ AQ9
  ◇ AKQ532   W     E       ◇ 764
  ♣ 1083        S          ♣ AK9
              ♠ Q85
              ♡ J10762
              ◇ —
              ♣ J7542
```

RECOMMENDED BIDDING

WEST	NORTH	EAST	SOUTH
		1 NT	No bid
3 NT	No bid	No bid	No bid

Bidding: Note West's three no trumps, not three diamonds. Aim for nine tricks rather than eleven, unless you have freakish distribution.

Lead: The six of hearts, fourth highest. When you have two equally long suits to lead, generally prefer the stronger. On this lead North must play the king of hearts, otherwise declarer would win the trick cheaply with the nine of hearts.

RIGHT PLAY Win the first trick and play on diamonds (your long suit). When South discards on the first lead of diamonds, you know North has all four missing diamonds. Play low from dummy and let North have his trick now. When you regain the lead, play out all your diamonds, then your heart and club winners, making nine tricks at least.

WRONG PLAY 1) Attacking any suit but diamonds after you win the lead. Suppose you cash your second heart winner before playing diamonds. Now when North wins his diamond trick, the enemy can take two spades, three hearts and a diamond, beating you by two tricks.
2) Failing to 'duck' a diamond. If you play the ace, king and queen of diamonds and then lose a diamond trick, dummy has two diamond winners, but there is no sure way of getting to dummy to cash them, as the ace of spades will capture the king. By losing a diamond on the first or second round of diamonds you preserve a *sure entry* to dummy in the diamond suit itself.

  Be prepared to lose a trick deliberately if this is necessary to set up winners in a long suit.

Hand 3: Bidding game in a suit—'finessing' to avoid a loser

Dealer South
East-West
vulnerable

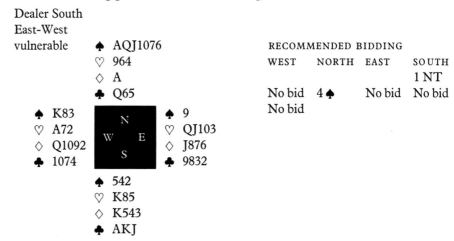

♠ AQJ1076
♡ 964
◇ A
♣ Q65

♠ K83
♡ A72
◇ Q1092
♣ 1074

♠ 9
♡ QJ103
◇ J876
♣ 9832

♠ 542
♡ K85
◇ K543
♣ AKJ

RECOMMENDED BIDDING

WEST	NORTH	EAST	SOUTH
			1 NT
No bid	4♠	No bid	No bid
No bid			

Lead: East leads the queen of hearts, top of a solid sequence. If the king is played from dummy, West plays the ace. If a low card is played from dummy, West must not play the ace, of course; instead he plays the *seven*, the start of a high-low signal to encourage a heart continuation. The defence should take three heart tricks and then switch to a minor suit.

RIGHT PLAY After losing three tricks, North cannot afford another loser in trumps, and to play the ace of trumps hoping that the king will drop is wishful thinking. The best chance is that West holds the king of spades and, if so, you can eliminate any spade loser in this way. Enter dummy and play a low spade. When West plays low, play your queen (*not* the ace). If West has the king (a 50-50 chance), your queen will win. Cross back to dummy with a club and repeat the manoeuvre ('finesse' again). Then play the ace of spades, capturing West's king, then cash your other winners, making ten tricks.

Note that if the lead were a club or a diamond you should not tackle trumps at once. It is better to win the ace of diamonds, cross to dummy with a club and then play the king of diamonds, *discarding a heart loser*. Then you can play trumps (and even afford a trump loser), making eleven tricks.

WRONG PLAY 1) Winning the fourth trick and playing the ace of spades. This will work only in the remote case where the king of spades is singleton.
2) Winning the fourth trick and playing three rounds of clubs. The enemy might trump one of your winners, and the effect of playing off all the clubs is that you cut out any entries to dummy to repeat the spade finesse if necessary.
3) Taking the spade finesse successfully but failing to repeat the finesse as often as necessary. Here two finesses are needed before the king falls under the ace.

Losers may be eliminated because of the favourable position of key cards by means of 'finesse' plays.

Hand 4: Eliminating losers by discarding them before drawing trumps

Dealer West
All vulnerable

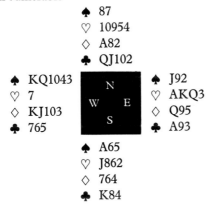

```
              ♠ 87
              ♡ 10954
              ◇ A82
              ♣ QJ102
  ♠ KQ1043           ♠ J92
  ♡ 7          N     ♡ AKQ3
  ◇ KJ103   W   E    ◇ Q95
  ♣ 765        S     ♣ A93
              ♠ A65
              ♡ J862
              ◇ 764
              ♣ K84
```

RECOMMENDED BIDDING

WEST	NORTH	EAST	SOUTH
No bid	No bid	1 NT	No bid
3 ♠	No bid	4 ♠	No bid
No bid	No bid		

Bidding: Despite his poor shape, East should feel obliged to raise spades since he has the requested three-card support. With only two spades East would bid three no trumps. Note that three no trumps could be beaten if the defence attacks clubs early.

Lead: North leads the queen of clubs, top of a solid sequence.

RIGHT PLAY Win the ace of clubs, then play the ace, king and queen of hearts, discarding your two losing clubs. Only after that, play trumps. On a club lead you see four losers: ace of spades, ace of diamonds and two clubs. If you play trumps at once, the enemy can cash four tricks straight away. You must eliminate some losers first, even though this involves a slight risk that the enemy will trump your heart winners.

On a heart or a diamond lead you should play trumps first. This is because when the enemy get the lead they cannot cash any clubs winners yet, since you still have the ace of clubs. You can discard the losing clubs on the hearts later, after the enemy teeth, their trumps, have been extracted.

WRONG PLAY Winning the ace of clubs and playing trumps or diamonds instead of immediately discarding club losers on dummy's good hearts.

With more losers than you can afford try to eliminate losers by discarding them on dummy's winners; if necessary, postpone drawing trumps to do this, but normally draw trumps as soon as possible.

Lesson 3

Part A: Raising partner's opening bid of one in a suit

TRUMP POINTS

If you have support for partner's suit, count for shortage in outside suits:
Void=5
Singleton=3
Doubleton=1

AUCTION	MEANING OF RESPONDER'S RAISE
1 ♡ : 2 ♡ or 1 ♠ : 2 ♠	Single raise=6—10 points + four-card support or better.
1 ♡ : 3 ♡ or 1 ♠ : 3 ♠	Double raise=11—12 points + four-card support or better.
1 ♡ : 4 ♡ or 1 ♠ : 4 ♠	Triple raise=less than an opening hand, usually five or more trumps, singleton or void (shut-out bid).
1 ♣ : 2 ♣ or 1 ◇ : 2 ◇	Single raise (minor)=6—10 points + four card support or better, no four-card major.
1 ♣ : 3 ♣ or 1 ◇ : 3 ◇	Double raise (minor)=11—12 points + four-card support or better, no four-card major.

COMMENTARY

To respond to an opening bid you should have 6 points or better (not necessarily HCP). With fewer than 6 points game is unlikely. You should not pass a 6 point hand since opener could be very strong, having 20 points or more, and a game could be missed.

Support for partner's suit depends on how many he has in the suit, but the combined total should be at least eight cards. For an opening bid of one in a suit opener is taken to have a four-card suit; if he rebids his suit, he has a five-card suit; if he makes a jump rebid in his suit or bids his suit a third time, he has a six-card suit.

Although you are expected to have four-card support for partner, you may give a single raise in a major suit with A x x, K x x or Q x x support, provided that you also hold a void or singleton. This is because when partner opens with one of a major he is likely to have a five-card suit or a *good* four-card suit, and with a singleton or void your trumps can be put to a useful purpose. The tough hands where you have support for partner are the 10 point hands. Usually a single raise is enough, but on a really good 10 count you might give a double raise.

You will have noticed that the immediate raises cover 6—10 and 11—12 point hands. What about hands of 13 points or more? With 13 points or more you know you have enough for game, but it would not be correct to jump straight to game. The 1 ♡ : 4 ♡ or 1 ♠ : 4 ♠ raises are based on good support and good shape but do not have much in high-card strength. Normally such a raise would not have more than 10 high-card points.

With 13—15 points and support for partner's major, bid a new suit and jump to game in partner's suit next time (for example, 1 ♡ : 2 ♣, 2 ◇ : 4 ♡). This *delayed game raise* shows a good hand. With 16 points or more and support for partner's major, jump-bid a new suit (forcing to game) and support partner's suit next time (for example, 1 ♡ : 3 ♣, 3 ◇ : 3 ♡).

With a strong hand and support for partner's minor you may have to bid delicately, partly in order to avoid bidding beyond three no trumps, which is often an easier contract than five in a minor, and partly to avoid making a bid partner might pass.

If your hand fits a major-suit raise, prefer that response to bidding a new suit or responding in no trumps; if your hand fits a minor-suit raise, prefer to bid a four-card or longer major to investigate a major-suit fit or respond in no trumps rather than raise the minor—you can always return to the minor suit later.

Use the 5—3—1 count when you have established a trump fit. Otherwise use 3—2—1 in assessing the value of semi-balanced or unbalanced hands.

Part B: Subsequent bidding after the opening suit bid has been raised

REVALUATION BY OPENER	RANGE OF OPENER'S HAND
After receiving a raise, opener revalues his hand, adding:	After revaluation
Void = 5	12—15 points: minimum
Singleton = 3	16—19 points: strong
Doubleton = 1	20-points up: super

AUCTION	ACTION BY OPENER	EXAMPLE
1 ♡ : 2 ♡ or 1 ♠ : 2 ♠ ? ?	a) Minimum 12—15: pass b) Strong 16—19: invite game. c) Super 20-up: bid game.	1 ♡ : 2 ♡, No 1 ♡ : 2 ♡, 3 ♡ 1 ♡ : 2 ♡, 4 ♡
1 ♡ : 3 ♡ or 1 ♠ : 3 ♠ ? ?	a) Minimum: pass on 12—13, bid game on 14—15. b) Strong: bid game. c) Super: investigate slam.	1 ♠ : 3 ♠, No or 4 ♠ 1 ♠ : 3 ♠, 4 ♠ See Lesson 8
1 ♡ : 4 ♡ or 1 ♠ : 4 ♠ ? ?	a) Minimum or strong: pass. b) Super plus: investigate slam.	1 ♠ : 4 ♠, No
1 ♣ : 2 ♣ or 1 ♢ : 2 ♢ ? ?	a) Minimum: pass. b) Strong: invite game. c) Super: bid game.	1 ♠ : 2 ♣, No 1 ♣ : 2 ♣, 2 NT 1 ♣ : 2 ♣, 3 NT
1 ♣ : 3 ♣ or 1 ♢ : 3 ♢ ? ?	a) Minimum: pass on 12—13, bid game on 14—15. b) Strong: bid game. c) Super: investigate slam.	1 ♣ : 3 ♣, No or 1 ♣ : 3 ♣, 3 NT See Lesson 8

COMMENTARY

Opener's rebids are largely a matter of common sense. He adds his points to those shown by responder and passes if game is impossible, invites game if game is possible but not certain, and bids game if he can count about 26 points or more between the two hands. Similarly, opener will take action if he sees that a slam is possible, but this is taken up in detail in Lesson 8.

After a single major-suit raise, there are various possible invitations to game. The most simple is raising the suit again (for example, 1 ♡ : 2 ♡, 3 ♡), but a bid of two no trumps (for example, 1 ♡ : 2 ♡, 2 NT) or a new suit bid (for example, 1 ♡ : 2 ♡, 3 ♣) are also possible. Each of these invites responder to bid game if he is maximum. The rebid of two no trumps gives responder the choice of three no trumps as well as the major-suit game if he is maximum, or to pass or bid three of the major if he is minimum. A new suit rebid is forcing, asking responder to bid game if he is maximum or if he can assist in the suit bid, otherwise to bid three of the major. Assistance is a holding of ace, king, void or singleton in the suit bid.

After a raise in a minor, the more common game to reach, if any, is game in no trumps, but it is also possible to reach game in the minor suit if the hands are more suitable for suit play. N.B. If you have opened one club on a three-card suit (in a 4—3—3—3 hand) and partner raises you to two clubs, on no account should you bid again on a 12—14 point hand: *pass*!

EXERCISES

1) Partner opens one heart.
   i) How many points is each of these hands worth?
   ii) What is your response?

a) ♠ K83
   ♡ 8743
   ◊ 6543
   ♣ 95

b) ♠ K7432
   ♡ J832
   ◊ 765
   ♣ 9

c) ♠ 8
   ♡ Q9872
   ◊ A7
   ♣ 76532

d) ♠ 98
   ♡ KJ83
   ◊ A762
   ♣ 1062

e) ♠ 97
   ♡ KQ83
   ◊ A86
   ♣ KQ42

f) ♠ 98
   ♡ Q8543
   ◊ A7
   ♣ J632

g) ♠ 54
   ♡ AJ643
   ◊ KQ72
   ♣ K3

h) ♠ A43
   ♡ Q742
   ◊ 3
   ♣ K9853

i) ♠ AJ103
   ♡ K752
   ◊ Q43
   ♣ 86

j) ♠ A74
   ♡ KQ82
   ◊ 6
   ♣ AQJ95

2) Partner opens one club. What is your response?

a) ♠ A54
   ♡ 76
   ◊ 543
   ♣ K9432

b) ♠ 743
   ♡ KQ52
   ◊ 76
   ♣ J932

c) ♠ A73
   ♡ 53
   ◊ 942
   ♣ AQJ43

d) ♠ AQ73
   ♡ 75
   ◊ 43
   ♣ A9543

e) ♠ 9843
   ♡ A962
   ◊ 7
   ♣ KQJ6

3) You opened one spade and partner raised to two spades.
   i) What is your hand now worth?
   ii) What is your rebid?

a) ♠ AQJ7
   ♡ K843
   ◊ Q5
   ♣ 872

b) ♠ AQJ72
   ♡ KQ92
   ◊ 6
   ♣ AJ10

c) ♠ AQ1043
   ♡ K7
   ◊ A84
   ♣ A92

d) ♠ KQ1082
   ♡ 72
   ◊ AK93
   ♣ 86

e) ♠ AQ9743
   ♡ —
   ◊ AKJ4
   ♣ J72

4) You opened one spade and partner raised to three spades. What is your rebid?

a) ♠ AJ82
   ♡ 9742
   ◊ AK
   ♣ J73

b) ♠ AQ973
   ♡ 872
   ◊ KQ
   ♣ J95

c) ♠ AQ1043
   ♡ K7
   ◊ K92
   ♣ A96

d) ♠ AQ963
   ♡ 7
   ◊ AJ876
   ♣ 86

e) ♠ A976
   ♡ KQ10
   ◊ AJ3
   ♣ KJ10

5) You opened one club and partner raised to two clubs. What do you rebid?

a) ♠ KJ7
   ♡ 6542
   ◊ AJ3
   ♣ KQ5

b) ♠ AQ74
   ♡ 76
   ◊ K82
   ♣ K932

c) ♠ AQ986
   ♡ 6
   ◊ 8
   ♣ AKJ743

d) ♠ QJ4
   ♡ A63
   ◊ AQJ
   ♣ KQ42

e) ♠ A3
   ♡ A4
   ◊ Q94
   ♣ AK9853

6) You opened one club and partner raised to three clubs. What do you rebid?

a) ♠ AKQ
   ♡ Q53
   ◊ K42
   ♣ Q762

b) ♠ AQ72
   ♡ 6
   ◊ K43
   ♣ KQ872

c) ♠ AQJ4
   ♡ K6
   ◊ K8
   ♣ 98432

d) ♠ AJ73
   ♡ KJ
   ◊ 743
   ♣ K542

e) ♠ KJ32
   ♡ A9
   ◊ KQJ
   ♣ A873

Hand 1: Raising partner's minor suit opening—avoiding the error of blocking your long suit

Dealer North
Nil vulnerable

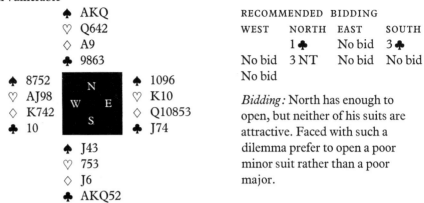

♠ AKQ
♡ Q642
◇ A9
♣ 9863

♠ 8752   ♠ 1096
♡ AJ98   ♡ K10
◇ K742   ◇ Q10853
♣ 10   ♣ J74

♠ J43
♡ 753
◇ J6
♣ AKQ52

RECOMMENDED BIDDING

WEST	NORTH	EAST	SOUTH
	1♣	No bid	3♣
No bid	3 NT	No bid	No bid
No bid			

Bidding: North has enough to open, but neither of his suits are attractive. Faced with such a dilemma prefer to open a poor minor suit rather than a poor major.

Lead: East leads the five of diamonds, fourth highest of his longest suit. Declarer should play dummy's jack on this, just in case East has led from KQxxx, because then the jack would win the trick and North would make two diamond tricks instead of one. However, West plays the king on the jack, and North wins with the ace.

RIGHT PLAY North has an easy nine tricks (three spades, one diamond and five clubs) unless he is careless. Win the ace of diamonds, and play the ace, king and queen of clubs, *being very careful to play the* 986 *of clubs from your own hand.* Then play the five of clubs, dropping your carefully preserved three of clubs under the five; then cash the two of clubs and the three spade tricks, making nine tricks.

WRONG PLAY 1) Playing the three of clubs on the first, second or third round of clubs. This means the fourth round of clubs will be won in the North hand instead of dummy. This would leave a club winner in dummy, but no way to get there to cash it, for you have *blocked* the clubs.
2) Winning the ace of diamonds and playing a heart or a diamond. This lets the enemy into the lead to cash four diamond tricks and two heart tricks defeating your contract.
3) Failing to cash the fifth club winner while in dummy. Again you will have a club winner stranded in dummy.

Be careful in the cards that you play. If you see that dummy has no entry outside its long suit, take care not to block the suit. Make sure that the lead is in dummy when you want to cash the long cards in that suit.

Hand 2: The triple raise, a shut-out bid—the cross-ruff

Dealer East
North-South
vulnerable

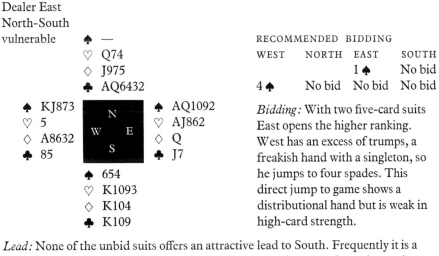

♠ —
♡ Q74
♢ J975
♣ AQ6432

♠ KJ873   ♠ AQ1092
♡ 5   ♡ AJ862
♢ A8632   ♢ Q
♣ 85   ♣ J7

♠ 654
♡ K1093
♢ K104
♣ K109

RECOMMENDED BIDDING

WEST	NORTH	EAST	SOUTH
		1 ♠	No bid
4 ♠	No bid	No bid	No bid

Bidding: With two five-card suits East opens the higher ranking. West has an excess of trumps, a freakish hand with a singleton, so he jumps to four spades. This direct jump to game shows a distributional hand but is weak in high-card strength.

Lead: None of the unbid suits offers an attractive lead to South. Frequently it is a good idea to lead a trump (by starting with a trump lead you cut down dummy's ruffing ability), and that is South's best lead here.

RIGHT PLAY Win the trump lead, play the ace of hearts and the ace of diamonds, and then ruff hearts in dummy and diamonds in your hand. You ruff backwards and forwards, making each of your trumps separately. This play is called a 'cross-ruff', because you do not draw trumps but use your trumps and dummy's trumps separately. This way you win the first spade lead, two red aces, four ruffs in dummy and four ruffs in your hand, making eleven tricks.

WRONG PLAY 1) Drawing three rounds of trumps to get rid of South's trumps. This would limit you to three top trumps, two ruffs in dummy, two ruffs in your hand and two red aces, one down (if the defenders play properly). On some hands your trumps are more valuable for ruffing than for drawing the enemy trumps.
2) Drawing two rounds of trumps. This will probably limit you to ten tricks on the same reasoning as above.

Where you are short in dummy's long suit and dummy is short in your long suit, you may profit by playing on a cross-ruff instead of drawing trumps.

Hand 3: Inviting partner to bid game—delaying drawing trumps—ruffing losers in dummy

Dealer South
Both vulnerable

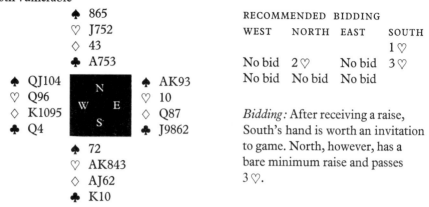

♠ 865
♡ J752
◇ 43
♣ A753

♠ QJ104
♡ Q96
◇ K1095
♣ Q4

♠ AK93
♡ 10
◇ Q87
♣ J9862

♠ 72
♡ AK843
◇ AJ62
♣ K10

RECOMMENDED BIDDING

WEST	NORTH	EAST	SOUTH
			1 ♡
No bid	2 ♡	No bid	3 ♡
No bid	No bid	No bid	

Bidding: After receiving a raise, South's hand is worth an invitation to game. North, however, has a bare minimum raise and passes 3 ♡.

Lead: West leads the queen of spades, top of a solid sequence. A diamond is also possible, but the spades, being solid, should be preferred. A trump lead or club lead would be poor. On the queen of spades East plays the nine, encouraging West to continue spades. The defence continues spades, and South ruffs the third round.

RIGHT PLAY South ruffs the third round of spades and plays *one* round of trumps, then ace and another diamond. When South next regains the lead, he will play a second round of trumps, then ruff a diamond in dummy, return to his hand and ruff his last diamond in dummy. He loses two spades, one heart and one diamond, and makes nine tricks. The key to the hand is giving up a diamond trick before drawing two rounds of trumps, so that you are able to make sure of ruffing two diamonds in dummy.

WRONG PLAY 1) Drawing three rounds of trumps as soon as you get the lead. This leaves only one trump in dummy to ruff your diamonds, but you need two trumps in dummy since you need to ruff two diamonds in dummy.

2) Drawing two rounds of trumps and then giving up a diamond trick. This will have the same effect as drawing three rounds of trumps, since if the defence is awake West will win the diamond trick and play his good queen of trumps, drawing two of your trumps.

Where you need dummy's trumps to ruff your losers, be careful neither to draw too many rounds of trumps yourself nor to let the enemy draw your trumps. If necessary, give up a trick before playing trumps.

Hand 4: The delayed raise—ruffing losers in dummy—setting up winners in dummy to obtain a discard

Dealer West
Both vulnerable

North-South have
part-score of 90

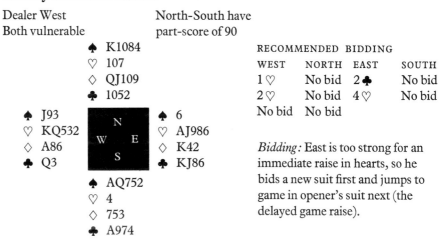

	♠ K1084	
	♡ 107	
	◇ QJ109	
	♣ 1052	
♠ J93	N	♠ 6
♡ KQ532	W E	♡ AJ986
◇ A86	S	◇ K42
♣ Q3		♣ KJ86
	♠ AQ752	
	♡ 4	
	◇ 753	
	♣ A974	

RECOMMENDED BIDDING

WEST	NORTH	EAST	SOUTH
1 ♡	No bid	2 ♣	No bid
2 ♡	No bid	4 ♡	No bid
No bid	No bid		

Bidding: East is too strong for an immediate raise in hearts, so he bids a new suit first and jumps to game in opener's suit next (the delayed game raise).

Lead: North would lead the queen of diamonds, top of a solid sequence. In choosing your lead, first choose which suit to lead, next the correct card in the suit. Normally you would steer away from a suit bid by the enemy.

RIGHT PLAY Win the ace of diamonds (or the king) and draw trumps. Unless you have a good reason not to draw trumps, draw trumps as soon as possible. Two rounds of trumps is enough. Then play the queen of clubs, and if the enemy do not take the ace of clubs, continue with clubs. This establishes club winners in dummy, and when you regain the lead, you can discard your losing diamond on the third round of clubs. Next give up a spade trick and trump two spades in dummy later, making eleven tricks.

WRONG PLAY 1) Failing to draw trumps.
2) Drawing trumps but failing to play clubs at once. You will still make ten tricks but by setting up a club winner to discard the losing diamond you can make eleven tricks.
3) Playing more than three rounds of trumps. You have three spades in your hand, two of which you have to ruff in dummy. If you draw more than three rounds of trumps, you will not have enough trumps in dummy to ruff your spade losers. If you combine mistakes (2) and (3), you could even go down.

One way to get rid of losers is to discard them on dummy's winners: this may require you to set up winners in dummy in order to obtain the discards. Another way is to ruff losers in dummy: to do this you must not draw too many of dummy's trumps.

Lesson 4

Part A: No trump responses to partner's opening bid of one in a suit

RESPONSE	SHOWS	EXAMPLE
1 NT	6—10 points and no support for partner (exceptionally 1 ♣ : 1 NT shows 8—10 points and a flat hand).	1 ♡ : 1 NT 1 ♠ : 1 NT
2 NT	11—12 points + balanced hand.	1 ◇ : 2 NT
3 NT	13—15 points + balanced hand + stoppers in the unbid suits (stoppers = Jxxx, Qxx, Kx or better).	1 ♣ : 3 NT 1 ♡ : 3 NT

COMMENTARY

Where partner opens with one of a suit and you have 6—9 points, you have two basic options: you may raise partner's suit (if you have support), *or* you may make a bid at the one-level. If you have no suit you can bid at the one-level and you have the 6—9 point minimum responding hand, your last available bid is one no trump.[1] That is why the response of one no trump is not necessarily always a balanced hand.

The sequence 1 ♣ : 1 NT, however, is the exception. Firstly it shows 8—10 points (not 6—10), and secondly responder will be balanced. The reason is that if responder has 6—7 points or an unbalanced hand there will always be some other bid available. He must have a four-card suit he can bid or have support for opener's suit.

The 10 point hand is a problem. If you have a reasonable suit, it is preferable to bid the suit rather than one no trump, and if your hand is well packed with intermediate cards (tens and nines), it is reasonable to upgrade it and respond two no trumps. However, with 10 points in a 4—3—3—3 hand you will generally find that the more conservative one no trump is the winning action. The 4—3—3—3 hand is a very poor playing hand, and you need your full quota of high-card strength to make a game or a slam with such a hand.

The response of two no trumps shows a goodish hand with balanced shape and denies support for partner if he opened with a major-suit bid. Ideally, the response of two no trumps should have stoppers in the unbid suits, but this cannot be guaranteed. Where you have a suit unguarded, it is often better to bid a suit of your own rather than jump to two no trumps, and with 11—12 points there is no restriction on bidding your suit: you have ample strength to introduce a new suit at the two-level.

The response of three no trumps is a wasteful bid because it uses up three levels of bidding and inhibits partner from investigating other possible game contracts. It is best restricted to 4—3—3—3 hands of 13—15 points with the unbid suits guarded. With other balanced hands of 13—15 points a better approach is to bid a new suit and listen to what partner has to say. A new suit by responder is a forcing bid, and you need not fear that partner will pass. After his rebid, you can still jump to three no trumps if you then judge that to be the best contract.

Where you hold 16 or more high-card points, you alert partner to the good news by making a jump bid in a new suit (for example, 1 ◇ : 2 ♡ or 1 ◇ : 3 ♣). When you later follow up with a bid of no trumps, partner will know you have a powerful balanced hand.

[1] With 8—9 points and a very good suit you may bid it at the two-level.

Part B: Subsequent bidding after a no trump response to an opening suit bid

After a response of one no trump: for example, 1: ♡ 1 NT

1) *Pass.* With a minimum hand not unsuitable for no trumps opener should pass (for example, 1 ♡ : 1 NT, No bid). Even with a minimum 5—4—2—2 shape it is not attractive to remove one no trump. With 5—3—3—2 shape it is best to pass one no trump—do *not* rebid your five-card suit.

2) *Raise no trumps.* With 17—18 points in a no trumpish hand invite game via two no trumps (for example, 1 ♠ : 1 NT, 2 NT). With a good 16 points (5—3—3—2 shape or good intermediate cards) the invitation raise to two no trumps is the expert move. With a balanced hand of 19 points you have enough to justify raising to three no trumps (for example, 1 ♡ : 1 NT, 3 NT).

Note that after the 1 ♣ : 1 NT you may raise to three no trumps on 17 points or better since responder promises 8—10.

3) *Rebid own suit.* At the two-level (for example, 1 ♠ : 1 NT, 2 ♠) with a *one-suiter* unsuitable for no trumps and 12—15 points. Usually the suit will be a six-card suit, but occasionally an excellent five-card suit is acceptable if the hand is unsuitable for no trumps (or if you have a minimum two-suiter with the second suit higher ranking than the first).

At the three-level (for example, 1 ♠ : 1 NT, 3 ♠) with a *one-suiter* unsuitable for no trumps and 16—18 points. The suit will be a very good six-card suit, and responder should raise with a doubleton or better support.

At game-level (for example, 1 ♠ : 1 NT, 4 ♠) with a one-suiter unsuitable for no trumps and usually 19 points or more. If the suit is longer than six cards, you can jump to game with even fewer points.

4) *Bid a new suit.* At the two-level (for example, 1 ♡ : 1 NT, 2 ♣) with a two-suiter unsuitable for no trumps and 12—18 high-card points. The refusal to play in no trumps indicates a holding of at least 5—4 in the suits bid, and responder should be quick to support the first bid suit with three-card support. If opener's second suit is higher-ranking than the first (for example, 1 ♡ : 1 NT, 2 ♠), opener will have 15—18 high-card points and his first suit will be longer than his second. Bidding at the two-level in a suit higher than the suit opened is termed 'reversing'.

At the three-level (for example, 1 ♠ : 1 NT, 3 ♣) with a two-suiter unsuitable for no trumps (at least 5—4 in the suits bid) and 19 or more points. This jump bid in a new suit is called a 'jump shift' and is forcing to game. Responder will take suitable action but will not pass below game.

After a response of two no trumps: for example, 1 ♡: 2 NT

With 13 points or less opener has two weak actions available: he may pass two no trumps or he may rebid his suit (for example, 1 ♡ : 2 NT, 3 ♡), which responder should pass. With 14 or more points opener should go to game, bidding three no trumps with a balanced hand (for example, 1 ♡ : 2 NT, 3 NT) or jumping to game in his major with a six-card suit (for example, 1 ♡ : 2 NT, 4 ♡).

Where you have a known eight-card fit, do not forget to count any void, singleton or doubletons on the 5—3—1 scale.

Where opener has an unbalanced two-suiter, he should bid his second suit over 2 NT (for example, 1 ♡ : 2 NT, 3 ♢ or 1 ♡ : 2 NT, 3 ♠). This bid of a new suit at the three-level is forcing for one round and indicates that opener is not keen on trying for game in no trumps.

After a response of three no trumps: for example, 1 ♡ : 3 NT

Opener will usually pass unless his hand is seriously unbalanced or he has hopes for slam. If opener bids game in his major (for example, 1 ♡ : 3 NT, 4 ♡), he has no further ambitions on the hand and responder must pass. With 19—20 points and balanced shape opener should raise to four no trumps, inviting responder to bid six no trumps with a maximum hand.

EXERCISES

1) Partner opens one heart. What do you respond on each of these hands?

a) ♠ K43	b) ♠ KQ6	c) ♠ A62	d) ♠ KQ62	e) ♠ 74
♡ Q6	♡ A43	♡ J83	♡ 76	♡ 83
◇ 9843	◇ 7432	◇ KJ7	◇ Q983	◇ AJ843
♣ J976	♣ 854	♣ J842	♣ 984	♣ Q432

f) ♠ K87	g) ♠ J95	h) ♠ AQ43	i) ♠ 87	j) ♠ KJ10
♡ A83	♡ K432	♡ 76	♡ QJ4	♡ 87
◇ Q963	◇ AJ86	◇ K87	◇ A982	◇ QJ103
♣ QJ2	♣ Q8	♣ Q942	♣ KJ43	♣ K1092

2) What would your answers to Exercise 1 have been if partner had opened one spade?

3) Partner opens one heart. What do you respond on each of these hands?

a) ♠ KJ4	b) ♠ KJ43	c) ♠ KJ4	d) ♠ KQ	e) ♠ K83
♡ 873	♡ 87	♡ 87	♡ 843	♡ AQ43
◇ AQ4	◇ AQ4	◇ AQ43	◇ AQ42	◇ K9
♣ K1065	♣ K1065	♣ AK106	♣ K1065	♣ Q762

4) What would your answers to Exercise 3 have been if partner had opened one spade?

5) You opened one spade, and partner responded one no trump. What do you now bid on these hands?

a) ♠ KJ43	b) ♠ KQ632	c) ♠ KQ8643	d) ♠ KQ8643	e) ♠ AQ843
♡ 8742	♡ A7	♡ A92	♡ A92	♡ K72
◇ AQ	◇ QJ4	◇ 7	◇ 7	◇ A98
♣ K97	♣ J98	♣ QJ2	♣ AQ7	♣ A7

f) ♠ AKQ4	g) ♠ A9762	h) ♠ AQ1043	i) ♠ KJ843	j) ♠ KQ63
♡ J1032	♡ A8	♡ 7	♡ Q7	♡ AJ10
◇ KQ9	◇ QJ432	◇ AQJ4	◇ J732	◇ J65
♣ A8	♣ Q	♣ AQ2	♣ AQ	♣ AK9

6) You opened one heart, and partner responded two no trumps. What action do you now take on these hands?

a) ♠ K8	b) ♠ 873	c) ♠ A83	d) ♠ KJ43	e) ♠ 4
♡ QJ93	♡ AQ86	♡ A983	♡ AQ863	♡ AQ862
◇ 764	◇ KQ9	◇ KQ4	◇ KJ8	◇ 76
♣ AQ107	♣ KQ2	♣ KQJ	♣ 6	♣ AK943

f) ♠ QJ4	g) ♠ KQ	h) ♠ A105	i) ♠ Q6	j) ♠ A62
♡ K109862	♡ AJ10743	♡ 97643	♡ AJ743	♡ AJ743
◇ 7	◇ 6	◇ KQ8	◇ KQ82	◇ KQ83
♣ AJ4	♣ KJ42	♣ AQ	♣ 87	♣ 6

7) What action would you take on the hands in Exercise 6 if partner's response had been three no trumps?

Hand 1: Play at trick one—entries—finessing

Dealer North
Nil Vulnerable

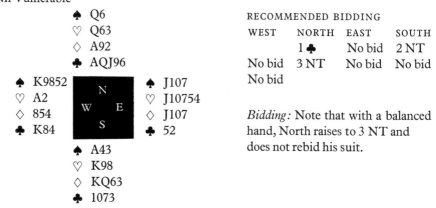

	♠ Q6		
	♡ Q63		
	♢ A92		
	♣ AQJ96		

♠ K9852   ♠ J107
♡ A2   ♡ J10754
♢ 854   ♢ J107
♣ K84   ♣ 52

    ♠ A43
    ♡ K98
    ♢ KQ63
    ♣ 1073

RECOMMENDED BIDDING

WEST	NORTH	EAST	SOUTH
	1 ♣	No bid	2 NT
No bid	3 NT	No bid	No bid
No bid			

Bidding: Note that with a balanced hand, North raises to 3 NT and does not rebid his suit.

Lead: West leads the five of spades, fourth highest of his longest suit. When East gets the lead, he should return his partner's suit. Make it a rule to return partner's suit, *unless you have a good reason to switch.*

RIGHT PLAY On the lead South should play the queen of spades from dummy. South must hope West has led away from the king of spades in which case the queen of spades will win the trick. (However, if South's spades were A103 or K103, it would be correct to play low in dummy as this makes sure of two tricks—check it!).

After the queen of spades wins, South should play a diamond to his hand to take the club finesse. When the club finesse works, South can knock out the ace of hearts for a heart trick and the diamonds split 3—3, so South makes two spades, one heart, four diamonds and five clubs, a total of twelve tricks.

WRONG PLAY 1) Failing to play the spade queen at trick one. This limits you to one spade trick, and were the club finesse to lose, you would go down.
2) Winning with the queen of spades and then playing a heart. This is very risky, because if West wins the heart and plays back a heart you would again go down if the club finesse lost.
3) Failing to take the club finesse. If you play the ace of clubs and give up a club, you make only ten tricks. If you fail to play the queen of spades at trick one and fail to take the club finesse, you go down.
4) If you discard a diamond on the good clubs, you will in fact make only three diamond tricks instead of four.

Work out the situations where you should play low in dummy at trick one and where you should play high.

Hand 2: Play at trick one—combining a number of chances

Dealer East
North-South vulnerable

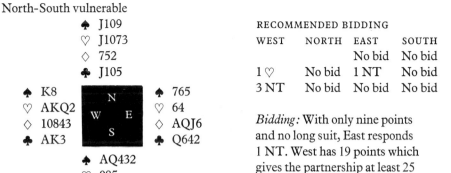

```
              ♠ J109
              ♡ J1073
              ◇ 752
              ♣ J105
  ♠ K8                    ♠ 765
  ♡ AKQ2      N           ♡ 64
  ◇ 10843   W   E         ◇ AQJ6
  ♣ AK3       S           ♣ Q642
              ♠ AQ432
              ♡ 985
              ◇ K9
              ♣ 987
```

RECOMMENDED BIDDING

WEST	NORTH	EAST	SOUTH
		No bid	No bid
1 ♡	No bid	1 NT	No bid
3 NT	No bid	No bid	No bid

Bidding: With only nine points and no long suit, East responds 1 NT. West has 19 points which gives the partnership at least 25 points together, so he raises to 3 NT.

Lead: South leads the three of spades, fourth highest. It is best to lead your longest suit unless the enemy have bid that suit. If North gets the lead, he should return partner's suit.

RIGHT PLAY East must play the king of spades from dummy at trick one. It is his only chance to make a trick with the king, and he has to hope the ace is with South.

After the king of spades wins, East can count eight tricks for sure (one spade, three hearts, three diamonds and one club). The ninth trick could come from a successful finesse in diamonds, *or* from a 3—3 split in clubs so that the thirteenth club is a winner.

It is vital to tackle these chances in the right order. If you take the diamond finesse first and it loses, the enemy take four spade tricks, defeating you, and you don't have an opportunity to try the clubs. But if you try for the 3—3 club break first and that doesn't come off, you can still try the diamond finesse.

In fact, clubs are 3—3, so the thirteenth club is a winner. Do *not* take the diamond finesse, for if it loses you may go down in your contract which is now certain.

WRONG PLAY 1) Failing to play the king of spades from dummy at trick one. North wins, returns a spade, and the defence takes the first five tricks.
2) Winning with the king of spades but playing diamonds before clubs. South wins the king of diamonds and cashes four more spade tricks.
3) Winning the king of spades and playing three rounds of clubs but forgetting whether the last club is high or not.
4) Winning the king of spades, playing the top hearts and discarding a club on the third round of hearts. This throws away your ninth trick.

Where you have a number of chances for your contract, try and combine as many chances as possible rather than stake everything on one chance.

Hand 3: Play at trick one—hold-up play—finessing

Dealer South
Both vulnerable

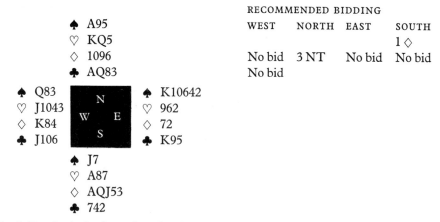

♠ A95
♡ KQ5
◇ 1096
♣ AQ83

♠ Q83
♡ J1043
◇ K84
♣ J106

♠ K10642
♡ 962
◇ 72
♣ K95

♠ J7
♡ A87
◇ AQJ53
♣ 742

RECOMMENDED BIDDING

WEST	NORTH	EAST	SOUTH
			1◇
No bid	3 NT	No bid	No bid
No bid			

Lead: East leads the four of spades, fourth highest. West plays the queen. West should return partner's suit when he gets the lead.

RIGHT PLAY When West plays the queen of spades at trick one, North must play low (hold-up play). West plays another spade, and again North plays low. The third spade is won by the ace. North now leads the ten of diamonds for a finesse, which loses. But because of North's precaution in holding-up twice with the ace of spades West has no more spades to give his partner the lead.

If West now plays a club, North must play the ace of clubs, not the queen. North makes one spade, three hearts, four diamonds and one club.

WRONG PLAY 1) Failing to play the jack of spades from dummy at trick one. This does not cost on the actual hand but would cost a trick if East had led from ♠KQxxx (but if North held A10x, playing low in dummy would guarantee two tricks).

2) Winning the ace of spades on the first or second round of spades. Now when the diamond finesse loses to West, he still has a spade left and can put East into the lead. The defenders would thus make the king of diamonds and four spade tricks.

3) Holding up the ace of spades until the third round but then playing three rounds of hearts before tackling diamonds. This sets up a heart trick for the defence and would set up two heart tricks for them if they split 5—2.

4) Holding up the ace of spades until the third round, tackling diamonds next, but falling for the club finesse trap.

Unless you fear a switch to some other suit, it often pays to hold up a winner in the enemy long suit in order to exhaust one defender of his cards in that suit; if your contract is secure do not jeopardize it for the sake of an overtrick.

Hand 4: Handling a trump suit to guard against adverse distributions

Dealer West
Nil vulnerable

```
                 ♠ A765
                 ♡ J972
                 ◇ 9652
                 ♣ 3
       ♠ 8                    ♠ Q43
       ♡ AK86      N          ♡ Q1043
       ◇ 73     W   E         ◇ KQ8
       ♣ AQJ842    S          ♣ K97
                 ♠ KJ1092
                 ♡ 5
                 ◇ AJ104
                 ♣ 1065
```

RECOMMENDED BIDDING

WEST	NORTH	EAST	SOUTH
1 ♣	No bid	2 NT	No bid
3 ♡	No bid	4 ♡	No bid
No bid	No bid		

Bidding: With an unbalanced two-suiter, West rebids in his second suit. East has support for hearts and raises to game.

Lead: Sometimes a singleton is a good lead against a suit contract but not where you hold four or more trumps. In such a case you should lead your long suit, trying to force declarer to ruff. North should lead a diamond or a spade. If he leads a spade, he should lead the ace, not a low one. Against a suit contract it is poor tactics to lead a low card away from an ace.

RIGHT PLAY If the enemy lead ace and another spade, you ruff, play the ace of hearts and the king of hearts, discovering that South started with only one heart, then a low heart, and if North plays low, you play dummy's ten (as South has no more hearts), then draw North's last trump and play out all your clubs. You make one ruff, four hearts and six clubs. If the lead is a diamond, the play is essentially the same, making eleven tricks.

WRONG PLAY 1) Ruffing the second spade and failing to draw trumps. Suppose you play clubs: North ruffs the second club, plays a diamond to South's ace, and South plays another club for North to ruff. One down.
2) Tackling trumps the wrong way. If you play the queen of hearts on the first or second round of trumps, North must make a heart trick. The ace and king first guards against the given situation and is a cost-nothing precaution.
3) Failing to draw all the trumps. If you leave North with one or more trumps, he may ruff clubs and beat the contract.
4) Drawing all the trumps and trying to set up a diamond trick. South wins the ace of diamonds and cashes all his spade tricks. If you have no trumps left to guard you against spades, you must cash all your club winners.

When drawing trumps take whatever precautions you can to guard against unfavourable splits.

Lesson 5

Part A: Responding in a new suit after an opening suit bid

	EXAMPLES
The one-over-one response (new suit at the one-level) shows:	1♣ : 1◇
	1♣ : 1♡
a) 6—15 points;	1♣ : 1♠
	1◇ : 1♡
b) at least a four-card suit and is forcing for one round.	1◇ : 1♠
	1♡ : 1♠

	EXAMPLES
The two-over-one response (new suit at the two-level) shows:	1◇ : 2♣
	1♡ : 2♣
a) 8—15 points;	1♡ : 2◇
	1♠ : 2♣
b) at least a four-card suit and is forcing for one round.	1♠ : 2◇
	1♠ : 2♡

	EXAMPLES
The jump shift response (jump bid in a new suit) shows:	1♣ : 2◇
	1◇ : 2♡
16 points or more and is forcing to game.	1♡ : 3♣
	1♠ : 3◇

WHICH SUIT TO BID IN RESPONSE
a) With a long suit bid it.
b) With two long suits bid the longer first. With two five-card suits bid the higher ranking first.
c) With four-card suits only bid them 'up-the-line', i.e., cheapest first.

N.B. The rule requiring at least 8 points for a new suit at the two-level overrides the above rules.

	EXAMPLES
A double or triple jump in a new suit shows the same values as a	1♣ : 3♡
non-vulnerable three- or four-opening (showing a weak hand	1♣ : 4♠
with a very long suit—see Lesson 6), and any subsequent	1◇ : 3♠
bidding is the same as after such an opening.	1◇ : 4♡
	1♡ : 3♠
	1♡ : 4♠
	1♠ : 4♡

COMMENTARY

Note the wide range of both the one-over-one and the two-over-one response. Since responder may have enough points for game, opener is obliged to bid again. As far as responder is concerned there are no restrictions on the quality of the suits he is allowed to bid; he may bid any four-card (or longer) suit.

Sometimes as responder you may have two or three possible responses available. Give preference as follows:

If partner opened a major, prefer:

a) to raise his major;

b) to bid no trumps;

c) to bid a minor.

If partner opened a minor, prefer:

a) to bid a major;

b) to bid no trumps;

c) to raise his minor.

This assumes that your hand fits the possible responses and that you do have a choice as to which response to make. If you have only one possible response, you have no problem.

Where you have 8 or 9 points, prefer a response of one no trump to a two-over-one response, unless you have a very good five-card or longer suit. In other words, the two-over-one response is usually based on 10 points or more. With a 10 point hand and 4—3—3—3 shape it is occasionally best to respond one no trump where your suit is poor and you have no intermediate cards.

You should note that in the sequence 1 ♠ : 2 ♡ responder guarantees a five-card heart suit at least, so that opener may raise hearts with any three-card support.

The jump-shift response showing 16 or more points can be based on your own good suit or suits, *or* on a balanced hand, *or* a hand with support for partner. In these last two cases you should make your jump bid in a powerful three-card minor suit rather than a weakish four-card suit. You will clarify your hand with your next bid and in the meantime you are bidding where your strength lies.

Part B: Subsequent bidding after a response in a new suit. N.B. Opener cannot pass; he must rebid to describe his hand

REBIDDING AFTER A ONE-OVER-ONE RESPONSE

TYPE OF ACTION	EXAMPLES AUCTION	SHOWING
Rebid own suit		*Using 3—2—1 scale*
Simple rebid	1 ♡ : 1 ♠ 2 ♡	Minimum hand (12—15)+likely six-card suit.
Jump rebid	1 ♡ : 1 ♠ 3 ♡	Strong hand (16—19)+strong six-card suit.
Game rebid	1 ♡ : 1 ♠ 4 ♡	Super hand (20-up)+excellent six- or seven-card suit.
Raise responder's suit		*Using 5—3—1 scale*
Simple raise	1 ◇ : 1 ♠ 2 ♠	minimum hand (12—15)+three- or four-card support.
Jump raise	1 ◇ : 1 ♠ 3 ♠	Strong hand (16—19)+four-card support.
Game raise	1 ◇ : 1 ♠ 4 ♠	Super hand (20-up)+four-card support.
Bid no-trumps at one-level	1 ♣ : 1 ♡ 1 NT	*High-card points only* 12—14 (if using a strong no trump)+balanced shape. 15—16 (if using a weak no trump)+balanced shape.
Jump no trumps	1 ♣ : 1 ♡ 2NT	17—18+balanced shape.
Game in no trumps	1 ♣ : 1 ♡ 3NT	19 points+balanced shape.
Bid a new suit at one-level	1 ♣ : 1 ♡ 1 ♠	*High-card points only* Ambiguous (12—18), at least 4—4 in the suits bid.
At two-level a) Lower ranking than suit opened	1 ♡ : 1 ♠ 2 ♣	Ambiguous (12—18), first suit bid usually five-cards long.
b) Higher ranking than suit opened	1 ♣ : 1 ♠ 2 ♡	Strong (15—18 points), first suit (at least five-cards long) is longer than the second suit.
Jump shift	1 ♣ : 1 ♡ 2 ♠	Super hand (19-up). Forcing to game. The jump shift is the only forcing bid by opener after a one-over-one response.

TYPE OF ACTION	EXAMPLES	SHOWING
Rebid own suit		*Use 3—2—1 scale*
Simple rebid	1 ♡ : 2 ♣ 2 ♡	Minimum hand (12—15)+five-card suit.
Jump rebid	1 ♡ : 2 ♣ 3 ♡	Strong hand (16—17)+strong six-card suit.
Game rebid	1 ♡ : 2 ♣ 4 ♡	Powerful hand (18-up)+excellent six-or seven-card suit.
Raise responder's suit		*Use 5—3—1 scale*
Simple raise	1 ♠ : 2 ♣ 3 ♣	Minimum hand (12—15)+support for responder.
Jump raise	1 ♠ : 2 ♣ 4 ♣	Powerful hand+excellent support for responder. Forcing to game.
Game raise	1 ♠ : 2 ♡ 4 ♡	Strong hand enough for game opposite 10 points.
Bid no trumps		*High-card points only*
2 NT	1 ♡ : 2 ♣ 2 NT	15—16 HCP+balanced hand (likely to have a five-card major).
3 NT	1 ♡ : 2 ♣ 3 NT	17—19 HCP+balanced hand.
Bid a new suit At two-level		*High-card points only*
a) Lower ranking than suit opened	1 ♡ : 2 ♣ 2 ♢	Ambiguous (12—16), at least 4—4 in suits. Responder will usually bid again.
b) Higher ranking than suit opened	1 ♡ : 2 ♣ 2 ♠	Strong hand (15—18), first suit longer than second (at least 5—4). Responder cannot pass.
At three-level	1 ♡ : 2 ♢ 3 ♣	Strong hand (15-up), at least 5—4 in suits bid. Responder cannot pass.
Jump shift	1 ♡ : 2 ♣ 3 ♢	Strong or super hand (17-up), at least 5—4 in suits bid. Forcing to game.

COMMENTARY

Subsequent bidding after a suit response is quite a complex area. It is not easy to provide simple rules since judgment plays a considerable part, but the two foregoing tables cover the most important areas.

Whenever responder bids a new suit, opener's aim should be to find a descriptive bid, showing his point range and distribution, if possible. It is important to note that after a one-over-one response only the jump shift is technically forcing (although many jump rebids are highly encouraging and rarely passed in practice).

The following guides will help you in the many situations that occur in later bidding not covered by the charts.

1) AFTER A JUMP SHIFT

If partner responded with a jump shift, say to yourself, 'What would my rebid have been if partner had simply responded with a change of suit?' Then make the same rebid, but one level higher. For example, you open one diamond and partner jump shifts with two hearts. Ask yourself what rebid you would have made over a response of one heart from partner. If the answer is one spade, bid now two spades. If the answer is two hearts, bid now three hearts. If the answer is one no trump, bid now two no-trumps, and so on.

2) FORCING BIDS

Although the charts appear complicated as to which sequences are forcing, the following rule is very simple and very logical.

If the bidding has shown that the partnership must have enough points for game, you cannot pass below game.

If partner's bids show that there may yet be enough points for game, you cannot pass.

A bid is droppable (i.e., not forcing) only if it is clear that there *cannot* be enough points for game. To say that a bid is not forcing does not mean that you have to pass; it just means that you are not compelled to bid again. You may pass if you feel the best contract has been reached. Thus, suppose partner opens one heart and you respond one no trump. If partner rebids two clubs, you are not forced to bid, but you would be expected to bid two hearts if you prefer hearts to clubs, etc.

Some handy rules: *A bid in a new suit at the three-level is forcing. A bid of the fourth suit is forcing. Any new suit after suit agreement is forcing.*

3) 'THE REVERSE'

The following bidding sequences constitute a 'reverse' by opener.

1♣ : 1♡	1♣ : 1♠	1♣ : 1 NT	1♢ : 1♠	1♢ : 1 NT	1♡ : 2♢
2♢	2♡	2♢	2♡	2♡	2♠

Therefore, a reverse by opener is a simple (not a 'jump') rebid at the two-level in a new suit higher ranking than the suit opened. A reverse shows 15 high-card points up, and the first suit bid must always be longer than the second suit bid.

4) BIDDING SUITS TO SHOW DISTRIBUTION

Where partner bids two suits, you will usually find that his hand is unbalanced, and usually he will have five cards in his first suit bid. This is not invariably so but it is, nevertheless, a good guide. After partner bids two suits, you may support the first suit with three cards but you need four cards to support the second suit. In any event partner will know that you probably have only three-card support for his first suit, since you did not raise his first suit immediately. *Delayed* support below game implies three trumps.

5) BIDDING NO TRUMPS

Where either partner bids no trumps at the two-level or the three-level, this shows stoppers in the unbid suits. A rebid of one no trump by either partner makes no such promise.

Two no trumps and three no trumps show balanced hands as: (a) opening bids; (b) responses to the opening bid; (c) opener's first rebid. After that they no longer guarantee balanced shape.

6) SUBSEQUENT BIDDING BY RESPONDER

a) *How often should responder bid where opener has not forced a further bid?*

    0— 5 points: Not at all, pass.

    6— 9 points: Once (unless giving simple preference on your rebid).

    10—12 points: Twice; invite game over opener's minimum rebid.

    13—15 points: Insist on reaching game; do not make a droppable bid below the game level.

    16 or more: Jump shift at once to force to game and suggest slam possibilities.

b) *Accepting or declining an invitation.*

Where partner invites you to bid game, pass if you are minimum for your previous bidding but accept the invitation and bid game if you are better than a minimum.

For example, partner opens one heart, you bid one spade, and partner bids three spades, inviting game. With a bare 6—7 points, (minimum response) you would pass, but with any more you would bid game.

Again, partner opens one heart, you bid one no trump, and partner bids two no trumps, inviting game. With a minimum 6—7 points you pass, while with the maximum 8—10 points you would bid three no trumps. With 8—10 points you could also bid three hearts which would show three-card support for his suit and invite him to bid three no trumps or four hearts, whichever he prefers. He will bid four hearts only if he has a five-card suit, or course.

Suppose, partner opens one spade, you bid two hearts, and partner bids three hearts, inviting game. Your bid of two hearts already showed 10 points, so with a minimum 10—11 you would pass, while with 12 or more you would bid game.

c) *Giving partner a preference.*
Where partner bids two suits, he is asking you to give preference to the suit for which you have better support.
 i) *Prefer the suit in which you have more cards.*
 ii) *With the same number of cards in each suit prefer partner's first suit bid, irrespective of the quality of the cards involved.*

Where partner's last bid does not force you to bid again, you may indicate your preference for the last suit bid by passing.

Simple preference means that you revert to partner's first suit bid at the lowest possible level (for example, 1 ♡ : 1 ♠, 2 ◇ : 2 ♡). Simple preference shows that you prefer partner's first suit bid *but you may have no extra values.*[1] In the examples given responder would have 6—9 points with heart preference.

Jump preference means that you revert to partner's first suit bid but skip one level in doing so (for example, 1 ♡ : 1 ♠, 2 ◇ : 3 ♡). Jump preference shows that you prefer partner's first suit bid *but you do have extra values.*

7) THE SKIP-OVER PRINCIPLE
Where opener at his rebid skips over a suit, he does not hold that suit. For example, after 1 ◇ : 1 ♡, 1 NT, responder may infer that opener does not hold four spades. Similarly, after 1 ♣ : 1 ◇, 2 ♣, opener will not have a four-card major, but after 1 ♣ : 1 ♠, 2 ♣, opener may still hold four cards in diamonds or hearts.

---

[1] 'extra values': more than the minimum range already promised.

EXERCISES

1) Partner opens one club. What do you respond on each of these hands?

a)	b)	c)	d)	e)
♠ 87432	♠ KQ84	♠ AK93	♠ QJ543	♠ K8643
♡ 6	♡ J1072	♡ K5432	♡ AQ97	♡ 75
◇ Q52	◇ 83	◇ 7	◇ 75	◇ AQJ76
♣ K432	♣ 764	♣ AJ4	♣ 42	♣ 7

f)	g)	h)	i)	j)
♠ 9432	♠ 72	♠ A742	♠ Q854	♠ AQ5
♡ AQ5	♡ AJ65	♡ A742	♡ J1076	♡ K84
◇ J98	◇ J53	◇ 7	◇ 53	◇ QJ108
♣ Q87	♣ K942	♣ A742	♣ J87	♣ 763

2) Partner opens one heart. What is your response on these hands?

a)	b)	c)	d)	e)
♠ AQ843	♠ AQJ4	♠ K643	♠ 76	♠ 84
♡ 7	♡ 7	♡ 6	♡ 843	♡ 6
◇ 85	◇ A9863	◇ AQJ3	◇ KQJ8	◇ AQ432
♣ AJ864	♣ J32	♣ Q542	♣ AQ93	♣ AQ543

f)	g)	h)	i)	j)
♠ K843	♠ 5	♠ A	♠ AQ7	♠ 652
♡ 7	♡ A93	♡ 76	♡ 6532	♡ 10
◇ 542	◇ K8432	◇ Q5432	◇ KQ9	◇ AK10987
♣ A9863	♣ 9876	♣ 109643	♣ AQ10	♣ Q32

3) Partner opens one heart. On which of the following hands do you 'jump shift', i.e., jump-bid in a new suit?

a)	b)	c)	d)	e)
♠ AKQJ83	♠ AKJ	♠ 76	♠ AKQ3	♠ AK
♡ 76	♡ —	♡ AQ432	♡ 6	♡ A
◇ 542	◇ AJ42	◇ 84	◇ AQJ1092	◇ A8652
♣ AJ	♣ Q87432	♣ AKQ2	♣ 42	♣ 96543

4) Playing a strong no trump you opened the bidding with one club. Partner responded one diamond. What is your rebid on each of these hands?

a)	b)	c)	d)	e)
♠ AQJ4	♠ AQ53	♠ K43	♠ 9852	♠ 7
♡ K732	♡ 42	♡ J874	♡ AQ	♡ AQ42
◇ 6	◇ J63	◇ AQ9	◇ A42	◇ K3
♣ K864	♣ KQJ9	♣ KJ4	♣ K982	♣ AJ8762

f)	g)	h)	i)	j)
♠ 6	♠ KJ5	♠ A87	♠ 632	♠ 43
♡ AKQ9	♡ A62	♡ AQ2	♡ A54	♡ Q7
◇ K3	◇ 73	◇ K42	◇ K	◇ A83
♣ AQ8742	♣ KQ1087	♣ KQ86	♣ AQ7532	♣ AKQ976

5) Playing a weak no trump you open the bidding with one heart. Partner responds one spade. What is your rebid on these hands?

a)	b)	c)	d)	e)
♠ KQ	♠ A43	♠ K932	♠ K6	♠ K8
♡ A J1032	♡ AQ72	♡ AQ543	♡ AQ9532	♡ AQJ53
◇ 1063	◇ K94	◇ K6	◇ 532	◇ K8642
♣ K95	♣ Q62	♣ 72	♣ A7	♣ 5

f)	g)	h)	i)	j)
♠ 3	♠ AJ102	♠ 98	♠ 65	♠ A3
♡ AKJ953	♡ KQ9832	♡ AQ943	♡ AKQ93	♡ AKJ54
◇ AQJ	◇ KQ	◇ KQ4	◇ KQ2	◇ Q5
♣ J52	♣ 7	♣ AQ7	♣ AJ3	♣ KQ72

6) Playing a weak no trump you opened the bidding with one heart. Partner responded two clubs. What do you rebid on these hands?

a) ♠ K7
   ♡ AQ953
   ◇ A42
   ♣ 863

b) ♠ K832
   ♡ AJ874
   ◇ KQ
   ♣ 72

c) ♠ K2
   ♡ AK43
   ◇ AQ42
   ♣ 1086

d) ♠ AQ87
   ♡ KQJ62
   ◇ A9
   ♣ 85

e) ♠ K94
   ♡ AQ1032
   ◇ A843
   ♣ 7

7) For each of the following hands you are the opening bidder. What is your rebid in each of the given auctions?

i) ♠ KQ3
   ♡ AQJ42
   ◇ 542
   ♣ 76

  a) 1♡ 2♣   b) 1♡ 3♣
    ?   ?
  c) 1♡ 2♠   d) 1♡ 2NT
    ?   ?

ii) ♠ 7
   ♡ KJ1083
   ◇ AQ543
   ♣ A6

  a) 1♡ 2♣   b) 1♡ 3♣
    ?   ?
  c) 1♡ 1♠   d) 1♡ 2♠
    ?   ?

8) In which of the following auctions are you forced to bid again? Indicate also in which auctions a game-forcing situation has arisen.

(i) You	Partner	(ii) Partner	You	(iii) You	Partner
a) 1♡	1♠	a) 1♡	1♠	a) 1♡	2NT
?		2◇	?	3◇	3♡
				?	
b) 1◇	2♣	b) 1♡	2♣	b) 1♡	2♣
?		2◇	?	2◇	2♡
				?	
c) 1♡	2♠	c) 1♣	1♡	c) 1♡	2♣
?		1♠	?	2◇	3♡
				?	
d) 1◇	2NT	d) 1♣	1◇	d) 1♡	1♠
?		2♡	?	2◇	3♡
				?	
e) 1♡	4♡	e) 1♡	1♠	e) 1♣	1◇
?		3♡	?	1♠	2♡
				?	
f) 1♣	3♣	f) 1♡	2♣	f) 1♡	1♠
?		4♣	?	2◇	2NT
				?	
g) 1◇	3♣	g) 1♡	1NT	g) 1♡	1♠
?		3◇	?	2◇	3◇
				?	
h) 1♠	2♠	h) 1♡	2NT	h) 1◇	1♠
?		3♡	?	2♣	3♠
				?	
i) 1♡	3NT	i) 1♡	2◇		
?		3♣	?		
j) 1♠	3♠	j) 1♡	2◇		
?		2NT	?		

9) How many hearts? In each of the following auctions how many hearts should *South* have for his bidding?

a) S	N	b) S	N	c) S	N	d) S	N	e) S	N
1♡	1♠	1♡	1♠	1♡	1♠	1♡	2♣	1♠	2♣
2♡		2◇		3♡		2♠		2♡	

f) S	N	g) S	N	h) S	N	i) S	N	j) S	N
1♠	2♦	1♥	2♣	1♥	2♣	1♥	1♠	1♥	2♦
2♥	2NT	2♦	2NT	2♠	3♦	2♦	2NT	2♥	3♣
3♠		3♦		3♠		3♥		3♥	

k) S	N	l) S	N	m) S	N	n) S	N	o) S	N
	1♠		1♣		1♠		1♥		1♦
2♥		1♥	1♠	2♣	2♥	1♠	3♥	1♥	1♠
		2♦		4♥		3NT		2NT	3♥
								3NT	

10) What is South's next bid on these hands?

a) ♠ K6
♡ AQ943
♢ 743
♣ K52

b) ♠ KQ4
♡ 7
♢ AQ97
♣ K9432

c) ♠ 83
♡ Q2
♢ KQ94
♣ AK842

d) ♠ 86
♡ QJ10742
♢ K93
♣ 87

e) ♠ KJ7
♡ 74
♢ 876
♣ AQJ84

S	N	S	N	S	N	S	N	S	N
	1♣		1♥		1♥		1♣		1♥
1♥	2♥	2♣	2♥	2♣	2♥	1♥	1NT	2♣	2♦
?		?		?		?		?	

11)

i) 1♥ : 1NT
2NT : ?

a) ♠ KJ8
♡ 74
♢ AJ53
♣ 9642

b) ♠ Q93
♡ 764
♢ K762
♣ J87

c) ♠ 753
♡ K93
♢ KQ84
♣ 864

d) ♠ K7
♡ J94
♢ Q862
♣ 8642

ii) 1♥ : 1♠
3♥ : ?

a) ♠ KQ76
♡ Q8
♢ J9863
♣ 75

b) ♠ AQJ9
♡ 4
♢ Q873
♣ 8642

c) ♠ AQJ87
♡ 3
♢ J876
♣ 432

d) ♠ 98432
♡ K74
♢ 3
♣ A432

iii) 1♦ : 1♠
3♠ : ?

a) ♠ Q9832
♡ A6
♢ K43
♣ 765

b) ♠ K942
♡ J62
♢ 3
♣ J9743

c) ♠ AQ765
♡ 3
♢ 87
♣ 96532

d) ♠ AJ963
♡ 3
♢ A74
♣ KQ72

iv) 1♥ : 1♠
2♦ : ?

a) ♠ KJ954
♡ 76
♢ Q63
♣ 852

b) ♠ KJ954
♡ Q76
♢ 63
♣ 752

c) ♠ KJ954
♡ 863
♢ QJ8
♣ 42

d) ♠ KJ954
♡ A87
♢ Q9
♣ 642

v) 1♥ : 2♣
2♦ : ?

a) ♠ KQ2
♡ 43
♢ Q6
♣ A86432

b) ♠ 87
♡ 42
♢ K95
♣ AQJ853

c) ♠ 972
♡ K64
♢ 94
♣ AQJ74

d) ♠ AJ32
♡ K9
♢ 7
♣ AJ8543

12)

i)

N	E	S	W
1♥	1♠	No	No
2♣	No	?	

What should South now bid on these hands?

a) ♠ 863
♡ 942
♢ 97642
♣ 87

b) ♠ 932
♡ 76
♢ Q9852
♣ J73

c) ♠ 8643
♡ Q98
♢ 763
♣ AJ9

d) ♠ 973
♡ 96
♢ QJ9854
♣ Q7

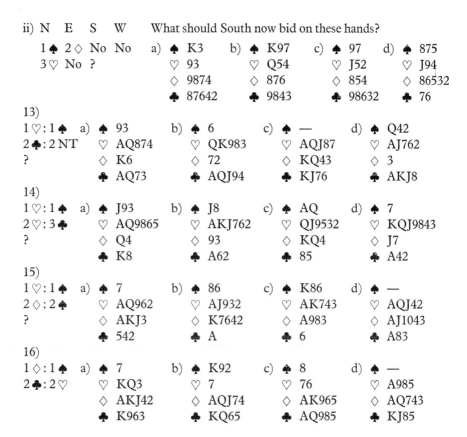

ii) N   E   S   W   What should South now bid on these hands?

1♠ 2◇ No No   a) ♠ K3   b) ♠ K97   c) ♠ 97   d) ♠ 875
3♡ No ?   ♡ 93   ♡ Q54   ♡ J52   ♡ J94
                        ◇ 9874   ◇ 876   ◇ 854   ◇ 86532
                        ♣ 87642   ♣ 9843   ♣ 98632   ♣ 76

13)
1♡:1♠   a) ♠ 93   b) ♠ 6   c) ♠ —   d) ♠ Q42
2♣:2NT   ♡ AQ874   ♡ QK983   ♡ AQJ87   ♡ AJ762
?   ◇ K6   ◇ 72   ◇ KQ43   ◇ 3
             ♣ AQ73   ♣ AQJ94   ♣ KJ76   ♣ AKJ8

14)
1♡:1♠   a) ♠ J93   b) ♠ J8   c) ♠ AQ   d) ♠ 7
2♡:3♣   ♡ AQ9865   ♡ AKJ762   ♡ QJ9532   ♡ KQJ9843
?   ◇ Q4   ◇ 93   ◇ KQ4   ◇ J7
             ♣ K8   ♣ A62   ♣ 85   ♣ A42

15)
1♡:1♠   a) ♠ 7   b) ♠ 86   c) ♠ K86   d) ♠ —
2◇:2♠   ♡ AQ962   ♡ AJ932   ♡ AK743   ♡ AQJ42
?   ◇ AKJ3   ◇ K7642   ◇ A983   ◇ AJ1043
             ♣ 542   ♣ A   ♣ 6   ♣ A83

16)
1◇:1♠   a) ♠ 7   b) ♠ K92   c) ♠ 8   d) ♠ —
2♣:2♡   ♡ KQ3   ♡ 7   ♡ 76   ♡ A985
             ◇ AKJ42   ◇ AQJ74   ◇ AK965   ◇ AQ743
             ♣ K963   ♣ KQ65   ♣ AQ985   ♣ KJ85

Hand 1: Delaying drawing of trumps—ruffing loser in dummy

Dealer North
Nil vulnerable

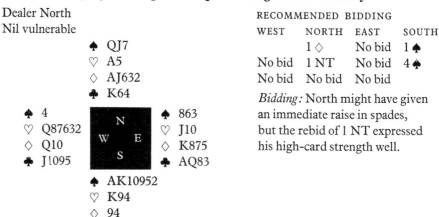

♠ QJ7
♡ A5
◇ AJ632
♣ K64

♠ 4
♡ Q87632
◇ Q10
♣ J1095

♠ 863
♡ J10
◇ K875
♣ AQ83

♠ AK10952
♡ K94
◇ 94
♣ 72

RECOMMENDED BIDDING

WEST	NORTH	EAST	SOUTH
	1 ◇	No bid	1 ♠
No bid	1 NT	No bid	4 ♠
No bid	No bid	No bid	

Bidding: North might have given an immediate raise in spades, but the rebid of 1 NT expressed his high-card strength well.

Lead: West should lead the jack of clubs, preferring the solid clubs rather than the broken hearts. If declarer plays low in dummy, East should play the eight of clubs, encouraging West to continue. If South plays the king from dummy, East, of course, plays the ace.

RIGHT PLAY Ruff the third club, spade to the queen, spade seven back to the ace (in case trumps are 2—2), then ace of hearts, king of hearts, a heart ruffed with dummy's top trump, then ace of diamonds and another diamond and draw the last trump when you regain the lead, making ten tricks.

WRONG PLAY 1) Ruffing the third round of clubs and then drawing three rounds of trumps. This leaves dummy without a trump to ruff the third round of hearts, and you will go one down.

2) Ruffing the third round of clubs, then playing three rounds of hearts and ruffing the third round with the seven of spades. East will overruff dummy, and you will go one down. Since you have an excess of high trumps, there is no need to be stingy; ruff as high as you can afford. In any case it is safer to draw two rounds of trumps before going for the heart ruff.

3) Ruffing the third club, then drawing two rounds of trumps with dummy's queen and jack of spades. Again when you try to ruff the third round of hearts, you will be overruffed by East.

Do not draw trumps if you need dummy's trumps for ruffing losers. When ruffing, ruff as high as you can afford to avoid the danger of being overruffed.

Hand 2: Play at trick one—drawing trumps—ruffing loser in dummy—suit-preference signal

Dealer East
North-South vulnerable

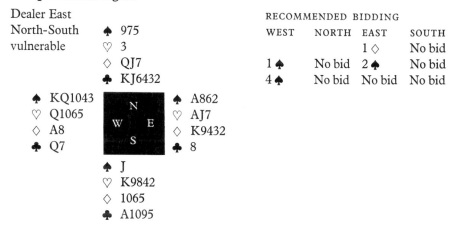

♠ 975
♡ 3
♢ QJ7
♣ KJ6432

♠ KQ1043
♡ Q1065
♢ A8
♣ Q7

♠ A862
♡ AJ7
♢ K9432
♣ 8

♠ J
♡ K9842
♢ 1065
♣ A1095

RECOMMENDED BIDDING

WEST	NORTH	EAST	SOUTH
		1♢	No bid
1♠	No bid	2♠	No bid
4♠	No bid	No bid	No bid

Lead: A good lead here is the singleton heart. If partner happens to have the ace, he can give you a ruff at once.

If declarer plays low in dummy, South wins the king and returns the two of hearts for North to ruff. The two of hearts is a *suit-preference* signal, asking partner to return a club. It works this way: *when you are giving partner a ruff,* a high card asks partner to return the higher suit, a low card asks for the lower suit (the trump suit and the suit being led are always excluded). Suit preference can arise in other circumstances but its most common use is when giving partner a ruff.

North ruffs the two of hearts and returns a club; South wins the ace of clubs and plays another heart. North ruffs and defeats the contract one trick. However, if after ruffing North plays a diamond instead of a club, West wins, draws trumps and makes his contract. See the importance of the club return and hence the value of the suit-preference signal. If South happened to have the ace of diamonds instead of the ace of clubs, he would win the king of hearts and play back the *nine* of hearts for North to ruff, a high card asking for the higher suit (hearts and spades being excluded here).

RIGHT PLAY West must not play low on the heart lead. He should win the ace of hearts, draw trumps and give up a heart trick and a club trick, then ruff a club in dummy, making eleven tricks.

Beware of a finesse at trick one if the lead could be a singleton: decide whether the finesse is necessary for your contract. If not, don't take it; draw trumps as soon as possible unless you need dummy's trumps. In defence note when you can use a suit-preference signal to indicate to partner which suit to play (do not confuse with encouraging-discouraging signals).

Hand 3: Handling suit combination—discarding loser—ruffing losers

Dealer South
Both vulnerable

	♠ 72	
	♡ KQ5	
	◇ K8762	
	♣ Q43	

♠ J109		♠ K63
♡ A843	N	♡ J10976
◇ 9	W E	◇ Q10
♣ 98762	S	♣ KJ5

	♠ AQ854
	♡ 2
	◇ AJ543
	♣ A10

WEST	NORTH	EAST	SOUTH
			1♠
No bid	2◇	No bid	4◇
No bid	5◇	No bid	No bid
No bid			

Lead: East's best lead is the jack of hearts. West wins the ace of hearts. Looking at dummy, West sees there is no future in hearts and should switch to a club. If North plays low, East plays the jack, while if North plays the queen, East covers with the king.

RIGHT PLAY When the ace of clubs is taken, North should play a trump to the king (rather than the ace and then a trump to the king). This is to guard against the chance that East has all three trumps. Trumps will probably split 2—1, in which case it doesn't matter how you play, while if West has all three, you have to lose a trick no matter what you do. But if East has all three trumps, by playing the king first you can capture East's queen via a finesse (check it!). On winning the king of diamonds play a diamond to the ace, back to hand with a low diamond, king and queen of hearts, discarding dummy's losing club and also a spade, take the spade finesse and then the ace of spades, cross-ruff the last four tricks, making twelve tricks.

WRONG PLAY 1) Failing to win the club switch with the ace of clubs. This loses a club trick and a heart trick, and makes everything depend on the spade finesse.
2) Winning the ace of clubs and playing the ace of diamonds instead of a diamond to the king. This costs a trick if East began with Q 10 9 in trumps but it doesn't cost on the actual hand since trumps are 2—1. Notice that, as in life, not all wrongs are punished.
3) Winning the ace of clubs, drawing trumps but forgetting to discard dummy's losing club on a top heart. This costs a trick unnecessarily.
4) Failing to take the spade finesse. This also costs a trick unnecessarily.

Draw trumps before discarding losers if safe to do so.

Hand 4: Handling a nine-card trump suit—discarding losers without drawing all trumps

Dealer West
Nil vulnerable

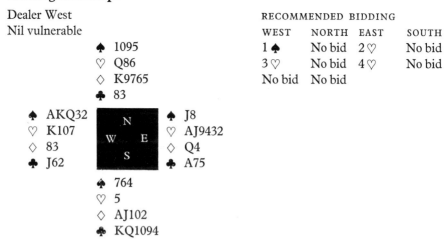

♠ 1095
♡ Q86
◇ K9765
♣ 83

♠ AKQ32
♡ K107
◇ 83
♣ J62

♠ J8
♡ AJ9432
◇ Q4
♣ A75

♠ 764
♡ 5
◇ AJ102
♣ KQ1094

RECOMMENDED BIDDING

WEST	NORTH	EAST	SOUTH
1 ♠	No bid	2 ♡	No bid
3 ♡	No bid	4 ♡	No bid
No bid	No bid		

Lead: South should lead the king of clubs, top of a semi-solid sequence.

RIGHT PLAY East should win the ace of clubs, play the ace of hearts, king of hearts, jack of spades, ace of spades and the other six spades, discarding his two losing diamonds. North will trump the fourth spade with ♡Q as East discards his last diamond. Later, East leads a club towards dummy's jack. By this line East should lose only one trump trick and one club trick.

WRONG PLAY 1) Failing to win the ace of clubs at trick one. If South switches to a diamond the defence can cash two diamond tricks and may defeat you.
2) Playing the trumps wrongly by playing the king of hearts and then finessing the jack. This is successful on the actual hand, but were the finesse to lose, the enemy could cash two diamonds and a club, beating you by one trick. The key play is the discard play on the spades, not the trump play.
3) Playing the king of hearts and the ace of hearts and a third round of hearts. This gives the enemy the lead and they can cash two diamonds and a club.
4) Failing to place the queen of clubs with South and hence not taking the club finesse. It is important to try and work out what cards are held by the enemy, and the opening lead often tells quite a story.

With nine trumps missing the queen play for the drop unless there is a good reason not to. If the last trump held by the enemy is high, it usually does not pay to draw it. Where the opening lead is the king of an unbid suit, the leader will usually hold either AK or KQ in that suit.

Lesson 6

Part A: Opening two-bids

HOW TO COUNT TRICKS

When you have a six-card or longer suit, count:
1) Each card in your long suit past the top three cards as one trick.
2) For the top three cards one trick for the ace, one for the king, half for the queen and half for the jack (but AKQ obviously counts three tricks).
3) In other suits A=1, AK=2, AQ=$1\frac{1}{2}$, KQ=1, K=$\frac{1}{2}$ and QJx=$\frac{1}{2}$. A fourth card in a side suit is worth half a trick, and a fifth card is a full trick.

You may also use this method when you have a 5—5 shape. Treat the stronger suit as your long suit and the weaker suit as your side suit.

OPENING TWO DIAMONDS, TWO HEARTS, TWO SPADES

These show eight or more playing tricks. (The point count can be as little as 14 up to a maximum of 21.) Where you have a choice of suits to open, apply the same rules as for a one-opening. An opening bid of two diamonds, two hearts or two spades is forcing for one round.

Responses: Negative: two no trumps—denies two tricks, usually 0—7 points.
Positive: Any other bid—shows two or more tricks, 7 or more points; any positive bid commits the partnership to game.

OPENING TWO CLUBS

An opening of two clubs is forcing to game (except for the sequence 2 ♣ : 2 ◇, 2 NT). The opening of two clubs is artificial, saying nothing about clubs, but showing a gigantic hand (21 points or more, $9\frac{1}{2}$ or more playing tricks).
Response: Weak response—2 ◇ : 0—7 points; any shape.
Strong responses: any other response, 8 or more points, slam very likely.

COMMENTARY

Counting points is an accurate guide to the value of a hand where it is balanced or an ordinary semi-balanced or unbalanced shape (for example, 5—4—2—2, 5—4—3—1). Where you have a long suit or two long suits, counting tricks is a more reliable guide. The more freakish a hand, the less reliable it is to count points.

Where you have a good long suit and can count eight or more tricks in your own hand, you should open with a bid of two in your long suit (not two clubs). This forces partner to bid no matter how weak his hand and enables you to describe hands too strong for a one-opening (which partner could pass).

In responding to an opening of two diamonds, two hearts or two spades you should again count tricks (A=1, AK=2, KQ=1, K=$\frac{1}{2}$, QJx=$\frac{1}{2}$, K or Q in suit opened=1 each). With less than two tricks respond two no trumps, regardless of your shape. With two or more tricks make some other bid. In general with 8 or more points you are worth some positive bid. A jump to three no trumps shows a balanced hand of about 10—12 points. In raising opener's major bid two no trumps with less than 8 points; raise one level with 8 points and at least one ace; raise to game with 8 or more points, no ace, but either two kings or one king and a singleton.

After a response of two no trumps to two diamonds, two hearts or two spades, responder may pass opener's next bid unless opener bids a major at the three-level higher ranking than the suit opened (for example, 2 ◇ : 2 NT, 3 ♡) or opener jumps to four of a minor (for example, 2 ♡ : 2 NT, 4 ♣). After any response other than two no trumps, the partnership must keep bidding until at least game is reached.

An opening of two clubs shows a monster of a hand, either 23 or more points in a balanced hand or 9½ tricks or more in hand which is not balanced. The opening of two clubs will generally have more than 20 points in high cards. With less high-card strength prefer to open two diamonds, two hearts or two spades. Where your dominant suit is clubs, some leeway must be allowed, as two clubs is an artificial opening saying nothing at all about your club suit but merely showing strength.

The weakness response (0—7 points) to two clubs is two diamonds, again an artificial bid saying nothing about your diamonds or your shape but simply limiting the strength of your hand. Other bids are natural, showing a five-card suit or good four-card suit and 8 points up. Specifically the responses of two no trumps and three no trumps show balanced hands of 7—9 and 10—12 points respectively.

After responder's bid, opener bids his dominant suit or bids two no trumps with a balanced 23—24 or three no trumps with a balanced 25 points or more. Bidding continues normally with the stipulation that the partnership must reach at least game, with one exception: the sequence 2 ♣ : 2 ◇, 2 NT (=23—24 balanced) is droppable by responder, but if responder makes another bid, the partnership will not stop below game.

EXERCISES

1) How many tricks are each of these suits worth?

a) AKQxxxxx   g) AQxxxxxx   m) KJxxxxxx
b) AKQxxxx   h) AKxxxxx   n) Kxxxxxx
c) AKQxxx   i) AJxxxx   o) QJ10xxxx
d) AKJxxxxx   j) Axxxxxx   p) Qxxxxxx
e) AKJxxxx   k) KQJxxxx   q) Jxxxxxx
f) AQJxxxx   l) KQxxxxxx   r) xxxxxxxxx

2) What is your opening bid?

a) ♠ A6   b) ♠ A   c) ♠ AKQ84   d) ♠ —
   ♡ AKJ1062   ♡ AKJ10652 ♡ AKJ987   ♡ AKQ8654
   ◇ AQ   ◇ AKQ   ◇ A   ◇ AQJ873
   ♣ K83   ♣ 83   ♣ 4   ♣ —

3) What is your response if partner opened: (i) two hearts? (ii) two clubs?

a) ♠ 754 b) ♠ K87 c) ♠ A87 d) ♠ AJ7 e) ♠ K84
   ♡ 642   ♡ 64   ♡ Q98   ♡ 64   ♡ Q753
   ◇ 5432   ◇ K653 ◇ 54   ◇ QJ106 ◇ 42
   ♣ 765   ♣ 9864 ♣ KJ543 ♣ Q962 ♣ K864

4) The bidding has gone 2♠ : 2 NT. What is your rebid as opener on:

a) ♠ AKQJ7 b) ♠ AKQJ876 c) ♠ AKJ1086 d) ♠ AQJ10865
   ♡ AK943   ♡ 65   ♡ AQJ65   ♡ AKQJ64
   ◇ 43   ◇ A43   ◇ 8   ◇ —
   ♣ 6   ♣ 8   ♣ 5   ♣ —

5)

2♠ : 2 NT a) ♠ 987 b) ♠ 987 c) ♠ 72   d) ♠ 65   e) ♠ K43
3♡ : ?   ♡ 76   ♡ 4   ♡ Q963 ♡ 43   ♡ Q87
        ◇ QJ654 ◇ KQ65 ◇ A843 ◇ J8743 ◇ 76542
        ♣ 632   ♣ 87543 ♣ 765 ♣ 9842 ♣ 86

6)

2♡ : 2 NT a) ♠ J7654 b) ♠ 6432 c) ♠ 87   d) ♠ J5   e) ♠ 764
6◇ : ?   ♡ 986   ♡ 43   ♡ 96   ♡ K86   ♡ 3
        ◇ 43   ◇ 876   ◇ 96   ◇ 43   ◇ K874
        ♣ 642   ♣ 5432 ♣ 8765432 ♣ J87642 ♣ 76432

7) You open two clubs. What is your rebid if partner responds: (i) two diamonds?
(ii) two no trumps?

a) ♠ AQJ b) ♠ AKJ   c) ♠ AKJ83 d) ♠ AQ   e) ♠ —
   ♡ K873 ♡ A1096 ♡ AKQ42 ♡ AKQ864 ♡ AQJ8
   ◇ AKJ   ◇ AKQ   ◇ AK   ◇ AJ8   ◇ AKJ84
   ♣ KQ4 ♣ KQ2 ♣ 7   ♣ A9   ♣ AQJ9

8) Partner opens two clubs, you respond two diamonds. What is your rebid if
partner rebids: (i) two no trumps? (ii) two spades?

a) ♠ 87   b) ♠ Q87 c) ♠ 8   d) ♠ 94   e) ♠ 6
   ♡ 9654 ♡ K9   ♡ QJ8643 ♡ QJ7   ♡ AJ843
   ◇ 8752 ◇ 8732 ◇ 743   ◇ Q1043 ◇ 9652
   ♣ 932   ♣ 9865 ♣ 862   ♣ J986 ♣ 764

9) Which of these hands would you say is most likely to be opener's?

2♣	2◇	a)	♠ AKJ	b)	♠ A5	c)	♠ KQ	d)	♠ KQ	e)	♠ —
2♡	2 NT		♡ KQJ4		♡ AKQ7		♡ AKJ76		♡ AK854		♡ AQJ876
3♣	3♡		◇ AQ		◇ KQ		◇ 4		◇ AQ		◇ AK
4♡	No		♣ AQ64		♣ AQJ76		♣ AKQJ3		♣ AQJ3		♣ AKQ52

10) Furnish appropriate bidding sequences for each of these pairs of hands.

a) Opener	Responder	b) Opener	Responder	c) Opener	Responder
♠ AKQ9	♠ 643	♠ AKQJ5	♠ 93	♠ AK108	♠ Q76543
♡ Q6	♡ J10752	♡ AKQ5	♡ J874	♡ AK	♡ 987
◇ AQJ985	◇ 43	◇ AK	◇ 63	◇ KQ109732	◇ 4
♣ A	♣ K63	♣ K2	♣ Q7643	♣ —	♣ Q72

Part B: Opening three-bids, four-bids and five-bids

An opening three-bid is weak and shows:
a) Less in HCP than an opening one-bid;
b) A good six-card suit but more usually a seven-card suit;
c) Five-six tricks, not vulnerable;
seven tricks, vulnerable.

An opening bid of three no trumps shows a *solid* six- or seven-card minor suit and almost no outside strength. It is a gambling bid and is called 'the gambling three no trumps'.

An opening four-bid is weak and shows:
a) Usually less in HCP than an opening one-bid;
b) A seven- or eight-card suit;
c) Seven tricks not vulnerable;
Eight tricks vulnerable.

Opening five clubs or five diamonds is weak and shows:
a) usually less in HCP than an opening one-bid;
b) an eight-or nine-card suit, hence an extremely freakish distribution;
c) eight tricks not vulnerable,
nine tricks vulnerable.

RESPONDING TO OPENING THREES, FOURS AND FIVES
Rule of two and three: an opening three or more is two tricks short of the contract when vulnerable, three tricks short when not vulnerable.
a) Add tricks in your hand to the number promised by partner.
b) If total is less than contract or just enough for contract, pass.
c) If total is more than enough for contract, pass if already in game (unless there are enough tricks for slam) or bid game in partner's suit.
d) With enough strength for game you may choose three no trumps over a three-bid with cover in the unbid suits.
e) Avoid bidding a suit of your own (unless you are happy for partner to support with a doubleton).

RESPONDING TO AN OPENING BID OF THREE NO TRUMPS
Pass: with a reasonable hand and stoppers in the majors.
Bid four clubs: with a weak hand and no stoppers in both majors (opener will bid four diamonds if diamonds is his suit).
Bid five clubs (or five diamonds): with a good unbalanced hand.
Look for slam: if you can envisage twelve tricks opposite the seven which opener should hold.

HOW TO COUNT TRICKS OPPOSITE A SHUT-OUT BID
In side suit: $AK=2$; $AQ=1\frac{1}{2}$; A or $KQ=1$; $Kxx=\frac{1}{2}$.
In trumps: A, K, or $Q=1$.
Three or more trumps$+$singleton$=1$.
Three or more trumps$+$void$=2$.

74

COMMENTARY

While opening two bids show power-houses, opening bids of three or more in a suit are the absolute opposite. Good bridge is not merely bidding to your own best contract; bridge is a battle, and good players harass the enemy whenever possible to try and make it difficult for the opposition to find their best contract.

Even experts are, more often than not, guessing at what to do after a shut-out bid has robbed them of three or more levels of bidding. And if experts admit to being at sea, how much more so must the average player be? The high pre-emptive openings are a powerful weapon when properly used: the enemy is often unsure whether to enter the bidding at all at such a high level, what the best contract is, whether to stop in game or to go on to a slam, etc. By making them guess you will often make them guess wrongly.

However, you are not prepared to enter the bidding with a high bid without some sort of a built-in safety factor. It is obviously silly to open with a bid like, say, four diamonds and wind up being doubled for penalties, losing 1,700 or so in the process. You should be prepared to risk losing 500 points (the approximate value of an enemy game, whether they are vulnerable or not) if you are doubled and partner does not provide any tricks for you. So you should apply the rule of two and three:

If vulnerable, you should be within two tricks of your contract in your own hand.
If not vulnerable, you should be within three tricks of your contract in your own hand.

You may loosen this up slightly when not vulnerable but be strict when vulnerable. Usually, partner will provide a trick or so for you even when you are doubled, so that —500 should be the worst possible result. And if partner provides no tricks, it is of course very likely that the enemy have missed a slam.

The key to the shut-out openings is to have a long, good suit. The higher your opening bid, the more freakish the hand.

Usually a pre-emptive opening is less than an opening bid, but when partner has already passed, there is no need to keep to the right requirements especially for the bids of four hearts and four spades. For example, you hold:

♠ : AKJ10765   ♡ : 3   ◇ : A103   ♣ : 87

First or second to speak, you would open one spade, but if partner has already passed, you can judge that slam is very unlikely so that an opening bid of four spades in third or fourth position is quite in order (whether vulnerable or not). This makes it even harder for the enemy who do not know whether you have a poor hand or a reasonably strong one.

When partner opens with a shut-out bid, the most important thing to remember is that he has an excellent suit and is most unlikely to hold support for any suit of yours. Doubleton support for his suit is more than adequate, and you may raise on a singleton and sometimes even on a void! Do not bid a suit of your own unless you are prepared to be raised on a small doubleton.

Responding to partner's pre-emptive opening is merely a matter of working out how many tricks he should have and adding the number of tricks in your hand to that. Over a three-opening, especially three clubs or three diamonds, you may try three no trumps if you have a fit with partner plus stoppers in the outside suits.

In responding to partner's gambling opening of three no trumps you should count on him to produce seven tricks. As he has little or no strength outside his long suit, you are the one who has to gauge whether to stay in three no trumps or remove it to four or five in his minor suit.

Often you can tell from your own hand which minor suit partner holds. Where you cannot tell and you want to remove three no trumps, you simply bid four clubs (or five clubs). If partner's suit is diamonds, he will correct to four diamonds (or five diamonds). If three no trumps is doubled, it is the partner of the opener of three no trumps who should judge what action to take. If he passes the double or if he redoubles, the opener of three no trumps should pass.

EXERCISES

1) You are dealer. What is your opening bid: (i) not vulnerable? (ii) vulnerable?

a) ♠ QJ108765 b) ♠ 8   c) ♠ K3   d) ♠ KJ107654 e) ♠ 5
   ♡ 6   ♡ KQJ97654   ♡ 54   ♡ 6   ♡ 43
   ◇ AK3   ◇ 43   ◇ 862   ◇ QJ1096   ◇ 9752
   ♣ 54   ♣ 32   ♣ AQJ986   ♣ —   ♣ AKQ764

f) ♠ KQJ87   g) ♠ AK9875   h) ♠ J98654 i) ♠ Q876   j) ♠ 7
   ♡ 5   ♡ A7   ♡ AK5   ♡ 6   ♡ AKQ98653
   ◇ QJ106   ◇ J86   ◇ Q54   ◇ AQJ976   ◇ 654
   ♣ 432   ♣ 65   ♣ 3   ♣ 54   ♣ 3

2) Partner opens three hearts. What is your response: (i) not vulnerable?
(ii) vulnerable?

a) ♠ AJ987   b) ♠ AJ9874 c) ♠ AK54 d) ♠ AKJ1086 e) ♠ 7
   ♡ 43   ♡ 3   ♡ —   ♡ 3   ♡ Q853
   ◇ QJ76   ◇ QJ7   ◇ J8743   ◇ AQJ   ◇ AK876
   ♣ 52   ♣ 652   ♣ 9762   ♣ J32   ♣ K32

f) ♠ AQ5   g) ♠ AK8764 h) ♠ AKJ43 i) ♠ 2   j) ♠ K832
   ♡ 874   ♡ 43   ♡ 97   ♡ K87   ♡ 5
   ◇ KQ103   ◇ A7   ◇ AK762   ◇ AK7   ◇ A32
   ♣ AJ9   ♣ 863   ♣ 2   ♣ 987643   ♣ AKQ54

3) Which hand does opener have? Neither side is vulnerable.

i) Opener Responder a) ♠ 76   b) ♠ 5   c) ♠ 97
    3♡   3♠   ♡ AKJ765   ♡ KQJ8762   ♡ AK87432
    4♠   No   ◇ AQ4   ◇ Q86   ◇ 1086
                          ♣ 62   ♣ 43   ♣ 4

ii) Opener Responder a) ♠ 6   b) ♠ 964   c) ♠ 87
    3♡   3 NT   ♡ AQJ8764   ♡ QJ1097654   ♡ AKQJ764
    No   ◇ 864   ◇ 3   ◇ 3
                          ♣ 62   ♣ 3   ♣ 543

iii) Opener Responder a) ♠ 76   b) ♠ QJ3   c) ♠ Q97
    3♣   3♡   ♡ Q5   ♡ 4   ♡ 3
    3 NT   No   ◇ 43   ◇ Q87   ◇ K64
                          ♣ AQJ8763   ♣ KQJ876   ♣ AKJ874

PLAYING HANDS

Hand 1: Shut-out bids—establishing winners after drawing trumps

Dealer North
Nil vulnerable

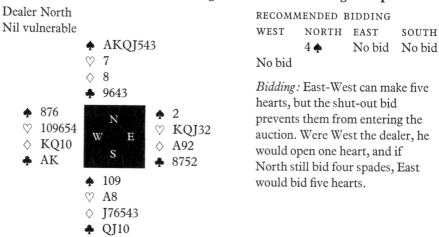

♠ AKQJ543
♡ 7
◇ 8
♣ 9643

♠ 876   ♠ 2
♡ 109654   ♡ KQJ32
◇ KQ10   ◇ A92
♣ AK   ♣ 8752

♠ 109
♡ A8
◇ J76543
♣ QJ10

RECOMMENDED BIDDING

WEST	NORTH	EAST	SOUTH
	4♠	No bid	No bid
No bid			

Bidding: East-West can make five hearts, but the shut-out bid prevents them from entering the auction. Were West the dealer, he would open one heart, and if North still bid four spades, East would bid five hearts.

Lead: East will lead the king of hearts, top of a solid sequence.

RIGHT PLAY North wins the ace of hearts in dummy and draws trumps in three rounds. He then plays clubs, regains the lead and plays clubs again, knocking out the ace and king and setting up two winners in clubs. He loses only one diamond and two clubs, making ten tricks.

In fact, four spades can be defeated if East finds the unlikely lead of a club. In practice four spades will make, but had North timidly opened only three spades, South would pass.

WRONG PLAY 1) Winning the ace of hearts but failing to draw trumps. If North attacks clubs first, West can play the ace and king of clubs, put East in with the ace of diamonds and get a club ruff, defeating the contract.
2) Winning the ace of hearts, drawing trumps but keeping on with trumps instead of setting up the clubs. Suppose North plays six rounds of trumps before attacking the clubs. West will then win the club lead and play a heart or a diamond. North will have to ruff with *his last trump*. When he loses the next club trick, the enemy can cash heart and diamond tricks to beat the contract two tricks.
3) Playing the nine of clubs on any of the first three rounds of clubs. This sets up East's eight as a winner.

Draw only as many trumps as necessary. After trumps have been drawn, establish winners rather than continue trumps aimlessly.

Hand 2: High-level shut-out bidding and support—establishing a suit by ruffing

Dealer East

North-South vulnerable

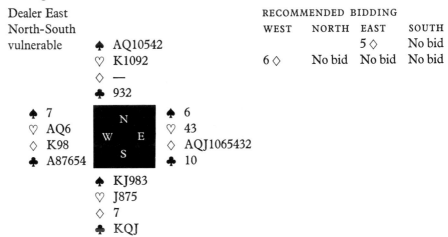

♠ AQ10542
♡ K1092
♢ —
♣ 932

♠ 7
♡ AQ6
♢ K98
♣ A87654

♠ 6
♡ 43
♢ AQJ1065432
♣ 10

♠ KJ983
♡ J875
♢ 7
♣ KQJ

RECOMMENDED BIDDING

WEST	NORTH	EAST	SOUTH
		5 ♢	No bid
6 ♢	No bid	No bid	No bid

Lead: South leads the king of clubs.

RIGHT PLAY East sees eleven tricks. The twelfth can come from a finesse in hearts or by setting up dummy's club suit. It is correct to win the ace of clubs and ruff a club with a high trump, play a low trump to dummy (dummy's king, nine and eight of diamonds are all equal), ruff another club high. Since clubs split 3—3, the enemy have no more. Dummy's three clubs are now winners, so cross over to dummy with a diamond or a heart to the ace and discard your spade and heart losers on the good clubs.

It is important to keep track of the clubs as you ruff. If clubs split 4—2, you would have had to ruff an extra round of clubs before getting your discards. This method would also succeed if clubs broke 5—1. In fact, you make thirteen tricks.

WRONG PLAY 1) Winning the ace of clubs, playing a trump to your hand and taking the heart finesse. When this loses, North cashes the ace of spades to beat the slam. The finesse is a 50% shot; the right play, setting up the club suit, is foolproof. 2) Winning the ace of clubs and playing a couple of rounds of trumps. This is wrong because you may need all of dummy's trumps as *entries*, while you are ruffing the clubs. If you take away the entries, you may succeed in setting up the clubs as winners but have no way of getting to dummy to cash them. Operation successful, but the slam died.

When you have more losers than you can afford, see if you can set up a long suit and discard your losers on the winners thus established. Prefer this to a finesse (which you can take later if the establishment play fails).

Hand 3: Opening two-bid—setting up a second suit by ruffing—timing the play

Dealer South
All vulnerable

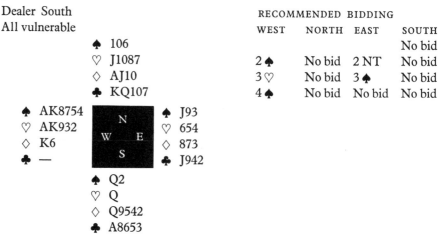

♠ 106
♡ J1087
◇ AJ10
♣ KQ107

♠ AK8754   ♠ J93
♡ AK932   ♡ 654
◇ K6   ◇ 873
♣ —   ♣ J942

♠ Q2
♡ Q
◇ Q9542
♣ A8653

RECOMMENDED BIDDING

WEST	NORTH	EAST	SOUTH
			No bid
2♠	No bid	2 NT	No bid
3♡	No bid	3♠	No bid
4♠	No bid	No bid	No bid

Lead: King of clubs.

RIGHT PLAY West wins the opening lead, plays two rounds of trumps only and then plays ace of hearts, king of hearts and a third round of hearts. If the hearts had been 3—2 and the opposition continue clubs, declarer would win, play out his hearts and discard two diamonds from dummy. He would then give up a diamond and trump his second diamond in dummy, making eleven tricks.

As it is, hearts are 4—1, and North wins the third round. If North switches to a diamond, this sets up declarer's king. If North continues with a club, declarer trumps and plays another heart, trumping in dummy. This eliminates the hearts and makes declarer's fifth heart a winner.

The lead is now in dummy, and declarer should lead a diamond towards his king. As the ace of diamonds is with North, the king does not score. This makes ten tricks.

WRONG PLAY 1) Failing to draw two rounds of trumps. If declarer first starts with ace and king of hearts, South trumps the second round.

2) Drawing three rounds of trumps. This leaves dummy without any trumps to ruff the fourth round of hearts.

3) Failing to play a diamond while in dummy. This does not cost here but could cost an overtrick if South held the ace.

Draw trumps to prevent the opponents from trumping your winners, but do not draw too many. You may need to keep some trumps in dummy to take care of your losers.

Hand 4: Shut-out opening—establishing long suit—defensive hold-up—change in plans

Dealer West
Nil vulnerable

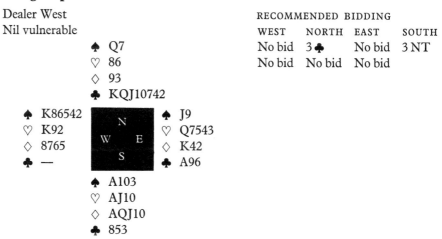

RECOMMENDED BIDDING

WEST	NORTH	EAST	SOUTH
No bid	3♣	No bid	3 NT
No bid	No bid	No bid	

Lead: West leads the five of spades, fourth highest.

RIGHT PLAY Play low in dummy, thus ensuring two spade tricks (check it!). With Qx opposite Axx it is correct to play the queen (cf. Hand 1 p. 52), but with Qx opposite A10x it is normally correct to play low in dummy. East's jack forces your ace and you naturally lead a club, attacking your long suit first. West's club void is a bitter blow, for if clubs were 2—1, the contract would be simple.

East may make matters easy for you by taking the ace of clubs. That would be poor defence, allowing you to make easily.

Assuming East plays low, do not give up hope. Since East will not let you enjoy dummy's clubs, turn your attention to the next best suit, diamonds. Play a diamond from dummy and finesse your queen. That wins. Play another club to dummy. East must hold up again, otherwise your clubs are good. Play another diamond from dummy and finesse your jack. That wins. Next the ace of diamonds, and luckily the king of diamonds falls, making your ten a winner. Play the ten of diamonds, then a low spade. West will capture dummy's queen with his king, but your ten of spades is a winner, making nine tricks.

WRONG PLAY 1) Playing dummy's queen of spades on the opening lead. This works, but if East had the king of spades, this play could cost the contract.
2) Winning the spade lead and playing anything but clubs.
3) Winning the spade lead, playing a club to dummy and, if East plays low, playing a second club. Once East plays low, you should realize that clubs are not going to provide the tricks you need. It is then better to attack diamonds. A second round of clubs destroys the entry to dummy to repeat the diamond finesse.

In defence note when you can cut declarer off from dummy's long suit by a hold-up play.

Lesson 7

Part A: Bidding by a passed hand

A passed hand cannot make a forcing bid.
A new suit by a passed hand can be passed.
A passed hand cannot hold 13 high card points, so all bids have an upper limit of 12; a one-over-one response has a 6—12 range; a two-over-one response has an 8—12 range with a rebiddable suit.

COMMENTARY

When you have passed originally, it is important to realize that partner may pass any response you make. It is therefore vital to describe your hand as accurately as possible with one bid: you should try to indicate your strength and where that strength lies. In particular steer away from four-card suits in two-over-one responses —there is always some better bid available.

Most rebids retain their normal meaning, but the change-of-suit response is limited to a maximum of 12 points. The jump shift after passing (for example, Pass: 1 ♡, 2 ♠) shows a maximum pass (10-11 points) four-card support for partner and a good five-card suit. Partner will sign off in his suit or bid game.

EXERCISES

1) You pass and partner opens one club. What is your response?

a)	♠ AQ82	b)	♠ AQ87	c)	♠ AQ975	d)	♠ KJ8
	♡ K54		♡ K962		♡ K852		♡ A54
	◇ 43		◇ 432		◇ 762		◇ QJ103
	♣ 9872		♣ 75		♣ 3		♣ 764

2) You pass and partner opens one heart. What is your response?

a)	♠ KJ4	b)	♠ 432	c)	♠ A8	d)	♠ 6
	♡ A3		♡ 54		♡ K963		♡ K10964
	◇ Q532		◇ AQ		◇ 43		◇ A5432
	♣ 7654		♣ KJ9643		♣ QJ542		♣ 76

e)	♠ KQ6	f)	♠ J542	g)	♠ Q543	h)	♠ AQ653
	♡ J72		♡ A83		♡ J92		♡ 76
	◇ 10873		◇ 6		◇ A84		◇ K9
	♣ AJ8		♣ Q6432		♣ 863		♣ J642

3)
a) ♠ AJ74   Partner passes. You open one diamond. b) ♠ AK   Partner
   ♡ K43   What is your rebid if partner now bids: ♡ Q9543 passes. You
   ◇ KQ965 (i) 2 ♡? (ii) 2 ♠? (iii) 1 ♠? (iv) 2 NT? ◇ Q43   open one
   ♣ 6   (v) 1 NT?   ♣ J52   heart. What
                                      is your rebid if partner
                                      now bids: (i) 2 ♣?
                                      (ii) 2 ◇? (iii) 2 ♠?
                                      (iv) 2 NT? (v) 3 ♡?

Part B: Defensive bidding

The enemy opens the bidding and you hold a balanced hand:

12 HCP or less: Always pass;

13—15 HCP: usually pass;

16—18 HCP with stopper in enemy suit: bid one no trump (bidding proceeds as after an opening of one no trump);

16—18 HCP with no stopper in enemy suit: make a take-out double (see Lesson 8);

19 HCP or more: make a take-out double (see Lesson 8).

SIMPLE OVERCALLS

At the one-level			At the two-level		
If the enemy open the bidding and you bid a suit at the one-level:	EXAMPLES N E		If the enemy open the bidding and you bid a suit at the two-level (not a jump-bid):	EXAMPLES N E	
Range: 8—13 HCP+good suit, i.e., a very good five-card suit or a decent six-card suit (if in doubt, apply rule of two and three—see page 74).	1♣ 1♣ 1♣ 1♦ 1♦ 1♥	1♦ 1♥ 1♠ 1♥ 1♠ 1♠	Range: 8—13 HCP+excellent suit (super five-card suit or good six-card suit (if in doubt, apply rule of two and three).	1♦ 1♥ 1♥ 1♠ 1♠ 1♠	2♣ 2♣ 2♦ 2♣ 2♦ 2♥

RESPONSES TO SIMPLE OVERCALLS

1) Raise partner's suit (Three-card support is adequate)

	EXAMPLES W N E S	or W N E S	or W N E S
a) Single raise=8—10 +support	1♦ 1♠ No 2♠	1♥ 2♣ No 3♣	1♠ 2♥ No 3♥
b) Double raise=11—13 +support	1♦ 1♠ No 3♠	1♥ 2♣ No 4♣	1♠ 2♥ No 4♥
c) Triple raise=14 +support (or fewer points but excellent shape)	1♦ 1♠ No 4♠	1♥ 2♣ No 5♣	

2) Bid no trumps (Denying support but promising stopper in enemy suit)

a) Minimum no trump =8—10 HCP	1♦ 1♠ No 1 NT	1♥ 2♣ No 2 NT	1♠ 2♥ No 2 NT
b) Jump no trumps= 11—13 HCP (or more than 13 HCP after a two-level overcall)	1♦ 1♠ No 2 NT	1♥ 2♣ No 3 NT	1♠ 2♥ No 3 NT
c) 3 NT over one-level overcall=14+HCP	1♦ 1♠ No 3 NT		

3) Bid a new suit
   (Denying support)
   a) Minimum＝9—15
      HCP＋excellent suit
      (not forcing)

1◇ 1♠ No 2♡	1♡ 2♣ No 2◇	1♠ 2♡ No 3◇

   b) Jump bid＝16＋HCP
      ＋excellent suit
      (forcing)

1◇ 1♠ No 3♣	1♡ 2♣ No 3◇	1♠ 2♡ No 4◇

   c) Double jump＝Pre-
      emptive, weak with
      good, long suit

1◇ 1♠ No 4♣	1♡ 2♣ No 4♠	1♠ 2♣ No 4◇

4) Bid enemy suit＝
   artificial, forcing

1◇ 1♠ No 2◇	1♡ 2♣ No 2♡	1♠ 2♡ No 2♠

JUMP OVERCALLS

A jump overcall one level higher than a simple overcall shows a strongish hand: Range: 14＋HCP and a very strong rebiddable suit (the bid is not forcing but highly encouraging).

EXAMPLES

N	E
1♣	2♡
1◇	2♠
1♡	2♠
1♡	3♣
1♠	3◇
1♠	3♡

A jump overcall two or three more than a simple overcall is pre-emptive, weak with a very long suit. Further bidding, if any, is the same as after a shut-out opening.

N	E
1♣	3♠
1♣	3◇
1◇	4♡
1♠	4♣
1♡	5◇

RESPONSES TO SINGLE JUMP OVERCALLS

Pass＝0—5 HCP

Single raise＝6—9 HCP ＋support (support＝Qx or xxx or better)

Double raise＝10＋HCP ＋support

No trumps＝6＋HCP＋ no support＋stopper in enemy suit (Over two-level jump overcall, 2 NT＝6—9 HCP and 3 NT＝10＋ HCP)

New suit＝6＋HCP＋ strong rebiddable suit

Enemy suit＝artificial, game-force

EXAMPLES

W	N	E	S
1♡	2♠	No	No
1♡	2♠	No	3♠
1♣	2♡	No	4♡
1◇	2♠	No	2 NT
1♠	3◇	No	3 NT
1♣	2♡	No	3 NT
1♠	3♣	No	3♡
1♡	3♣	No	3♠

COPING WITH INTERFERENCE FROM ENEMY OVERCALLS AFTER PARTNER OPENS

1) If the enemy overcall does not stop you making the bid you would have made without the interference, make your normal bid.
2) You are no longer forced to keep the bidding open on 6 HCP; except for the single raise of partner's suit (still 6—10 points), other bids (new suit, no trumps) show 8 points or better.
3) No trump bids promise a stopper in the enemy suit.
4) Consider doubling the enemy bid for penalties where you have 8—12 HCP＋ strong holding in the enemy suit. Be more careful when this involves doubling the enemy suit into game (doubles of two hearts or higher). If you have enough for game opposite partner's opening, you need a penalty of 500 or better to compensate you for the game missed. You should double an enemy overcall of one no trump whenever your side has more than twenty points.

COMMENTARY

Defensive bidding (overcalls and take-out bids), covered in this lesson and the next, is at least as important as constructive bidding when your side opens the bidding. You should pay particular attention to these lessons and, bit by bit, try to absorb the principles of defensive bidding.

With balanced hands it is dangerous to enter the bidding because it is easy for the enemy to double you for penalties. Even with a strongish hand of 13—15 points, pass if the hand is balanced unless it qualifies for a take-out double (see next lesson). In general, if your main strength is in the enemy suit opened, prefer to pass rather than bid.

The overcall of one no trump is marginally stronger than a strong opening of one no trump, but the overcall of two no trumps is not used to show 20—22 HCP. The overcall of two no trumps is commonly used as 'unusual', showing a very distributional hand with both minor suits, at least 5—5 in clubs and diamonds. The overcall of three no trumps is still used as a gambling bid but shows a stopper in the enemy suit together with the solid six- or seven-card minor or better.

Simple overcalls show primarily a good suit—you do not need 12 points to bid but the suit must be good. This is to indicate a good lead to partner and to minimize the risk of being penalized. A simple overcall at the two-level can be expected to be better than a minimum overcall at the one-level; similarly, you may overcall non-vulnerable on weaker values than when vulnerable since the risk of a hefty penalty is not as great. Later, when you have gained experience, you will recognize the rare occasions when a one-level overcall on a powerful four-card suit is permissible, but for the time being keep your overcalls to at least good five-card suits. When in doubt whether to bid your suit or whether to pass, the rule of two and three is a reasonable guide.

In responding to simple overcalls note that:

1) Three-card support for partner is adequate since his suit must be rebiddable.
2) Since the top limit of a simple overcall is about 13 HCP, you need not bid on less than 8 points since game is beyond reach.
3) You have only two forcing bids available in response to a simple overcall: a jump bid in a new suit and a bid of the enemy suit.
4) Avoid 'rescuing' partner even if he has been doubled. If he is doubled in his overcall, do not rescue if you hold a doubleton or better in his suit. If you hold a singleton or void in his suit, you should 'rescue' only if you hold a strong six-card or longer suit yourself.
5) Your sole aim in responding to partner's overcall should be to reach game if possible, not to improve the part-score position. Aim for major-suit or no trump games rather than minor suit games.

SINGLE-JUMP OVERCALL

This is a strong bid although not forcing. It is frequently based on a single very powerful suit or on a two-suiter. Partner should strive to keep the bidding open, particularly when support is held.

EXERCISES

1) Your right-hand opponent opens one club. What do you bid?

a) ♠ KQ9743   b) ♠ KQJ76   c) ♠ KQ97   d) ♠ 7
    ♡ K82   ♡ 7   ♡ 3   ♡ AJ62
    ◇ 764   ◇ A542   ◇ A872   ◇ AQJ93
    ♣ 6   ♣ 765   ♣ 7632   ♣ 763

e) ♠ AQ942   f) ♠ AKJ754   g) ♠ KQ   h) ♠ 7
    ♡ 72   ♡ AQ   ♡ AQJ84   ♡ KQJ98643
    ◇ AJ1083   ◇ Q43   ◇ KQ873   ◇ A7
    ♣ 6   ♣ 63   ♣ 4   ♣ 43

i) ♠ Q   j) ♠ 53   k) ♠ 53   l) ♠ A7
    ♡ A943   ♡ 762   ♡ A62   ♡ K4
    ◇ QJ76   ◇ KQ43   ◇ KQ43   ◇ J532
    ♣ A643   ♣ AKJ9   ♣ AKJ9   ♣ KQJ98

2) Your right-hand opponent opens one spade. What do you bid?

a) ♠ K7   b) ♠ Q63   c) ♠ J432   d) ♠ 76
    ♡ 64   ♡ AQ543   ♡ 76   ♡ K4
    ◇ AQJ1043 ◇ Q852   ◇ A8   ◇ A54
    ♣ 763   ♣ 4   ♣ AK854 ♣ AKQJ75

e) ♠ AQ   f) ♠ 7   g) ♠ 765   h) ♠ AK10964
    ♡ 853   ♡ A109862 ♡ A   ♡ K
    ◇ A5   ◇ AKJ5   ◇ K872   ◇ K54
    ♣ AKQJ84 ♣ 83   ♣ QJ843 ♣ 763

3)

W N E S   a) ♠ K843   b) ♠ 6   c) ♠ 64
1♣ 1♡ No ?   ♡ 76   ♡ K8432   ♡ K843
What should South ◇ K763   ◇ AK865   ◇ A8542
bid on these hands? ♣ 943   ♣ 74   ♣ 72

    d) ♠ Q6   e) ♠ A4   f) ♠ A97   g) ♠ AQ9743
       ♡ K84   ♡ 7   ♡ 76   ♡ 72
       ◇ AK853 ◇ K9432 ◇ K1086 ◇ K84
       ♣ 752   ♣ J8764 ♣ QJ84 ♣ 63

    h) ♠ AQ8   i) ♠ A96   j) ♠ A96   k) ♠ KQ873
       ♡ K7   ♡ 3   ♡ 3   ♡ A86
       ◇ QJ107 ◇ KQJ642 ◇ AKQJ74 ◇ 763
       ♣ KQ86 ♣ 763   ♣ 842   ♣ J3

4)

NORTH	a) W N E S	b) W N E S	c) W N E S
♠ KQJ86	1♣ 1♠ No 2♠	1◇ 1♠ No 1NT	1♡ 1♠ No 2♡
♡ A87	No ?	No ?	No ?
◇ 43			
♣ 985	d) W N E S	e) W N E S	f) W N E S
	1◇ 1♠ No 2◇	1♡ 1♠ No 3♣	1♣ 1♠ No 3♡
	No ?	No ?	No ?

5)

W N E S   a) ♠ 9743   b) ♠ 1076   c) ♠ K742   d) ♠ A83
1♡ 2♠ No ?   ♡ 53   ♡ Q9   ♡ 4   ♡ 87632
             ◇ Q64   ◇ A8742 ◇ QJ95   ◇ K5
             ♣ Q1095 ♣ 543   ♣ 8752   ♣ Q42

e) ♠ 76
♡ KQ10
♢ 87642
♣ J103

f) ♠ 7
♡ AJ10
♢ QJ1043
♣ Q984

g) ♠ Q8753
♡ —
♢ 87643
♣ 762

h) ♠ 6
♡ 432
♢ AK9876
♣ J43

6)

W	N	E	S
1♡	3♣	No	?

a) ♠ QJ76
♡ 875
♢ Q762
♣ 43

b) ♠ 8764
♡ KJ9
♢ J872
♣ Q8

c) ♠ AJ10854
♡ 6
♢ J873
♣ 75

d) ♠ 8
♡ 9654
♢ A8763
♣ Q85

7)

W	N	E	S
1♣	1♠	?	

What should East
bid on these hands?

a) ♠ KJ5
♡ Q987
♢ QJ83
♣ 76

b) ♠ 86
♡ KQ9876
♢ J96
♣ Q3

c) ♠ AJ10854
♡ QJ4
♢ 987
♣ 5

d) ♠ 84
♡ AJ86
♢ 743
♣ KJ54

8) What would your answers in Exercise 7 have been if North's overcall had been one diamond?

9)

W	N	E	S
1♡	2♣	?	

What should East
bid on these hands?

a) ♠ 75
♡ K854
♢ 65
♣ Q8762

b) ♠ AQ7
♡ 5
♢ 87642
♣ KJ105

c) ♠ AJ64
♡ 76
♢ 9875
♣ J86

d) ♠ QJ107
♡ 432
♢ KQ86
♣ AQ

10)

W	N	E	S
1♠	2♢	No	No
2♡	No	?	

a) ♠ 643
♡ 76
♢ 9862
♣ 7642

b) ♠ 6
♡ K8743
♢ 76542
♣ J3

c) ♠ 9
♡ 42
♢ 874
♣ QJ109764

d) ♠ 653
♡ KQ8
♢ 4
♣ 875432

PLAYING HANDS

Hand 1: Defensive bidding—inferences from the bidding

Dealer North

Nil vulnerable

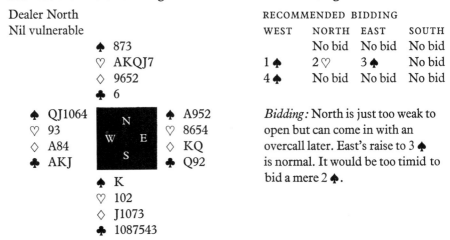

♠ 873
♡ AKQJ7
♢ 9652
♣ 6

♠ QJ1064   ♠ A952
♡ 93   ♡ 8654
♢ A84   ♢ KQ
♣ AKJ   ♣ Q92

♠ K
♡ 102
♢ J1073
♣ 1087543

RECOMMENDED BIDDING

WEST	NORTH	EAST	SOUTH
	No bid	No bid	No bid
1 ♠	2 ♡	3 ♠	No bid
4 ♠	No bid	No bid	No bid

Bidding: North is just too weak to open but can come in with an overcall later. East's raise to 3 ♠ is normal. It would be too timid to bid a mere 2 ♠.

Lead: North leads the king of hearts, the standard lead from an AK combination against a suit contract.

North continues with the ace of hearts and after two rounds he knows that South and West are both out of hearts. A switch to the singleton club is more attractive than a heart continuation, offering the best chance to beat the contract.

RIGHT PLAY The *normal* play in the spade suit is to take the finesse; but West should play the ace of spades, spurning the finesse.

After the second heart trick, West should reason that North must have five hearts for his overcall; he therefore started with AKQJx, since South followed low twice; but North passed originally; with even a queen extra he would have opened; therefore, after the second trick West 'knows' that South has the king of spades.

The correct play is the ace of spades on the first round.

WRONG PLAY Winning the club at trick three and taking the spade finesse (unless North passed with 13 HCP, the finesse must lose). South would win the king of spades and return a club for North to trump. One down.

That the king of spades falls singleton is just lucky. Declarer should play ace and another spade, making ten tricks always and making eleven tricks when the king of spades is singleton. The risk of a club ruff is another reason to draw as many trumps as possible: *the spade finesse is unnecessary for the contract.*

A passed hand cannot have 13 high-card points; do not take a finesse that is sure to fail.

Hand 2: Overcalls—counting—inferences from the bidding

Dealer East
North-South
vulnerable

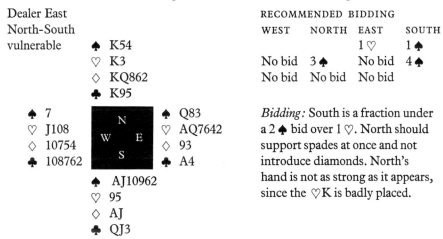

♠ K54
♡ K3
◇ KQ862
♣ K95

♠ 7
♡ J108
◇ 10754
♣ 108762

♠ Q83
♡ AQ7642
◇ 93
♣ A4

♠ AJ10962
♡ 95
◇ AJ
♣ QJ3

RECOMMENDED BIDDING

WEST	NORTH	EAST	SOUTH
		1 ♡	1 ♠
No bid	3 ♠	No bid	4 ♠
No bid	No bid	No bid	

Bidding: South is a fraction under a 2 ♠ bid over 1 ♡. North should support spades at once and not introduce diamonds. North's hand is not as strong as it appears, since the ♡K is badly placed.

Lead: West leads the jack of hearts. When leading partner's suit, lead the top card when you hold two or more honours in sequence.

RIGHT PLAY South sees that he will lose two hearts and a club. Therefore he must avoid a spade loser. Counting his points and dummy's, he sees 27 HCP. West has led the jack of hearts, so that leaves only 12 HCP unaccounted for. East opened the bidding, so he should have all 12 missing points. Thus on the opening lead South 'knows' where all the points are. The correct trump play is to place the queen of spades with East—low spade to the king and a low spade back. If East follows low on the second round, South must play the jack (not the ace) to finesse for the queen, making ten tricks.

WRONG PLAY 1) Not drawing trumps as soon as you obtain the lead. On most hands it is proper to draw trumps at once, unless dummy's trumps are needed to ruff losers. If you fail to draw trumps here, East may defeat you by ruffing the third round of clubs.

2) Playing the ace and king of trumps instead of finessing East for the queen. The queen is marked in the East hand because of his opening bid.

An opening bid will normally include 12 or more HCP. Where one opponent is known to hold more HCP than his partner, any missing high card is more likely to be with the one who holds more points.

With nine trumps missing the queen it is normally correct to play the ace and king, hoping the queen will drop. This does not apply when you have additional information about the enemy hands, when you 'know' which hand has the queen.

Hand 3: Overcall of one no trump—penalty doubles—leading partner's suit

Dealer South
All vulnerable

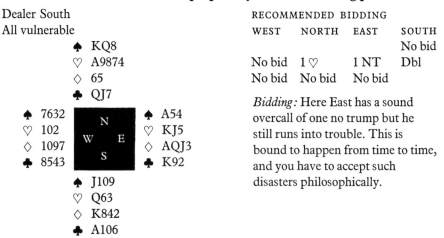

```
              ♠ KQ8
              ♡ A9874
              ◇ 65
              ♣ QJ7
  ♠ 7632              ♠ A54
  ♡ 102      N        ♡ KJ5
  ◇ 1097   W   E      ◇ AQJ3
  ♣ 8543     S        ♣ K92
              ♠ J109
              ♡ Q63
              ◇ K842
              ♣ A106
```

RECOMMENDED BIDDING

WEST	NORTH	EAST	SOUTH
			No bid
No bid	1 ♡	1 NT	Dbl
No bid	No bid	No bid	

Bidding: Here East has a sound overcall of one no trump but he still runs into trouble. This is bound to happen from time to time, and you have to accept such disasters philosophically.

Lead: South should lead his partner's suit. From Q63 the correct card is the three. Note here that the lead of the queen would give declarer two heart tricks. On the lead of the three North wins with the ace, returns a heart, and South's queen will always capture declarer's jack, holding East to only one trick in hearts.

There are several lines of play and defence. On best play and defence East is likely to be held to five tricks, two down, −500. This is where the defenders set up North's heart suit and next attack spades. East, as soon as he wins the lead, should go after diamonds, since this is where he will make most of his tricks. To start with North-South should keep playing hearts until North's hearts are set up. Then, if South has the lead, he should play spades, not clubs. It is important to resist playing the ace of clubs. If South plays the ace of clubs, East's king becomes a winner, but if South holds on to his ace of clubs, East can never make a trick with the king.

Double an overcall of one no trump when your side has the balance of strength. In leading partner's suit lead top of a doubleton, but with three cards lead the lowest from an honour (Kxx, Qxx, Jxx, 10xx; from Axx lead low against no trumps, but lead the ace against a suit contract), lead M.U.D.—middle-up-down from three rags and lead the top honour where you have honours in sequence (KQx, QJx, J10x, 109x, but lead the king from AKx).

Hand 4: Simple overcall—penalty double—suit preference signal

Dealer West
All vulnerable

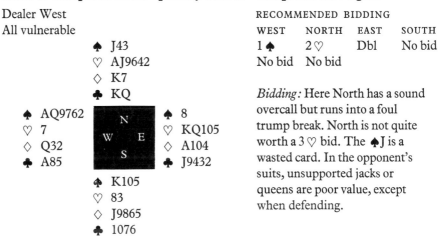

♠ J43
♡ AJ9642
♢ K7
♣ KQ

♠ AQ9762
♡ 7
♢ Q32
♣ A85

♠ 8
♡ KQ105
♢ A104
♣ J9432

♠ K105
♡ 83
♢ J9865
♣ 1076

RECOMMENDED BIDDING

WEST	NORTH	EAST	SOUTH
1♠	2♡	Dbl	No bid
No bid	No bid		

Bidding: Here North has a sound overcall but runs into a foul trump break. North is not quite worth a 3♡ bid. The ♠J is a wasted card. In the opponent's suits, unsupported jacks or queens are poor value, except when defending.

Lead: East leads the eight of spades. Assuming South plays low, West wins the queen of spades, cashes the ace of spades and returns the two of spades for East to ruff. West knows that East is out of spades (he discarded on the second round), so when West plays a spade for East to ruff, West asks East to play back a club. He does this by playing the *two* of spades for East to ruff—*a low card for the low suit*. Had West wanted a diamond back, he would have played the *nine* of spades for East to ruff—*a high card for the high suit*. The suits here are diamonds and clubs, spades and trumps obviously being excluded. This method of telling partner which suit to play when you are giving him a ruff is called the 'suit-preference signal' (cf. Lesson 5, Hand 2). If East plays the ace of diamonds, North's king makes. But East returns a club, and best defence puts the contract three down for 800, ample compensation on a hand where East-West are unlikely to reach game. Note that in the last two deals the overcallers had good hands but still ran into trouble. Imagine how much worse it would have been with a poor hand or a poor suit!

Be quick to double an enemy suit overcall when your hand has good trumps (at least four trumps against a two-level overcall; five or more trumps against a one-level overcall), middling strength (8—12 high-card points) and a misfit with partner (singleton or void in his suit).

Lesson 8

Part A: Slam Bidding

For a small slam you need about 33 points; for a grand slam you need about 37 points.

If you go down in a small slam, you have missed a valuable score; you could have scored game. A small slam that depends on more than a finesse is not worth bidding. If you go down in a grand slam, you have missed a valuable score; you could have scored game and small slam. Do not bid a grand slam unless you are virtually sure that it is a laydown.

Four no trumps asking for aces: the Blackwood convention
Four no trumps over a suit bid asks: 'Partner, how many aces do you have?'

Replies: 5♣=0 or 4 aces
           5◇=1 ace
           5♡=2 aces
           5♠=3 aces

After a Blackwood bid of four no trumps for aces has been answered, five no trumps asks partner for kings.

Replies: 6♣=No kings
           6◇=1 king
           6♡=2 kings
           6♠=3 kings
           6 NT=4 kings

The bid of five no trumps for kings guarantees the partnership holds all the aces.

COMMENTARY

1) Do not use Blackwood four no trumps unless you are in the slam zone. It is very annoying to be in five hearts or five spades, one down. You should use Blackwood only to make sure you are not short of aces; it is no cure if you are short of points. The 33 points for a small slam or the 37 for a grand slam need not all be high-card points; the enemy may therefore hold enough aces to beat your contract. To make sure they don't, use Blackwood.

2) There can be no ambiguity over the response of five clubs showing no aces or four aces. You cannot be in the slam zone if the partnership is missing all four aces!

3) When replying to Blackwood, do not count a void as an ace.

4) If partner's reply to Blackwood shows that one ace is missing, bid a small slam—do not use five no trumps asking for kings. The bid of five no trumps for kings is a try for a grand slam and promises that the partnership holds all the aces. If you are not going past a small slam, for example, when you are missing one ace, there is no point in telling the opposition how many kings partner has.

5) If partner's reply to Blackwood shows that two aces are missing:

a) Pass if partner's reply was in the agreed trump suit.

b) Otherwise bid five of the agreed trump suit. If this is impossible (for example, the agreed suit is clubs and you have already passed five clubs), *bid a new suit at the five level*. This asks partner to bid five no trumps which you can then pass. Note that you cannot bid five no trumps yourself, because this would ask partner for kings. It should be clear that caution must be exercised in using Blackwood when the agreed trump suit is clubs or diamonds. If partner's reply is embarrassing, you may be unable to retreat to five clubs or five diamonds, while five no trumps may be a very risky proposition.

6) You cannot use the bid of five no trumps for kings without first using the bid of four no trumps for aces. (This is because a jump to five no trumps is 'the grand slam force', asking partner to bid seven of the agreed trump suit if he holds two of the top three honours in it. If there is no agreed suit, it is the last suit bid by partner. Do not worry about the grand slam force—it is a very rare bid.)

7) Avoid using Blackwood unless you know what to do with the answer. Blackwood tells you how many aces partner holds but not which aces they are. If it is vital to know which aces are held, for example, if you have a void, do not use Blackwood, use cue bidding (see Appendix II, page 107). Cue bidding is an advanced slam-bidding method and you need not worry about it yet; when you gain confidence, then you will want to learn how to cue-bid.

8) Sometimes you may want to be in slam only if partner has good trumps. A bid of five of a major suit asks partner to bid six if he has good trumps (for example, 1 ♡ : 2 ♣, 2 ♠ : 5 ♡, or 4 ♡ : 5 ♡, or even 1 ♠ : 5 ♠). If partner's trumps are poor, he just passes. It does not come up frequently, and you should note that it does not apply in a minor suit or after Blackwood has been used.

9) A bid of four no trumps is not Blackwood if it is a raise of partner's no trump bid (for example, 2 NT : 4 NT or 1 ◇ : 3 NT, 4 NT). Here the bid of four no trumps is an invitation to bid six no trumps if partner is maximum. Four no trumps is also not Blackwood when used by a player who has previously bid no trumps in the auction.

EXERCISES

1) In each of the following auctions you are South with the hand shown. What is your next bid in each of the auctions?

a)		b)		c)		d)		e)	
♠ 642		♠ K86		♠ AK8		♠ AJ83		♠ 7	
♡ Q8765		♡ AQ4		♡ KQ7		♡ A6		♡ K93	
◇ 3		◇ 763		◇ Q832		◇ AQJ42		◇ 7432	
♣ KQ83		♣ AK92		♣ AKJ		♣ 83		♣ AKQ76	

N	S	N	S	N	S	N	S	N	S
1♡	4♡		1 NT		2 NT		1◇	1♡	2♣
4 NT	?	3♠	4♠	4 NT	?	1♠	3♠	2♠	4♡
		4 NT	?			4 NT	?	4 NT	?

2) You hold: what is your next bid in each of these auctions?

		a) You	Ptnr	b) You	Ptnr	c) You	Ptnr	d) You	Ptnr	e) You	Ptnr
♠ KQ853		1♠	3♠	1♠	3♠	1♠	3♣	1♠	3♣	1♠	3♣
♡ AQJ2		4 NT	5◇	4 NT	5♡	3♡	3♠	3♠	3♠	3♡	3♠
◇ KQ4		?		?		4 NT	5♠	4 NT	5♠	4 NT	5♠
♣ 6						5 NT	6♣	5 NT	6◇	5 NT	6♡
						?		?		?	

3) You hold: what is your next bid?

		a) You	Ptnr	b) You	Ptnr	c) You	Ptnr	d) You	Ptnr
♠ A95		1♡	4 NT		1♠		2◇	1♡	3◇
♡ AJ632		5♡	6◇	2♡	4 NT	2♡	5 NT	3♡	5♡
◇ —		?		5♡	6◇	?		?	
♣ QJ876				?					

4) You hold: what is your next bid?

		a) You	Ptnr	b) You	Ptnr	c) You	Ptnr	d) You	Ptnr
♠ A8432		1♠	2♣	1♠	2◇	1♠	2♡		2◇
♡ KQ5		4♣	4 NT	3♣	5♠	4♡	5♡	2♠	5 NT
◇ 6		5◇	5♡	?		?		?	
♣ KQJ3		?							

94

Part B: Take-out doubles and other take-out bids

When is a double for take-out?

A double is for take-out if:

1) It is a double of a suit bid;
2) At the one-, two- or three-level; and
3) Partner has not bid anything (except pass).

A double is for penalties if:

1) It is a double of no trumps; or
2) It is at the four-level or higher; or
3) Partner has made any bid at all.

What do you need to make a take-out double?

1) An opening hand or better.
2) If balanced, 16 HCP or more with no stopper in the enemy suit, 19 HCP or more with or without a stopper in the enemy suit (with a stopper+16—18, bid one no trump).
3) If unbalanced, the major suits, unless you are very powerful. If the enemy opened a major suit, the double should promise the other major. If the enemy opened a minor suit, the double should promise support for both majors (no worse than 4—3)
4) Do not double on one-suited hands unless the hand is too strong for a jump overcall.

A take-out double is not used simply to show 12 or more HCP. It should also show the right shape. In the minimum zone (12—15 HCP) the doubler should be short in the enemy suit and guarantee support for any unbid major.

Responding to partner's take-out double

EXAMPLES

1) Pass

—don't; the only time you might consider passing partner's take-out double is when you have a long, solid holding in the enemy suit (for example, KQJ10xx, QJ109xx). Your pass converts the take-out into a penalty double, and partner should lead a trump.

N	E	S	W
1♣	Dbl	No	No

2) No trumps

1 NT—6—10 points+stopper in the enemy suit.
2 NT—11—12 points+stopper in enemy suit, not forcing
3 NT—13—15 points+solid stopper in enemy suit.

1♡	Dbl	No	1 NT
1♡	Dbl	No	2 NT
1♡	Dbl	No	3 NT

3) Suit bids

Cheapest level 0—8 points, weak hand, may even be three-card suit if no four-card suit held outside enemy suit. Doubler passes unless very strong.

1◇	Dbl	No	1♠
		or	
1♡	Dbl	No	2♣

Single jump—9—12 points, fair hand, suit will be genuine, not forcing; doubler will bid again if chance for game, i.e., unless absolutely minimum double.

1◇	Dbl	No	2♠
		or	
1♡	Dbl	No	3♣

Double jump—weak, shut-out bid; doubler not expected to bid again unless very strong.

1◇	Dbl	No	3♠

Game bid—values for game+confidence that this is the best spot (if in doubt about best spot, bid enemy suit).	1 ◇	Dbl	No 4 ♡
Enemy suit—artificial, forcing to game, 13 points or more, asks partner to describe hand.	1 ◇	Dbl	No 2 ◇

1) Redouble—any hand with 10 or more HCP—does not promise tolerance for partner's suit.
2) All bids other than redouble deny 10 points, even jump raises of partner's suit or jump bids in new suits.
3) 1 NT—6—19 points, balanced.
4) Pass—0—9 points+inability to raise partner, bid one no trump or bid long suit of your own.

COMMENTARY

When you bid a suit over an enemy opening, partner expects at least a five-card suit and usually a one-suited hand. When you have only four-card suits but a strong hand, or you have at least two suits and don't know which to bid, the solution is to make a take-out double. Suppose you hold ♠: AQJ4, ♡: KQ97, ◇: 3, ♣: K542, and your right-hand opponent opens one diamond. If you bid one heart or one spade. you not only misinform partner as to the length of your suit but you may pick the wrong suit. If you bid one heart, partner will not be inclined to introduce a four-card spade suit, while if you bid one spade, a possible heart fit might be lost. The solution is to 'double', asking partner to take out the double into his best suit.

The ideal shape for a double is 5—4—4—0 or 4—4—4—1 with a shortage in the enemy suit. The strength can be anything from an opening bid upwards. You can also make a take-out double after you have passed; then the strength would be just under an opening hand.

You should avoid making a take-out double on balanced hands under the strength of an overcall of one no trump. You will not always have the ideal doubling shape and may have to compromise, but the emphasis in take-out doubles is on the major suits. You should avoid making a take-out double of one club or one diamond without support for both majors and similarly avoid making a take-out double of one major suit without four-card support for the other.

In responding to partner's take-out double you should not pass—no matter how weak your hand is. The only time to pass is when you are long and strong in the enemy suit; your pass then converts the double into a penalty double and the doubler should lead a trump. With 0—8 points partner of the doubler just bids his best suit (i.e., his longest) at the cheapest level, *but prefer a four-card major to a longer minor*. With no four-card suit outside the enemy suit bid your cheapest three-card suit, unless your hand fits a response of one no trump (6—10 points and a stopper in the enemy suit; it is not a desperation bid but shows some values). If partner doubles and next opponent bids or redoubles, you may pass on a weak balanced hand.

The doubler will usually pass a weakness bid unless he still has some hopes for game opposite partner's known poor hand. Since the doubler knows that partner may have even zero points, any bid he makes will be based on strength. A no trump bid by the doubler after a weakness bid shows better than an overcall of one no trump, a good 18 to 19 points, while a jump in no trumps shows the equivalent of an opening of two no trumps.

With 9 points or more partner of the doubler should not make a weakness bid. A jump bid in a suit is called for, showing 9—12 points. Doubler is not forced to bid again but he will do so with any extra values.

The bid of the enemy suit by the defenders is forcing to game: this is so if partner has made an overcall, a take-out double, or has not bid at all. Where partner has not bid at all, the forcing-to-game bid of the enemy suit must be based on a gigantic hand, since game must be reached even if partner has a yarborough. If in doubt, ask yourself: 'If partner has a 4—3—3—3 shape but no points at all, have I enough for game?' If so, bid the enemy suit; if not, just make a take-out double.

When the enemy starts with a shut-out bid, your bidding can no longer be scientific and 100% accurate, since you have lost considerable bidding space. To come into the bidding at all you should have a better-than-minimum opening hand plus either a very good suit of your own or support for the unbid suits. You should assume that partner has about 6—7 points and if that is enough for game, bid game. If you need more than that, invite game (for example, by bidding your suit at the three-level). A bid of three no trumps would show about 18 points or more plus a stopper in the enemy suit. Sometimes you will be too high and you will be doubled, but that is part of the enemy's reward for their shut-out bidding.

EXERCISES

1) In the following auctions is South's double for take-out or penalties?

a)
W	N	E	S
No	No	1♡	Dbl

b)
W	N	E	S
1♡	No	2♣	Dbl

c)
W	N	E	S
1♡	No	2♡	Dbl

d)
W	N	E	S
1♡	No	4♡	Dbl

e)
W	N	E	S
No	No	1 NT	Dbl

f)
W	N	E	S
1♡	No	No	Dbl

g)
W	N	E	S
1♡	No	1♠	Dbl

h)
W	N	E	S
1♡	Dbl	1♠	Dbl

i)
W	N	E	S
No	1♣	1♠	Dbl

j)
W	N	E	S
1 NT	2♢	Dbl	

k)
W	N	E	S
	No	No	
1♢	No	1♠	Dbl

l)
W	N	E	S
No	4♣	Dbl	

2) You are East. North opens one club. What action do you take on these hands?

a)
♠ K843
♡ QJ42
♢ AQ72
♣ 5

b)
♠ AJ87
♡ KQ94
♢ A10743
♣ —

c)
♠ AQ87
♡ 6
♢ AK10432
♣ 62

d)
♠ AQ84
♡ AJ963
♢ K2
♣ 74

e)
♠ AQ875
♡ 6
♢ AK1043
♣ 43

f)
♠ AJ87
♡ KQ9
♢ A843
♣ 63

g)
♠ AJ74
♡ KQ7
♢ J96
♣ AQ5

h)
♠ AQ62
♡ A4
♢ AKQ6
♣ 542

3) You are East. North opens one heart. What action do you take on these hands?

a)
♠ KQ
♡ A43
♢ A832
♣ J754

b)
♠ KQ72
♡ A3
♢ A832
♣ J75

c)
♠ KQ43
♡ 7
♢ AK10962
♣ 62

d)
♠ AK8632
♡ 7
♢ KQ43
♣ 62

e)
♠ J832
♡ 6
♢ AK762
♣ KQ9

f)
♠ AJ1073
♡ 6
♢ AK1052
♣ 86

g)
♠ K
♡ AK10962
♢ A74
♣ J43

h)
♠ Q
♡ 432
♢ AQJ72
♣ KQ95

4)
W	N	E	S
1♢	Dbl	No	?

What should South bid on these hands?

a)
♠ K973
♡ Q5
♢ 7643
♣ 832

b)
♠ 9732
♡ 842
♢ 76
♣ 6432

c)
♠ Q9874
♡ Q865
♢ 43
♣ 62

d)
♠ 62
♡ Q865
♢ 43
♣ Q9874

e)
♠ 76
♡ 432
♢ A72
♣ J9875

f)
♠ 764
♡ 543
♢ 98743
♣ 32

g)
♠ 76
♡ Q43
♢ AQ82
♣ 7652

h)
♠ 4
♡ K8
♢ KQJ1032
♣ 8432

5)
W	N	E	S
1♣	Dbl	No	?

What should South bid on these hands?

a)
♠ K9843
♡ 6
♢ 642
♣ A742

b)
♠ K954
♡ AJ1075
♢ 43
♣ 62

c)
♠ 76
♡ K84
♢ AQJ42
♣ 653

d)
♠ 85
♡ A75
♢ AJ93
♣ Q1087

e)
♠ KQ8764
♡ A8
♢ 2
♣ 7643

f)
♠ AQJ42
♡ 6
♢ A87
♣ 6432

g)
♠ J104
♡ AJ7
♢ QJ43
♣ KQ8

h)
♠ QJ5
♡ K432
♢ A872
♣ A8

6) W N E S   What should South bid on these hands?
   1 ◇ Dbl 1 ♠ ?

	a)	b)	c)	d)	e)
♠	Q7	J85	7	9	KQJ85
♡	Q843	K3	QJ843	AJ986	A6
◇	764	AJ82	865	762	432
♣	8652	7654	K872	K872	542

7) W N E S   What should South bid on these hands?
   1 ♡ Dbl Rdbl ?

	a)	b)	c)	d)	e)
♠	Q952	87	86	AQ954	AQ6
♡	76	Q54	AQ8	643	Q7
◇	8532	862	J943	QJ7	Q943
♣	765	K9432	9873	54	KJ76

8)
i) NORTH

  ♠ AJ73
  ♡ KQ42
  ◇ 76
  ♣ K83

a) W N E S
   1 ◇ Dbl No 1 ♡
   No ?

b) W N E S
   1 ◇ Dbl No 1 NT
   No ?

c) W N E S
   1 ◇ Dbl No 2 ♣
   No ?

d) W N E S
   1 ◇ Dbl No 3 ♠
   No ?

e) W N E S
   1 ◇ Dbl No 2 NT
   No ?

f) W N E S
   1 ◇ Dbl No 2 ◇
   No ?

ii) NORTH

  ♠ AQJ7
  ♡ KQ83
  ◇ A962
  ♣ 6

a) W N E S
   1 ♣ Dbl No 1 ♡
   No ?

b) W N E S
   1 ♣ Dbl No 2 ♡
   No ?

c) W N E S
   1 ♣ Dbl No 1 NT
   No ?

d) W N E S
   1 ♣ Dbl No 2 NT
   No ?

e) W N E S
   1 ♣ Dbl No 1 ♠
   No ?

f) W N E S
   1 ♣ Dbl No 2 ♣
   No ?

iii) EAST

  ♠ AJ7
  ♡ AKQ7
  ◇ A1083
  ♣ Q5

North opens one diamond and East doubles. What should East bid next if West responds?
a) 1 ♡ b) 1 ♠ c) 2 ♣

iv) EAST

  ♠ AK4
  ♡ AK8
  ◇ QJ95
  ♣ AJ5

North opens one club and East doubles. What should East bid next if West responds?
a) 1 ♡ b) 1 ♠ c) 1 NT

9)
i) SOUTH

  ♠ 6
  ♡ J8653
  ◇ 762
  ♣ K942

a) W N E S
   1 ♣ Dbl No 1 ♡
   No 3 ♡ No ?

b) W N E S
   1 ♡ Dbl No 2 ♣
   No 2 ◇ No ?

ii) SOUTH

  ♠ K84
  ♡ Q985
  ◇ 75
  ♣ JQ942

a) W N E S
   1 ♣ Dbl No 1 ♡
   No 1 NT No ?

b) W N E S
   1 ♣ Dbl No 1 ♡
   No 3 ♡ No ?

10) W N E S   What should East bid over the double on these hands?
   1 ♡ Dbl ?

	a)	b)	c)	d)	e)
♠	876	432	3	KQ94	QJ5
♡	542	—	8743	J765	K98763
◇	Q943	J984	J9743	6	7
♣	QJ6	QJ9765	876	7432	872

	f)	g)	h)	i)	j)
♠	J632	AQ93	AJ7	A8	76
♡	AK8	6	76	3	K8
◇	KQ5	KQ84	QJ52	AK843	A976
♣	J64	J732	J987	J10753	76542

Hand 1: Take-out double and response—suit combinations—discarding and ruffing losers

Dealer North
Nil vulnerable

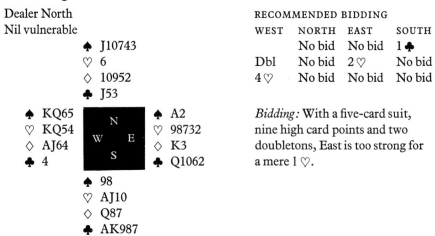

♠ J10743
♡ 6
♢ 10952
♣ J53

♠ KQ65   ♠ A2
♡ KQ54   ♡ 98732
♢ AJ64   ♢ K3
♣ 4   ♣ Q1062

♠ 98
♡ AJ10
♢ Q87
♣ AK987

RECOMMENDED BIDDING

WEST	NORTH	EAST	SOUTH
	No bid	No bid	1 ♣
Dbl	No bid	2 ♡	No bid
4 ♡	No bid	No bid	No bid

Bidding: With a five-card suit, nine high card points and two doubletons, East is too strong for a mere 1 ♡.

Lead: King of clubs. North plays a discouraging three of clubs, and South should switch to the nine of spades (top from a doubleton).

RIGHT PLAY After king of clubs and nine of spades switch, East should win with the ace of spades. As South should hold the heart ace (for his opening bid), East should lead hearts from his own hand towards the honours in dummy. South plays low and the king wins. Back to hand with the king of diamonds and another heart towards dummy. Say South wins and plays another spade. Win in dummy, cash the queen of hearts, drawing the last trump. Then play a top spade, discarding a club, ruff a spade, take a diamond finesse (it should work, since South opened), cash the ace of diamonds, discarding a club, ruff a diamond and ruff your last club, making eleven tricks. Even if the diamond finesse lost, you could still discard a club on the ace of diamonds and make ten tricks.

WRONG PLAY 1) Winning the spade switch in dummy and playing the king of hearts. This loses two heart tricks instead of one.
2) Winning the ace of spades but not playing trumps. If you play ace, king and queen of spades, South ruffs and again makes two heart tricks.
3) Winning ace of spades and ruffing a club. There is no urgency to ruff clubs.
You should draw trumps, planning to discard two clubs, one on the third spade and one on the third round of diamonds and then ruff your last club.

Take note of any opposition bidding: it usually pinpoints several key cards. In handling most suit combinations it usually pays to lead towards honours rather than lead the honours themselves.

Hand 2: Take-out double and response—discarding losers before drawing trumps—'marked' finesse

Dealer East
North-South vulnerable

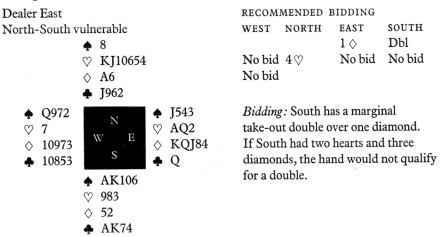

♠ 8
♡ KJ10654
♢ A6
♣ J962

♠ Q972   ♠ J543
♡ 7   ♡ AQ2
♢ 10973   ♢ KQJ84
♣ 10853   ♣ Q

♠ AK106
♡ 983
♢ 52
♣ AK74

RECOMMENDED BIDDING

WEST	NORTH	EAST	SOUTH
		1 ♢	Dbl
No bid	4 ♡	No bid	No bid
No bid			

Bidding: South has a marginal take-out double over one diamond. If South had two hearts and three diamonds, the hand would not qualify for a double.

Lead: East leads the king of diamonds. (East could also consider leading the singleton club, hoping that West might have an entry to give East a ruff.)

RIGHT PLAY North wins the ace of diamonds and plays ace and king of spades, discarding his losing diamond. He then plays a trump from dummy, playing the jack from his hand. Here East has both the ace and queen, but in handling this trump suit it will usually pay you to finesse for the queen. When North regains the lead, he plays trumps until they are drawn. He then plays a club to the ace, noting East's queen falling. On the king of clubs East shows out, so a low club from dummy is played, and if West plays low, North plays the nine, which must win, making eleven tricks.

WRONG PLAY 1) Winning ace of diamonds and playing trumps. This allows the enemy to gain the lead and cash a diamond.
2) Playing clubs before trumps are drawn. One way to go down is to win the ace of diamonds, then play ace of clubs and king of clubs. East ruffs with the two of hearts, cashes a diamond trick, and still must come to two heart tricks.
3) Failing to finesse the nine of clubs later in the hand.

Develop a habit of looking at all the cards played. If you don't see the cards, you cannot remember them. Practise counting the cards in a suit, starting with the trump suit and gradually extending it until you can count out all the suits. It will be difficult at first but it is just a matter of training.

Hand 3: Game-forcing take-out—Blackwood—establishing dummy's long suit

Dealer South
All vulnerable

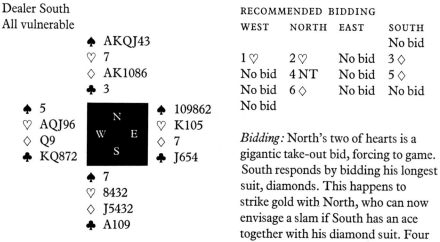

♠ AKQJ43
♡ 7
◇ AK1086
♣ 3

♠ 5
♡ AQJ96
◇ Q9
♣ KQ872

♠ 109862
♡ K105
◇ 7
♣ J654

♠ 7
♡ 8432
◇ J5432
♣ A109

RECOMMENDED BIDDING

WEST	NORTH	EAST	SOUTH
			No bid
1♡	2♡	No bid	3◇
No bid	4NT	No bid	5◇
No bid	6◇	No bid	No bid
No bid			

Bidding: North's two of hearts is a gigantic take-out bid, forcing to game. South responds by bidding his longest suit, diamonds. This happens to strike gold with North, who can now envisage a slam if South has an ace together with his diamond suit. Four no trumps asks South for aces; five diamonds answers 'one ace', so North bids six diamonds. Had South denied an ace with five clubs, North would have settled for five diamonds.

Six diamonds is on for North-South, and it is worth noting that East-West have a reasonable sacrifice in six hearts which costs less, even doubled, than the vulnerable slam. Six spades is a reasonable contract failing on the bad trump break.

Lead: West leads the king of clubs. Against a small slam it usually pays to try to build up a trick rather than cash an ace.

RIGHT PLAY South should win the ace of clubs, draw the trumps with the ace and king of diamonds, then play spades. On the spades South should discard hearts. The fifth round of spades has to be trumped, then a club is trumped in dummy, and South's last heart is discarded on the sixth spade. South's last club is trumped in dummy, and all thirteen tricks are made.

WRONG PLAY 1) Playing trumps after the enemy trumps have been drawn.
2) Discarding clubs on dummy's spades instead of hearts. The clubs can be trumped in dummy anyway, so there is no point in discarding them.
3) Playing spades before drawing trumps. West trumps the second spade and cashes the ace of hearts. One down.

With a powerful distributional hand be quick to look for a slam when you have a fit with partner: draw trumps as early as possible on most hands.

Hand 4: Bidding after an enemy take-out double—deceptive manoeuvres

Dealer West
Nil vulnerable

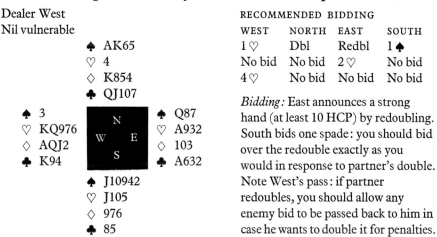

```
              ♠ AK65
              ♡ 4
              ◇ K854
              ♣ QJ107
    ♠ 3                      ♠ Q87
    ♡ KQ976      N           ♡ A932
    ◇ AQJ2    W     E        ◇ 103
    ♣ K94         S          ♣ A632
              ♠ J10942
              ♡ J105
              ◇ 976
              ♣ 85
```

RECOMMENDED BIDDING

WEST	NORTH	EAST	SOUTH
1♡	Dbl	Redbl	1♠
No bid	No bid	2♡	No bid
4♡	No bid	No bid	No bid

Bidding: East announces a strong hand (at least 10 HCP) by redoubling. South bids one spade: you should bid over the redouble exactly as you would in response to partner's double. Note West's pass: if partner redoubles, you should allow any enemy bid to be passed back to him in case he wants to double it for penalties.

The redoubler promises he will bid again.

Lead: North leads the king of spades, and South plays the two, warning North against continuing spades. If North continued with the ace of spades, West would ruff and now the queen of spades would be high. North realizes the danger and switches to the queen of clubs.

PLAY West should win with the king of clubs and draw trumps in three rounds, ending up in his own hand. The contract is safe, since West cannot lose more than one spade, one diamond and one club, but West may as well try for overtricks.

Since the king of diamonds must be with North (in view of his take-out double), there is no point in taking the diamond finesse. After drawing trumps, West might try a little skulduggery by leading the two of diamonds from his hand towards dummy. If North fails to play the king of diamonds, the ten will win and you have no diamond loser! Suppose North does win with the king of diamonds and plays the jack of clubs. You still make eleven tricks, because you win the ace of clubs, play three rounds of diamonds (all your diamonds are now high), discarding two clubs from dummy and ruffing your losing club in dummy.

When you know the location of key high cards, you can often bamboozle the defenders and steal tricks with low cards; when trying to steal a trick, play the lowest card that will do the job.

Appendix I: Opening leads

Part A: Which suit to lead

It is impossible to find the winning lead every time, but the following hints will keep you on the right track more often than not. Remember that this is only a general guide and circumstances may indicate a departure from the recommended approach.

1) **Lead partner's suit.** Unless you have a very, very good reason to choose another suit, prefer to lead partner's suit rather than anything else. Even if you have just a singleton and the opposition have bid no trumps over partner, still lead partner's suit unless you have a clear-cut better suit of your own. Leading partner's suit also has a considerable psychological benefit: if you lead his suit and it turns out another lead would have worked better, partner is all-forgiving; but if you lead something else and it turns out that partner's suit was the best lead, you have an irate partner on your hands. It is never pleasant to hear partner say after the hand is over: 'Sorry, partner, it was my fault for bidding diamonds. I should have bid spades. Then you might have led a diamond!'

2) **Listen to the bidding.** Good leaders have big ears. By working out declarer's and dummy's likely shapes from the bidding you will have a better idea of what to lead. It is usually undesirable to lead a suit bid by the opposition. If the opponents have bid three suits, it stands to reason that the best place to attack will be the unbid suit.

3) **Against no trumps lead your long suit.** But if partner has bid, prefer to lead his suit. Also if the opposition bidding has shown that they hold length in your suit, it may be best to direct your attack elsewhere, unless your long suit is solid.

4) **Against suit contracts different tactics apply.** A long suit is not the overwhelming favourite against a suit contract, because even if you establish the suit declarer is protected by his trumps. There are times to lead a singleton or doubleton; there are times to lead a trump; times to lead your long suit; times to make a passive lead.

i) Partner's suit: Still the first choice.

ii) Singleton leads: These are desirable when you hold two or three worthless trumps, possibly together with the ace or king, for example, 7 6 5, 4 3, A 5 2, K 4 3. By trumping in with a low trump you make a trick you wouldn't have made otherwise.

However, a singleton lead in declarer's second suit is best avoided, and a singleton lead in dummy's suit may also work out badly. A singleton lead is usually undesirable when you hold four or more trumps or you have very strong trumps which will produce tricks without the need to trump in.

What is said about singletons applies also to doubletons except that doubleton leads are far less attractive than singletons. It's a long time before you are able to trump in.

iii) Trump leads: These are worthwhile if: (a) the bidding is 'right'; and (b) your trump holding is 'leadable'.

a) Bidding: A trump lead is indicated if the trump suit has been raised by dummy or declarer has bid two suits and dummy has given a preference for one of them.

But if the trump suit has been bid only by declarer and dummy has not shown support for the suit, a trump lead is not indicated and is in general undesirable.

b) 'Leadable' trumps: From some holdings it is poor to lead a trump since you will very likely be costing your side a trick by a trump lead. Trump leads are best from two or three worthless trumps or from A x, A x x, or K x x or a solid holding. From A x x or K x x the low trump is led; from a doubleton trump lead the lower, while from three rags lead middle-down-up (high-low in trumps equals an odd number; low-high in trumps equals an even number).

Prefer not to lead a trump from J x, J x x, Q x, Q x x, K x, a singleton, or four trumps or more. With four or more trumps it is generally best to lead your long suit and avoid a short suit lead. Your aim should be to make declarer trump in and lose control of the trump suit. Your trump *length* is a serious threat to declarer, so a singleton or doubleton lead is undesirable because by trumping in you will be weakening your length and the threat to declarer.

With a singleton trump you should again lead your long suit for it may well be that partner has trump length and you will be assisting him by forcing declarer to trump.

iv) Other leads: Leading an enemy suit is not good for your side. You should be attacking where your strength is, not where theirs is. Leading out aces costs much more than it gains, for aces are best used to capture enemy high cards rather than low ones. Solid sequences (K Q J, Q J 10, J 10 9) are often the best leads, and A K suits also make good leads, for when you lead the king you retain the lead and still have control of the suit with the ace, while after you see dummy and partner's signal to your lead you will be better placed to decide whether to continue or whether to switch to another suit.

Doubleton honour leads (A x, K x, Q x, J x, 10 x) are likely to cost a trick and should be shunned except as desperation leads (unless, of course, it is partner's suit). However, a doubleton honour *in sequence* (KQ, QJ, J10) is much less likely to do damage and can be a good attacking lead.

Again, the bidding will often provide a reliable guide as to the best direction in which to attack. With nothing to go by a lead from three or four worthless cards may provide a safe passive lead.

5) **Leads against slams.** Against six of a suit an attacking lead is usually best (for example, from a king or a queen in an unbid suit). Ace leads against small slams are not more attractive than usual unless the lead is indicated by the bidding (it takes two tricks to beat a small slam). Trump leads usually don't work well here, though again the bidding may be the best guide. If the opposition have bid three suits, it will rarely be wrong to lead the unbid suit.

Against six no trumps or a grand slam a safe passive lead is called for, and leads from honour cards are generally not best.

6) **Leads against doubled contracts:** a) A take-out double is passed by partner, converting it into a penalty double. A trump lead is called for.

b) Three no trumps doubled: This demands the lead of any suit bid by the defenders or if the defenders have not bid, it calls for the lead of the first suit bid by dummy.

c) Slam doubled: This demands an *unusual* lead, usually the first suit bid by dummy.

Part B: Which card to lead

Doubleton: Lead the top card (except in trumps).

Three Cards: Lead *lowest* from three to an honour, *middle* from three worthless cards (no honour), *top* from two or three cards in *sequence* if the top card is an honour.

EXCEPTIONS

1) From A x x against a *suit* contract lead the ace if you must lead the suit.
2) From A K x lead the king.

EXAMPLES

Lead lowest from K 9 3, Q 8 7, J 8 2, 10 8 2.
Lead middle from: 9 6 5, 9 8 2, 6 4 2, 7 6 5.
Lead top from: K Q 3, Q J 8, J 10 2, 10 9 2.

Four cards or longer: Lead *fourth highest* unless the suit has a three-card sequence or near sequence with an honour at the top of the sequence, in which case lead top of the sequence.
K Q J, Q J 10, J 10 9, 10 9 8 are solid sequences.
K Q 10, Q J 9, J 10 8, 10 9 7 are near sequences.

EXAMPLES

KJ843	KQJ43	QJ62	QJ92	K10753	K10973
Lead the 4	Lead the K	Lead the 2	Lead the Q	Lead the 5	Lead the 10

EXCEPTIONS

1) From A K Q suits lead the king.
2) From A x x x suits *against a suit contract* lead the ace if you have to lead the suit.
3) From A K x x suits *against a suit contract* lead the king.
4) From K Q x x suits *against a suit contract* lead the king.

The card to lead is generally the same whether the contract is no trumps or trumps except for (2), (3) and (4) above.

There is no difference in which card to lead if the suit is partner's suit.

Appendix II: Bridge myths and fallacies

There are many popular maxims and jingles which all have one purpose in mind—*to avoid thinking*! But bridge is for humans, not for robots or parrots. You cannot play a good game of bridge simply by being able to recite more slogans than your fellow-parrot. Bridge is a thinking game.

Here are a few of the more common fallacies, some of which contain a grain of truth, some of which work now and then; but whatever value they might have is lost because they pretend to be and are usually treated as absolutes, 'always' or 'never' rules, universal principles. They are frequently dredged up at post-mortems in pinpointing blame or excusing guilt. If you have a partner whose favourite pastime is reciting parrot-cries, your best defence is a polite scoffing laugh without paying much attention.

At best, the following are reasonable guides to be discarded when the circumstances require. The hardest thing is to decide 'when the circumstances require'. What follows is not intended to replace one set of parrot cries with another but to indicate a more rational approach to many common situations.

1) 'Always lead top of partner's suit.'

No, no, no. This must be one of the worst slogans ever devised. It probably developed when good players were partnering weak players, and knowing that the weak players would be hard-pressed to know the proper lead, the good players would shrug, 'Oh, just lead top of my suit.'

The lead in partner's suit is just the normal lead as set out in Appendix I above. On occasion it may pay to depart from those principles, but if you do, you should have some good reason.

In the following situations leading the top card costs the defence a trick.

	84			J103			74	
Q63		A10975	Q72		A9865	K52		AJ1093
	KJ2			K4			Q86	

If West leads the queen, South makes two tricks. If West leads low, declarer makes one trick.

If West leads the queen, South makes two tricks. If West leads low, declarer makes one trick.

If West leads the king, South makes a trick. If West leads low, declarer makes no trick.

There are many similar situations. Mechanically leading top of partner's suit from three to an honour may not lose but it is only very rarely that it gains. Usually it's a case of heads you lose, tails you break even. So next time you hear 'Always lead top of my suit', be polite: you are dealing with a parrot, not a bridge player.

2) 'Always return partner's suit.'

This has at least some merit but it is far too wide. It is usually best to return partner's lead, but there are many situations where you should be able to recognize that a switch is called for. As your card-reading ability improves, so you will be able to recognize more easily when partner's suit is not best. Unless you have a definite reason to switch, it is reasonable to continue with partner's suit. But beware 'always'!

3) 'Never lead from a king.'

This is a favourite for the post-mortem. Partner's lead costs a trick, so out trots 'Never lead from a king.' Unlucky if you are on lead against four spades and you hold ♠—, ♡: K643, ◇: K6432, ♣: K643.

To lead from a king is not a particularly attractive lead, but then it is not too unattractive either. All things being equal, to lead from a king is less dangerous than to lead from a queen or a jack. Suppose you hold ♠: K, ♡: J643, ◇: Q643, ♣: K643, and the opponents bid 1 ♠: 3 ♠, 4 ♠. With nothing to go by, the club lead is more attractive than either red suit.

One reason to prefer a lead from a king than from a queen or a jack is that the king is more resilient: it may survive a poor lead. For example:

        1087   West leads the three, and South wins the queen. West may still
K643   952   make a trick later with the king, but a disastrous lead from a queen
        AQJ   or jack is likely to leave no second chance.

Far worse than leading from a king are the more popular leads of J x, or Q x in an unbid suit. If partner has bid the suit, leading J x or Q x is fine, but in some other suit it is usually calamitous.

4) 'Always cover an honour with an honour.'

Rubbish. It is correct to cover an honour with an honour if it will promote cards in your hand or if it may promote cards in partner's hand.

a)   Q6   b)   Q62   In (a) and (b) East should play the king in
8742   K1095   10987   K54   either case if the queen is led. In (a) East
    AJ3   AJ3   promotes his 10 9, while in (b) East promotes
c)   QJ109   d)   J109   partner's 10 9 8 7. *But it is wrong to cover an*
86   K542   Q876   K542   *honour with an honour if it will help to*
    A73   A3   *promote declarer's cards only*. When the queen
is led in (c), if East plays low, declarer can make only three tricks, but if East covers, declarer has four tricks. In (d) the jack is led. If East plays the king, declarer has two tricks, but if East plays low, declarer cannot make more than one trick.

In the trump suit in particular it is usually wrong to cover an honour unless you know partner has length in trumps.

5) 'Second hand low' and 'Third hand high.'

These are both good principles and apply in very many situations. However, it is important to remember *they do not always hold*. There are certain exceptions to both, and when you have experience in card reading, you will become familiar with the situations where it is correct to play second hand high and third hand low.

6) 'When in doubt, lead a trump.'

If this were a valid principle, some players would always be leading trumps. They are always in doubt. There are certain conditions under which a trump lead is indicated and others where a trump lead should be shunned. The principles were set out in Appendix I: Opening leads.

7) 'Lead through strength up to weakness.'

Again this principle has a modicum of sense and will often indicate the correct line of defence. But this principle does not apply to the opening lead (it is rarely correct to lead dummy's bid suit), and in the middle game, card reading and counting provide sounder guides to the defence. The slogan does players a disservice by substituting a mechanical reflex for the possibility of reasoning out the correct defence.

8) 'Eight ever, nine never.'

A maxim which refers to the method of handling eight- and nine-card suits when a key honour, usually the queen, is missing. The maxim suggests that with eight cards in the two hands you should finesse, while with nine you should play for the drop. It is a reasonable mathematical principle for the correct way to play a particular suit. But there are many other considerations when planning the play of a complete hand.

9) 'A bid of a new suit promises extra strength.'

There are too many exceptions to this to give it any credence. It depends on the situation. In some sequences a new suit will show extra strength; in others it will not and may even be a weakness-showing bid.

10) 'You need two stoppers in the enemy suit to bid no trumps.'

If this were really necessary, a good many games would be missed. It is, of course, nice to have a double stopper in their suit, but bidding no trumps after they have bid a suit merely promises one stopper, and that only applies to the member of the partnership that bids no trumps first. If they have bid a suit and your partner ventures no trumps, it is quite in order for you to raise his no trumps (with the required strength) even though you have no independent stopper.

11) 'If responder bids, he must have points and if he bids twice he has ten or more points.'

Again, not necessarily so, depending on the situation. An important limiting factor on responder's strength is the principle: '*Mere preference* by responder for opener's first suit does not promise more strength than responder *previously* showed.'

12) 'You must bid if you have 13 points.'

This is the general cry of a defender who has just suffered a disastrous penalty: 'But partner, I had to bid. I had 13 points.'

A defender doesn't bid simply because he has points; he needs the right *shape* also. With the right number of points you should *open*, virtually regardless of shape, but there is only one opening bid at the table. As soon as the first bid is made, the other side are the *defenders*, even though they may have more strength than the opening side. It is incorrect to talk of 'opening for your side', as some players do.

The principles of defensive bidding were set out in Lessons 7B and 8B. The hardest thing for many players to appreciate is that a defender with 13 or more points does not automatically bid and that a pass may be correct even on a very strong hand (especially when you are loaded in the enemy suit).

The aims of defensive bidding are not identical with the aims of the opening side, and in general, excluding a few peripheral possibilities, a defender has three primary choices for bidding.

a) To bid a suit: This requires a good *five*-card or longer suit (partner may support on three).

b) To bid one no trump: This requires 16—18 HCP plus a balanced hand plus a stopper in the enemy suit(s).

c) To double for take-out: This take-out double requires: (a) shortage in the enemy suit; (b) support for the unbid suits, especially unbid majors; *and* (c) 12 HCP or stronger (unless the doubler is a passed hand).

With a minimum double, 12—15 points, or a take-out double by a passed hand the *shape requirements* are most important. You would not open one no trump with a void (wrong shape), and similarly you do not double for take-out with length in the enemy suit (wrong shape).

When your hand doesn't fit (a), (b), or (c), the correct action is to pass. Benito Garozzo of Italy, a member of the virtually invincible Blue Team and considered by many to be the world's number one bridge player, held this hand in the 1974 World Teams' Championship: ♠: 9, ♡: Q J 8 5, ◇: A K Q 8, ♣: A K J 4. His partner passed; his right-hand opponent opened one heart. What would you have bid on Garozzo's hand?

Well, the hand didn't fit: (a) no five-card suit; (b) not balanced and wrong strength; or (c) not short in the enemy suit, no support for spades, so for all his twenty points Garozzo *passed*! The hand would have been ideal for a take-out double of one spade, but the length in the enemy suit militated against a take-out double of one heart.

13) 'You must rebid a suit to show five.'

Wrong again. It is possible to indicate a six-card suit, even though you only bid it once. For example, in the auction 1 ♡ : 2 ♣, 2 ♠ : 2 NT, 3 ♠ the opener has promised *six* hearts at least, while in the auction 1 ♡ : 2 ♣, 2 ♡ : 2 ♠, 2 NT : 3 ♠ the responder guarantees at least *six* clubs. If you cannot see why, go back to Lesson 5.

One reason why a five-card major need not be rebid is that it is responder's duty to show three-card major support *at his second bid*. In other words, opener doesn't need to show five; it is responder who should show *three* as a *check-back* in case opener has five.

With four-card major support responder raises at once.

With three-card major support responder shows this at his second bid.

Failure by responder to raise the major at once usually denies four-card support.

Failure by responder to support opener's major with his second bid denies three-card support.

For example:

1 ♡ : 1 ♠	1 ♡ : 2 ◇	1 ♡ : 2 NT	1 ♡ : 2 ♣	1 ♡ : 2 ◇
2 ♣ : 2 ◇	2 NT : 3 ♣	3 ◇ : 3 NT	2 ◇ : 2 NT	3 ♣ : 3 NT

In each of the above auctions responder will *not* have three-card support for opener's major.

The same check-back principle applies to opener's failure to support responder's major; if opener fails to support at once, he does not have four-card support; if opener fails to give delayed support, he does not have three-card support.

For example:

1 ♣ : 1 ♠	1 ♣ : 1 ♠	1 ♣ : 1 ♡	1 ◇ : 1 ♡
2 ◇ : 2 NT	2 ♣ : 2 ♡	1 NT : 2 NT	3 ◇ : 3 ♠
3 NT	2 NT	3 NT	3 NT

In each of the above auctions opener will not have three-card support for responder's first major.

So, don't rebid that five-card suit—just make sure that partner will check-back.

Appendix III: Cue bidding

Remember: You should bid a small slam if it has a 50% or better chance of success.
Until you are an experienced player avoid bidding a grand slam unless it is a sure thing.

Although slams do not come up too frequently, when they do occur a great deal hinges on the outcome because the slam bonuses are so valuable. Expert players are keen to make their slam bidding as accurate as possible.

Suppose you hold ♠: A K Q J 8 3 2, ♡: —, ♢: K Q J, ♣: A Q 5.

You open two clubs, and partner bids two hearts. You bid two spades, and partner bids three spades. What now? Clearly you are interested in a slam, but should you bid a small slam or the grand slam? If you bid Blackwood four no trumps now, you may land on your feet if partner shows two aces, but what if he responds five diamonds, showing just one ace? You are in a terrible dilemma because you do not know whether it is the ace of hearts or the ace of diamonds that he holds. The ace of hearts is completely wasted since you control the heart suit anyway, while the ace of diamonds would be worth its weight in gold. The answer is that Blackwood is not the answer. Blackwood can tell you only how many aces are held but not which ones (unless you hold the rest). When partner bids three spades, you should think to yourself that if he has the ace of diamonds and the king of clubs (or even a singleton club) you will make a grand slam. So your bidding should be aimed at finding out about these two key features. The way to do it is by cue bidding.

Example 1:

YOU	PARTNER	
♠ AKQJ832	♠ 10976	The dialogue between you and partner:
♡ —	♡ K5432	1) You say that you hold the ace of clubs.
♢ KQJ	♢ A7	2) Partner shows he has the ace of diamonds.
♣ AQ5	♣ KJ	3) You show you have the hearts under control.

4) Partner shows he has the king of clubs (or a singleton club).

YOU	PARTNER
2♣	2♡
2♠	3♠
4♣(1)	4♢(2)
4♡(3)	5♣(4)
7♠(5)	No bid

5) That's all you need to know.

Example 2:

YOU	PARTNER	
♠ AKQJ832	♠ 10976	The bidding here after three spades is identical with
♡ —	♡ 8643	the previous example. The same meanings apply
♢ KQJ	♢ A732	except that partner's bid of five clubs shows a
♣ AQ5	♣ 9	singleton club. You still bid the grand slam since you

can ruff your club losers in dummy (or discard one on the ace of diamonds).

YOU	PARTNER
2♣	2♢
2♠	3♠
4♣(1)	4♢(2)
4♡(3)	5♣(4)
7♠(5)	No bid

Example 3:

YOU	PARTNER
♠ AKQJ832	♠ 1097
♡ —	♡ KJ863
◇ KQJ	◇ A73
♣ AQ5	♣ 92

YOU	PARTNER
2 ♣	2 ♡
2 ♠	3 ♠
4 ♣(1)	4 ◇(2)
4 ♡(3)	5 ♡(4)
6 ♠(5)	No bid

1) You show first-round club control.

2) He shows first-round diamond control.

3) You show first-round heart control.

4) He shows second-round control in hearts *and no second-round control in clubs or diamonds.*

5) Since the king of clubs must be missing, you settle for the small slam.

Example 4:

YOU	PARTNER
♠ AKQJ832	♠ 10976
♡ —	♡ A9832
◇ KQJ	◇ 73
♣ AQ5	♣ K2

YOU	PARTNER
2 ♣	2 ♡
2 ♠	3 ♠
4 ♣(1)	4 ♡(2)
6 ♠(3)	No bid

1) Showing the ace of clubs.

2) Showing the ace of hearts *and denying the ace of diamonds.*

3) With the ace of diamonds missing the grand slam is impossible, so you settle for six spades.

Example 5:

YOU	PARTNER
♠ AKQJ832	♠ 10976
♡ —	♡ AKJ32
◇ QJ10	◇ 85
♣ AK5	♣ 98

YOU	PARTNER
2 ♣	2 ♡
2 ♠	3 ♠
4 ♣(1)	4 ♡(2)
5 ♣(3)	5 ♡(4)
5 ♠(5)	No bid

1) Showing ace or void in clubs.

2) Showing ace in hearts *and denying ace of diamonds.*

3) Showing second-round control in clubs.

4) Showing second-round control in hearts *and denying second-round control in diamonds and clubs.*

5) You give up on the slam since you know the enemy have the ace and king of diamonds with which they can defeat the slam.

When a trump suit has been agreed and either game has already been reached or a game-forcing situation exists, any bid in a new suit is a cue bid showing first-round control.

1) First-round control is usually the ace of the suit but it may also be a void. No distinction is drawn in cue bidding between aces and voids.

2) Note that you must have trump agreement; if you have not agreed on a trump suit, a new suit is just a new suit, not a cue bid.

3) Note that the partnership must be committed to game at least. If no game force exists, a new suit is not a cue bid. For example after 1 ♠ : 2 ♠, although you have agreed on trumps, a bid of three clubs would not be a cue bid (it would be a try for game), since no game-forcing situation exists. But after 1 ♠ : 3 ♠, a bid of four clubs would be a cue bid, since the bidding cannot now die below game.

4) When making a cue bid you make the cheapest cue bid available. After 1 ♡ : 3 ♡ four clubs shows not only ace or void in clubs but also denies first-round control in

spades, since the bid of three spades has been bypassed. Similarly, after 1 ♠ : 3 ♠ a bid of four hearts would show first-round control in hearts and deny first-round club or diamond control.

5) After first-round controls have been cue-bid, later cue bids show second-round control in the suit bid (and no cheaper second-round controls). Second-round control equals king or singleton. No distinction is drawn between kings and singletons.

6) You can never cue-bid your trump holding. If it is not obvious that you have no losers in trumps, Blackwood four no trumps is available even after cue bidding has started to check on the ace of trumps, while after cue bidding a bid of five no trumps would be the grand slam force to check on two of the top three honours in trumps.

7) Blackwood four no trumps for aces and then five no trumps for kings can be used even after cue bidding has taken place. You make your normal reply, even though you may have already cue-bid one or more of your aces. Partner may be using four no trumps to check whether your cue bids were aces or voids.

8) A bid in the agreed suit is a sign-off, saying 'I have nothing more to show at this stage'. It may be because you have nothing to show or because you do not want to show anything extra yet. A sign-off will often end the auction but not necessarily so.

9) Remember that you must always return to your agreed trump suit sooner or later. Never make the serious blunder of passing partner in a cue bid.

10) Cue bidding is far superior to, and far more sophisticated than, Blackwood. If all you want to know is how many aces and kings partner holds, by all means use Blackwood. But if you want to know which ones he holds, particularly where you hold a void or you fear that one suit may be wide open (you hold two or three small cards in one suit), prefer to use cue-bidding. *But make sure your partner understands cue bidding.* It is very dangerous to start a cue bidding sequence with a strange partner. If you discover partner does not understand cue bidding, give him a copy of this book.

Appendix IV: Tournament bridge

The main kinds of competitive bridge are pairs events, teams events and individual events. Bridge is played internationally, and every second year there is a World Teams Championship (called the Bermuda Bowl) in which five or six teams representing different geographical zones compete. Every four years there is a Bridge Olympiad in which there is a far greater number of teams competing. Also every four years is the World Pairs Championship and the World Mixed Pairs Championship.

In general, pairs events are more common than the other types of events. The advantage of tournament bridge is that the element of luck (of having good cards or bad cards) is reduced to a minimum, since all players play exactly the same hands. Another advantage is that you can compete against the top players merely by playing in the same tournament. In few other sports could a novice play against a world champion in competition. Tournament bridge also improves your game, since the hand records are available to check afterwards how and where you may have gone wrong.

There are some differences between tournament bridge and ordinary bridge, particularly in regard to pairs events. Except at the first table you will not shuffle and deal the cards. The cards come to you in a tray, called a 'board', and you must put the cards back in the correct slot after the board has been played. The board is marked N, E, S, and W, and must be placed properly on the table; it also states which side is vulnerable and who is the dealer. During the play the cards are not thrown into the middle of the table, but each person, including dummy, puts his his own cards in front of him, turning them face down after the trick has been completed. Each card is placed so as to point in the direction of the side that wins the trick. After the hand is over, you can see at a glance how many tricks have been won and how many have been lost.

Each board in tournament bridge is scored separately. While in rubber bridge you have an advantage for the next hand if you make a part-score, in tournament bridge you do not carry forward part-scores. You enter the score for the hand you have just played, and the next board is completely fresh, totally unrelated to what has happened on the previous hand. Because of this you have scoring differences in tournament bridge.
(1) Unless otherwise stated by the tournament conditions, honours do not count.
(2) For bidding and making a part-score add 50 to the trick total.
(3) For bidding and making a game, not vulnerable, add 300 to the trick total.
(4) For bidding and making a game, vulnerable, add 500 to the trick total.
   All other scoring remains the same.

The result you obtain on the board is entered on the 'travelling score-sheet' at the back of the board. You may not look at that until the hand is over, since it contains a record of the hand and also how other pairs fared on the board. Your score on each board is compared with the scores of every other pair that played the board. If you are sitting North-South, then your real opponents are all the other North-South pairs competing, not the particular pair you play each time. On each board a certain number of match-points are awarded (usually one less than the number of pairs who play the board). If fifteen pairs play a board, the best score receives 14 match-points, a 'top', the next best score receive 13 match-points, and so on down to the worst score which receives 0 match-points, a 'bottom'. An average score would receive 7 match-points. The scoring is done once for North-South pairs and then for the East-West pairs. Obviously, if a North-South pair gets a top, the corresponding East-West pair against whom they played the board gets a bottom. Each pair's points over all the boards are added up, and the pair with the highest number of match-points wins.

Tactics in pairs events differ from those in rubber bridge. Careful declarer play and defence are the order of the day. Every overtrick and every undertrick may be vital, making the difference between a good and a bad score. In rubber bridge declarer's aim is to make his contract; the defenders' aim is to defeat it; at pairs the aim is to obtain the best possible score which may mean from declarer's viewpoint that making the contract is a secondary consideration, while from the defender's viewpoint the risk of giving away an overtrick in trying to defeat the contract may be unwarranted.

Aggressiveness in competitive bidding is essential. Almost always force the opposition to the three-level. Be quick to reopen the bidding. In pairs events reopening the bidding occurs ten times more often than at rubber bridge.

Minor suit contracts, especially at the game zone, should be avoided. Prefer three no trumps to five clubs or five diamonds, even if three no trumps is riskier, since any overtrick in no trumps scores more than minor-suit games. On the other hand, it is not necessary to bid close games or close slams. The reward for success is not so great in pairs events as to justify 24 point games or 31 point slams. You should be in game or in slam if it has a 50% or better chance; if less, you will score better by staying out of it.

Penalty doubles are far more frequent at pairs since players are anxious to improve their score. The rule about having a two-trick safety margin is frequently disregarded since one down, doubled, vulnerable may be enough for a top score, while one down, undoubled, vulnerable may be below average.

Safety plays which involve sacrificing a trick to ensure the contract almost never apply in pairs, unless the contract you have reached is an unbelievably good one.

In the tournament world you will run up against a remarkable number and variety of systems and conventions and gradually you will come to recognize them. A most important point to remember is that a bidding system is not some secret between you and your partner. You and your partner are not allowed to have any secret understanding about your bids. That is *cheating*. A bidding system is not a secret code. The opponents are entitled to know as much about what the bidding means as you or your partner. If they ask you what you understand by a certain bid of your partner's, you must tell them truthfully. Of course, your partner's bid may be meaningless and you may understand nothing by it. All you can do then is to be honest and tell the opposition that you do not know what his bid means.

Similarly, if you do not understand the opposition bidding, you are entitled to ask. When it is your turn to bid but before you make your bid, you ask the partner of the bidder: 'What is the meaning of your partner's bid?' Unless it affects your making a bid, prefer to wait until the auction is over—after all, the opposition might not understand their bidding either, and when you ask they may well realize their mistake.

Appendix V: Ethics and etiquette

Bridge is an extremely ethical game. All good players strive to ensure that their bridge ethics are impeccable, and no more serious charge, other than outright cheating, can be made than to accuse a player of bad ethics. Unlike poker in which all sorts of mannerisms, misleading statements and bluff tactics are part and parcel of the game, bridge is played with a 'poker-face'! Beginners are, of course, excused for their lapses, and in social games nobody minds very much, but in serious competition your bridge demeanour must be beyond criticism.

When you are dummy, it is poor form to look at either opponent's hand or at declarer's. Do not stand behind declarer to see how he plays the contract. As a kibitzer (onlooker) try to watch only one hand and, above all, do not comment or talk, even between hands; if the players want the benefit of your views, they will ask for them.

Conversation at the table in serious games is generally unwelcome. Post-mortems after each hand, if limited, can be useful as long as they seek to be constructive, but it is preferable to keep all post-mortems until after the session is over and you can go over the score-sheets with your partner at your leisure rather than at a time when you should be conserving your energies to do battle at the next table. It is in extremely poor taste to abuse or criticize partner or an opponent. Never try to 'teach' anyone at the table. Never let a harsh word pass your lips and you will be a sought-after rather than a shunned partner. Prefer to say too little than too much. If partner has bid or played the hand like an idiot, say 'bad luck' and leave it at that. Do not continually harp on past errors.

Use only the proper language of bridge. Prefer to say 'no bid' rather than 'pass' (which sounds like 'hearts'). Do not say 'content', 'O.K.', 'by me'—say 'no bid'. Do not say 'I'll double one heart'—just say 'double'. Do not say 'spade' when you mean 'one spade'.

Never vary the intonation in your bidding—softly on weak hands, loud on good ones. Never put a question mark at the end of your bid to make sure that partner understands that your four no trumps is Blackwood or that your double is for take-out. That would be quite atrocious. You are supposed to convey messages to partner by what you bid, not the way you bid it. Frowns, scowls, smiles, raised eyebrows, etc., are out.

If your partner has a good sense of humour, you may be able to make clever remarks in repartee such as: 'When did you learn to play? I know, this afternoon, but what time this afternoon?'; or in reply to 'How should I have played that hand?', 'Under an assumed name'; or in reply to 'How did I play that hand?', 'Like a millionaire'; or in reply to 'Could I have done any better?', 'I suppose double dummy you could have gone one more down'. In general, however, bridge players are a proud lot with sensitive egos. Politeness and courtesy should be your watchword at the bridge table as in other areas of life.

Long pausing before bidding is also to be avoided; for example, the pause followed by 'no bid' tells everyone that you have 11—12 points, not quite good enough to open. Make all your bids at the same pace if you can. Sometimes, of course, you will have a serious problem which takes you some time to resolve, but where this happens the obligation falls on to the partner of the 'pauser', who must never take advantage of the information received from the pause. Play your cards as a defender always at the same speed. Fumbling or hesitating with the intention of deceiving declarer is cheating. You must not try to mislead your opponents by your manner.

In tournament bridge always call the tournament director if you are ever in doubt as to the correct procedure. Do not let other players tell you what the correct laws are; they are wrong more often than not. Nobody familiar with the tournament scene minds the director being called. It is not considered a slight, an insult, or a rebuff to the opposition.

Above all, remember that bridge is primarily a game and is meant to be enjoyed.

Answers to exercises and quizzes

Lesson 1

page 17 Quiz: (1) Spades; (2) Both score the same; (3) 100; (4) 8; (5) No;
(6) Spades and hearts; (7) Yes; (8) No; (9) No; (10) No; (11) Nil;
(12) No; (13) Vulnerable; (14) Yes, 100; (15) Nil

Exercises

page 20: 1)(a) 4; (b) 7; (c) 5; (d) 6; (e) 9; (f) 3; (g) 7; (h) 3; (i) 10; (j) 5;
(k) 6; (l) 2; (m) 4; (n) 8; (o) 1
2) Balanced: (a), (c), (e); semi-balanced: (d), (f); unbalanced:
(b), (g), (h)
3)(a) 17; (b) 17; (c) 16; (d) 15; (e) 16; (f) 19; (g) 17; (h) 17; (i) 17;
(j) 18. Only (e) and (g) are not balanced

page 24: 1)(i)(a) 1 NT; (b) 1 ◇; (c) 1 ◇; (d) 1 NT; (e) 2 NT
(ii)(a) 1 ♣; (b) 1 NT; (c) 1 ◇; (d) 1 ♣; (e) 2 NT
2)(i)(a) No bid; (b) No bid; (c) 3 NT; (d) No bid; (e) 3 NT;
(f) No bid; (g) No bid; (h) 3 NT—a reasonable gamble; (i) No bid;
(j) 3 NT
(ii)(a) No bid; (b) 2 NT; (c) 3 NT; (d) No bid; (e) 6 NT; (f) 3 NT;
(g) 2 NT; (h) 3 NT; (i) No bid; (j) 4 NT
3)(a) No bid; (b) 3 NT; (c) 3 NT; (d) 6 NT; (e) 3 NT
4)(a) Opener's 6 NT (after 1 NT: 3 NT, opener must pass)
(b) Responder's 2 NT (he should pass 1 NT) and opener's 3 NT
(with a minimum he should pass 2 NT)
(c) Opener's 1 NT (with 15 points he is too strong to open 1 NT)
and responder's pass (with 11 points he should invite game with
2 NT)

Lesson 2

page 31:
1)(a) 1 ♡; (b) 1 ♣; (c) 1 ♠; (d) 1 ♠; (e) 1 ♡; (f) 1 ◇; (g) 1 ♡; (h) 1 ◇; (i) No bid; (j) 1 ♠. All the hands are two-suiters except for (f) which is a one-suiter

2)(i)(a) No, open 1NT; (b) No, 1 ♡; (c) No, 1 NT; (d) No, 1 ◇; (e) No, 1 ◇; (f) Yes; (g) No, 1 NT; (h) No, pass; (i) No, 1 NT; (j) No, 1 NT

(ii)(a) No, 1 ♠; (b) No, 1 NT; (c) No, 1 ♣; (d) Yes; (e) No, 1 ◇; (f) Yes; (g) No, prefer 1 ♣; (h) No, pass; (i) No 1 ◇; (j) No, 1 ♠

page 34:
1)(i)(a) 2 ◇; (b) 2 ♠; (c) 2 ♠; (d) 2 ♡; (e) No bid; (f) 4 ♡; (g) 3 ♡; (h) 3NT; (i) 4 ♠; (j) 3 ♠

(ii)(a) 2 ◇; (b) 2 ♠; (c) 4 ♠; (d) 2 ♡; (e) No bid; (f) 4 ♡; (g) 3 ♡; (h) 3 NT; (i) 4 ♠; (j) 3 ♠

2)(a) 3 ♠; (b) 3 NT; (c) 4 ♠; (d) 4 ♡; (e) No bid

3)(i)(a) 4 ♠; (b) No bid; (c) No bid; (d) 3 NT; (e) No bid; (f) No bid
(ii)(a) 3 NT; (b) No bid; (c) No bid; (d) 4 ♡; (e) No bid; (f) No bid;
(iii)(a) No bid; (b) 4 ◇; (c) 3 NT; (d) No bid; (e) 4 ♡; (f) 4 ♠

4) (i-c) (ii-b) (iii-d) (iv-f) (v-a) (vi-e)

5)(a) Opener is too strong for 1 NT, and responder too weak for 3 ♠; correct auction: 1 ♠ : 4 ♠; (b) Opener should pass 2 ♡; (c) Opener should pass 2 ♠; (d) Opener should bid 3 NT over 3 ♡ (3 ♡ forced to game); (e) Responder should bid 4 ♡, not 2 ♡; (f) Opener should pass 4 ♠

6)(a) 2 ♡; (b) 2 ◇; (c) 2 ♡; (d) 2 ♠; (e) 2 ♡

7)(i)(a) 3 ♣; (b) No bid; (c) No bid; (d) 3 ♡; (e) 4 ♡
(ii)(a) No bid; (b) No bid; (c) No bid; (d) 3 ♠; (e) 4 ♠
(iii)(a) 3 ♣; (b) 2 ♠; (c) No bid; (d) 2 NT; (e) 3 ♡

Lesson 3

page 43:   1)(a) 4, No bid; (b) 7, 2 ♡; (c) 10, 4 ♡; (d) 9, 2 ♡; (e) 15, 2 ♣;
(f) 9, 2 ♡; (g) 15, 2 ◇; (h) 12, 3 ♡; (i) 11, 3 ♡; (j) 19, 3 ♣.
2)(a) 2 ♣; (b) 1 ♡; (c) 3 ♣; (d) 1 ♠; (e) 1 ♡
3)(a) 13, No bid; (b) 20, 4 ♠; (c) 18, 3 ♠; (d) 14, No bid; (e) 20, 4 ♠
4)(a) No bid; (b) No bid; (c) 4 ♠; (d) 4 ♠; (e) 3 NT
5)(a) No bid; (b) No bid; (c) 4 ♠, offering partner a choice between
4 ♠; and 5 ♣; (d) 3 NT; (e) 3 NT, a much better chance than 5 ♣
6)(a) 3 NT; (b) 5 ♣; (c) 3NT; (d) No bid; (e) 3 NT

Lesson 4

page 51:   1)(a) 1 NT; (b) 1 NT; (c) 1 NT; (d) 1 ♠; (e) 1 NT; (f) 2 NT;
(g) 3 ♡; (h) 1 ♠; (i) 2 ♣; (j) 2 NT (justified by the three tens)
2)(a) 1 NT; (b) 1 NT; (c) 1 NT; (d) 2 ♠; (e) 1 NT; (f) 2 NT;
(g) 2 ◇; (h) 3 ♠; (i) 2 NT; (j) 2 ♣
3)(a) 3 NT; (b) 1 ♠; (c) 3 ♣; (d) 2 ♣; (e) 2 ♣
4)(a) 2 ♣; (b) 2 ♣; (c) 3 ♣; (d) 2 ♣; (e) 2 ♣
5)(a) No bid; (b) No bid; (c) 2 ♠; (d) 3 ♠; (e) 2 NT; (f) 3 NT;
(g) 2 ◇; (h) 3 ◇; (i) No bid; (j) 2 NT
6)(a) No bid; (b) 3 NT; (c) 3 NT; (d) 3 ♠; (e) 3 ♣; (f) 3 ♡; (g) 4 ♡;
(h) 3 NT; (i) No bid; (j) 3 ◇
7)(a) No bid; (b) No bid; (c) 4 NT; (d) No bid; (e) 4 ♡ (if partner
can be relied on to have 4—3—3—3 shape; if not, investigating via
4 ♣ is safer) (f) 4 ♡; (g) 4 ♡; (h) No bid; (i) 4 ♡ (if partner will
be 4—3—3—3; if not, pass) (j) 4 ♡

Lesson 5

page 62: 1)(a) 1 ♠; (b) 1 ♡; (c) 1 ♡; (d)1 ♠; (e)1 ♠; (f)1 NT; (g) 1 ♡;
(h) 1 ♡; (i) No bid; (j) 2 NT
2)(a) 1 ♠; (b) 2 ◊; (c) 1 ♠; (d) 2 ♣; (e) 2 ◊; (f) 1 ♠; (g) 2 ♡;
(h) 1 NT; (i) 3 ♣; (j) 2 ◊
3)(a) 2 ♠—rebid the spades next; (b) 2 ♣—don't jump-shift;
bid the diamonds next; (c) 3 ♣—support hearts next; (d) 3 ◊—
bid spades next; (e) 2 ◊—bid clubs next
4)(a) 1 ♡; (2) 1 ♠; (c) 1 NT; (d) 1 NT; (e) 1 ♡; (f) 2 ♡; (g) 1 NT;
(h) 2 NT; (i) 2 ♣; (j) 3 ♣
5)(a) 2 ♡; (b) 1 NT; (c) 2 ♠; (d) 2 ♡; (e) 2 ◊; (f) 3 ♡; (g) 4 ♠;
(h) 2 NT; (i) 3 NT; (j) 3 ♣
6)(a) 2 ♡; (b) 2 ♡; (c) 2 NT; (d) 2 ♠; (e) 2 ◊
7)(i)(a) 2 ♡; (b) 3 ♡; (c) 3 ♠; (d) No bid
(ii)(a) 2 ◊; (b) 3 ◊; (c) 2 ◊; (d) 3 ◊
8) Forcing: (i) a, b, c, g; (ii) d, f, g, i; (iii) e
Game-forcing: (i) c, g; (ii) d, f, g
9)(a) 5 or 6; (b) 5 or more; (c) 6; (d) 5 or more; (e) 4 or more;
(f) 4; (g) 5 or more; (h) 6; (i) 6; (j) 6 or 7; (k) 5 or more; (l) 5;
(m) 4; (n) fewer than 3; (o) 4
10)(a) 4 ♡; (b) 3 NT; (c) 3 ◊; (d) 2 ♡; (e) 2 NT
11)(i)(a) 3 NT; (b) No bid; (c) 3 ♡; (d) No bid
(ii)(a) 4 ♡; (b) 3 NT; (c) 3 ♠; (d) 4 ♡
(iii)(a) 4 ♠; (b) No bid; (c) 4 ♠; (d) 6 ♠ (or 4 NT—see Lesson 8)
(iv)(a) No bid; (b) 2 ♡; (c) 2 ♡; (d) 3 ♡
(v)(a) 2 NT; (b) 3 ♣; (c) 3 ♡; (d) 2 ♠
12)(i)(a) 2 ♡; (b) No bid; (c) 3 ♡; (d) 2 ◊
(ii)(a) 3 ♠; (b) 4 ♠; (c) No bid; (d) 3 ♠
13)(a) 3 NT; (b) 3 ♣; (c) 3 ◊; (d) 3 ♠
14)(a) 3 ♠; (b) 3 ♡; (c) 3 NT; (d) 4 ♡
15)(a) No bid; (b) No bid; (c) 3 ♠; (d) 3 ◊
16)(a) 3 NT; (b) 3 ♠; (c) 3 ♣; (d) 3 ♡

Lesson 6

page 72: 1(a) 8; (b) 7; (c) 6; (d) $7\frac{1}{2}$; (e) $6\frac{1}{2}$; (f) 6; (g) $6\frac{1}{2}$; (h) 6 (i) $4\frac{1}{2}$; (j) 5;
(k) 6; (l) $6\frac{1}{2}$; (m) $6\frac{1}{2}$; (n) 5; (o) 5; (p) $5\frac{1}{2}$; (q) 4—$4\frac{1}{2}$; (r) 6—7
2)(a) 2 ♡; (b) 2 ♣; (c) 2 ♡ and follow up with 3 ♠; (d) 2 ♡
3)(i)(a) 2 NT; (b) 2 NT; (c) 3 ♡; (d) 3 NT;) (e) 4 ♡
(ii)(a) 2 ◇; (b) 2 ◇; (c) 3 ♣; (d) 3 NT; (e) 2 NT
4)(a) 3 ♡; (b) 3 ♠; (c) 4 ♡; (d) 6 ♡
5)(a) 3 ♠; (b) 4 ♠; (c) 4 ♡; (d) 3 ♠; (e) 4 ♠
6)(a) 6 ♡; (b) No bid; (c) 6 ♡; (d) 7 ♡; (e) 7 ◇
7)(i)(a) 2 NT; (b) 3 NT; (c) 2 ♠; (d) 2 ♡; (e) 3 ◇
(ii)(a) 3 NT; (b) 6 NT; (c) 3 ♠; (d) 3 ♡; (e) 3 ◇
8)(i)(a) No bid; (b) 3 NT; (c) 4 ♡; (d) 3 NT; (e) 3 ♡
(ii)(a) 2 NT; (b) 3 ♠; (c) 3 ♡; (d) 3 NT; (e) 3 ♡
9) Hand; (c) On (a) opener bids 3 NT over 2 ◇; on (b) he bids 3 ♣
over 2 ◇; on (d) opener should try 3 NT over 3 ♡; on (e) opener is
worth one more move towards slam

10)

a)	b)	c)
2 ♣ : 2 ◇	2 ♣ : 2 ◇	2 ♣ : 2 ◇
3 ◇ : 3 ♡	2 ♠ : 3 ♣	3 ◇ : 3 ♠
3 ♠ : 3 NT	3 ♡ : 4 ♡	6 ♠ : No
No	6 ♡ : No	

page 77: 1)(i) Not vulnerable: (a) 4 ♠; (b) 4 ♡; (c) 3 ♣; (d) 4 ♠; (e) 3 ♣;
(f) No bid; (g) 1 ♠; (h) No bid; (i) No bid; (j) 4 ♡
(ii) Vulnerable: (a) 3 ♠; (b) 3 ♡; (c) No bid; (d) 4 ♠; (e) No bid;
(f) No bid; (g) 1 ♠; (h) No bid; (i) No bid; (j) 4 ♡
2)(i) Not vulnerable: (a) No bid; (b) No bid; (c) No bid; (d) 3 ♠;
(e) 4 ♡; (f) 4 ♡; (g) No bid; (h) 4 ♡; (i) 4 ♡; (j) 4 ♡
(ii) Vulnerable: (a) No bid; (b) No bid; (c) No bid; (d) 3 ♠; (e) 4 ♡;
(f) 4 ♡; (g) 4 ♡; (h) 5 ♡—worth a slam try; 5 ♡ asks opener to bid
6 ♡ with solid or near-solid hearts; (i) 4 ♡; (j) 4 ♡
3)(i) Opener has hand (c), on (a) opener would open 1 ♡ and on
(b) he would bid 4 ♡ over 3 ♠
(ii) Opener has hand (a), on (b) he would remove 3 NT to 4 ♡ and
on (c), not vulnerable, he would have opened 4 ♡
(iii) Opener has hand (b), on (a) he would raise 3 ♡ to 4 ♡ and on
(c) he would open 1 ♣

Lesson 7

Page 82: 1)(a) 1 ♠; (b) 1 ♡; (c) 1 ♠; (d) 2 NT

2) 1 NT; (b) 2 ♣; (c) 3 ♣; (d) 4 ♡; (e) 2 NT; (f) 2 ♡; (g) 1 NT—better than 1 ♠ which partner might pass; (h) 1 ♠

3)(a)(i) 4 ♡; (ii) 4 ♠; (iii) 2 ♠; (iv) 3 ◇—looks safer than 2 NT; (v) 2 ◇

(b)(i) No bid; (ii) No bid; (iii) 3 ♡; (iv) No bid; (v) No bid

page 86: 1)(a) 1 ♠; (b) 1 ♠; (c) No bid; (d) 1 ◇; (e) 1 ♠; (f) 2 ♠; (g) 2 ♡; (h) 4 ♡; (i) No bid; (j) No bid; (k) 1 NT; (l) No bid

2)(a) 2 ◇; (b) No bid—suit too poor for 2 ♡; (c) No bid—too many cards in enemy suit; (d) 3 ♣; (e) 3 NT; (f) 2 ♡; (g) No bid; (h) No bid

3)(a) No bid; (b) 4 ♡—very good shape; (c) 2 ♡; (d) 3 ♡; (e) No bid (f) 1 NT; (g) 1 ♠; (h) 3 NT; (i) 2 ◇; (j) 3 ◇; (k) 2 ♡

4)(a) No bid; (b) No bid; (c) 2 NT—you have a heart stopper; (d) 2 ♠; (e) 3 NT; (f) 4 ♡

5)(a) No bid; (b) 3 ♠; (c) 4 ♠; (d) 4 ♠; (e) 2 NT; (f) 3 NT; (g) 4 ♠—few points but excellent shape; (h) 3 ◇

6)(a) No bid; (b) 3 NT; (c) 3 ♠; (d) 4 ♣

7)(a) 1 NT; (b) 2 ♡; (c) Double; (d) 2 ♣

8)(a) 1 NT (though 1 ♡ would be quite acceptable); (b) 1 ♡; (c) 1 ♠; (d) 1 ♡

9)(a) 2 ♡; (b) Double; (c) No bid; (d) 3 NT

10)(a) 2 ♠; (b) 4 ♡—a reasonable gamble; (c) 3 ♣—since you passed last time partner knows you are weak; (d) 3 ♠—with an equal number of cards in each suit prefer partner's first suit. Since you passed last time, you are now worth a jump bid. Compare hand (a) where you had to bid 2 ♠

Lesson 8

page 94: 1)(a) 5 ♣; (b) 5 ♡; (c) 6 NT (4 NT was not Blackwood but an invitation to bid 6 NT if maximum); (d) 5 ♠; (e) 5 ◇

2)(a) 5 ♠; (b) 6 ♠; (c) 6 ♠; (d) 6 ♠; (f) 7 NT

3)(a) No bid (partner must have solid diamonds); (b) 6 ♠ (here partner opened 1 ♠ and his 6 ◇ is giving you a choice between 6 ◇ and 6 ♠); (c) 6 ♡ (5 NT asked you to bid 7 ♡ with A K, A Q or K Q in hearts, otherwise bid 6 ♡); (d) No bid (5 ♡ asked you to bid 6 ♡ with good trumps; your hearts are minimum for your bidding)

4)(a) 5 NT (a new suit at the five-level asks you to bid 5 NT); (b) No bid (trumps too poor for 6 ♠); (c) 6 ♡ (trumps are good enough)

(d) 6 ♠ (lacking two of the top three trump honours)

page 98: 1) Take-out: (a) (b) (c) (f) (g) (k)   Penalties: (d) (e) (h) (i) (j) (l)

2)(a) Double; (b) Double; (c) 1 ◇; (d) Double; (e) 1 ♠; (f) Double; (g) 1 NT; (h) Double

3)(a) No bid; (b) Double; (c) Double; (d) 1 ♠; (e) Double; (f) 1 ♠; (g) No bid; (h) 2 ◇

4)(a) 1 ♠; (b) 1 ♠; (c) 1 ♠; (d) 1 ♡; (e) 2 ♣; (f) 1 ♡; (g) 1 NT; (h) No bid

5)(a) 2 ♠; (b) 2 ♡; (c) 2 ◇; (d) 2 NT; (e) 4 ♠; (f) 4 ♠; (g) 3 NT; (h) 2 ♣—forcing to game; uncertain which is best game

6)(a) No bid; (b) 1 NT (partner for his double will have the spades covered); (c) 2 ♡; (d) 3 ♡; (e) Double

7)(a) 1 ♠; (b) 2 ♣; (c) 1 NT; (d) 2 ♠; (e) 2 ♡—forcing to game

In (d) and (e) something is odd and probably one of your opponents has made a bluff bid. Trust partner and make the same bid you would have made without the double

8)(i) (a) No bid; (b) No bid; (c); No bid; (d) No bid; (e) No bid; (f) 2 ♡ (cheapest suit)

(ii) (a) 2 ♡; (b) 4 ♡; (c) 2 NT; (d) 3 NT; (e) 2 ♠; (f) 2 ◇ (cheapest four-card suit) or 3 ♣ ('You pick the suit, please, partner').

(iii) (a) 3 ♡; (b) 1 NT; (c) 2 NT   (iv) (a) 2 NT; (b) 2 NT; (c) 3 NT

9)(i) (a) 4 ♡ (You could be considerably worse); (b) No bid

(ii) (a) 3 NT; (b) 4 ♡

10)(a) No bid; (b) 2 ♣; (c) 2 ♡; (d) 3 ♡; (e) 4 ♡; (f) Redouble; (g) Redouble; (h) 1 NT; (i) Redouble; (j) No bid

Scoring table

POINTS TOWARDS GAME
Points scored below the line for contract bid and made

Contract bid and made		ONE	TWO	THREE	FOUR	FIVE	SIX	SEVEN
Trick value 40 for	NT	40	70	100	130	160	190	220
1 NT, then 30 each								
30 each	♠ and ♡	30	60	90	120	150	180	210
20 each	◇ and ♣	20	40	60	80	100	120	140

BONUS POINTS
Points scored above the line, not counting towards game

FOR OVERTRICKS	UNDOUBLED	DOUBLED	REDOUBLED	FOR SLAMS BID AND MADE	
Not vulnerable	Trick value	100 each	200 each	*Small slam*	*Grand slam*
				Not vul. 500	1000
Vulnerable	Trick value	200 each	400 each	Vul. 750	1500

DEFEATING THE CONTRACT	DECLARER *Not vulnerable*			DECLARER *Vulnerable*		
	UNDOUBLED	DOUBLED	REDOUBLED	UNDOUBLED	DOUBLED	REDOUBLED
Down 1	50	100	200	100	200	400
Down 2	100	300	600	200	500	1000
Down 3	150	500	1000	300	800	1600
Down 4	200	700	1400	400	1100	2200
Then, per undertrick	50	200	400	100	300	600

FOR MAKING A DOUBLED OR REDOUBLED CONTRACT + 50 POINTS ('FOR THE INSULT')

For honours:	*For winning the rubber:*
Four trump honours in one hand + 100	By two games to nil 700
Five trump honours in one hand + 150	By two games to one 500
Four aces in one hand (only if contract is no trumps) + 150	(For one game if rubber is unfinished 300)

Capsule summary

ACTION BY RESPONDER OVER SUIT OPENING

Hand valuation after suit openings

If eight-card fit located: USE 5—3—1 SCALE

No eight-card fit located: USE 3—2—1 SCALE

When bidding no trumps, count HCP only. Don't count for shortage in *partner's* suit until eight-card fit located.

OPENING BID

ACTION BY RESPONDER	1♣ 12–20 HCP	1♢ 12–20 HCP	1♡ 12–20 HCP	1♠ 12–20 HCP
Pass	0–5	0–5	0–5	0–5
Cheapest raise four-card support	2♣ 6–10 no major	2♢ 6–10 no major	2♡ 6–10	2♠ 6–10
Jump raise four-card support	3♣ 11–12 no major	3♢ 11–12 no major	3♡ 11–12	3♠ 11–12
Double jump or greater raise, five or more trumps+singleton or void	4♣/5♣ no major weak	4♢/5♢ no major weak	4♡ weak	4♠ weak
Cheapest no trump	1 NT 8–10 balanced no major	1 NT 6–10 no major	1 NT 6–10 no four hearts no four spades	1 NT 6–10 no four spades
Jump no trump	2 NT 11–12 balanced	2 NT 11–12 balanced	2 NT 11–12 balanced	2 NT 11–12 balanced
Game no trump	3 NT 13–15 balanced	3 NT 13–15 balanced	3 NT 13–15 balanced	3 NT 13–15 balanced
One-over-one forcing	1♢/1♡/1♠ 6–15	1♡/1♠ 6–15	1♠ 6–15	—
Two-over-one forcing	—	2♣ 8–15	2♣/2♢ 8–15	2♣/2♢/2♡ 8–15
Jump new suit game force	2♢/2♡/2♠ 16+	2♡/2♠/3♣ 16+	2♠/3♣/3♢ 16+	3♣/3♢/3♡ 16+
Double jump new suit seven-card suit	3♢/3♡/3♠ weak	3♡/3♠/4♣ weak	3♠/4♣/4♢ weak	4♣/4♢/4♡ weak
Triple jump to game in new suit seven–eight cards	4♡/4♠/5♢ weak	4♡/4♠/5♣ weak	4♠/5♣/5♢ weak	5♣/5♢ weak

WORD 2000

in easy steps

Scott Basham

In easy steps is an imprint of Computer Step
Southfield Road . Southam
Warwickshire CV33 OFB . England

Tel: 01926 817999 Fax: 01926 817005
http://www.computerstep.com

Notice of Liability

Every effort has been made to ensure that this book contains accurate
and current information. However, Computer Step and the author shall
not be liable for any loss or damage suffered by readers as a result of
any information contained herein.

Trademarks

Microsoft® and Windows® are registered trademarks of Microsoft
Corporation. All other trademarks are acknowledged as belonging to
their respective companies.

Printed and bound in the United Kingdom

ISBN 1-84078-037-1

Contents

5 Styles and Themes   63

6 Tabulation   77

7 Automatic Features   83

▮ 11 On-line and Internet Documents   149

▮ 12 Advanced Topics   169

Index   187

Getting to Know Word

This chapter gets you started with Word 2000 quickly. It explains the screen layout, and introduces the various viewing modes that you can use to display your documents. It looks at new Word 2000 features, such as its personalised menus and docking toolbars, and the extensive Help facilities.

Covers

Chapter One

Introduction

Word-processing was one of the first popular applications for the modern personal computer. In the early days it provided little more than the ability to enter and change text on a computer monitor. As time went on software and hardware improved, and features such as spell-checking and various type effects were added. The number of users increased.

Microsoft Word 2000 for Windows is widely acknowledged as a leader in its field, and is one of the best selling packages in any software category.

Let's face it, with Word 2000 we're talking about a *big* package. It has retained the position as market leader by stuffing itself full of useful features, taking it from word-processing into the realms of graphical and data-oriented documents, and adding the capacity for Internet communications. At first it may seem to contain a bewildering array of options and controls, but many are there to make life easier – providing quick access to the most commonly used features.

A big package inevitably comes with a depressingly big reference manual, which will describe each and every function in minute detail. This book is not intended to replace the manual; instead you should view it as a more graphical teaching guide. Wherever possible, pictures and examples are used rather than pages of text to explain and demonstrate the concepts covered.

To gain maximum benefit from this book:

- Make sure that you are first familiar with the Windows operating environment (i.e. using a Mouse, icons, menus, dialog boxes etc.).

- It is important to experiment using your own examples; like many things you will find that practice is the key to competence.

The Word 2000 Screen

Start Word by selecting Programs>Microsoft Word from the Start menu. You should see the following screen.

Title and Document bar   Menus   Ruler

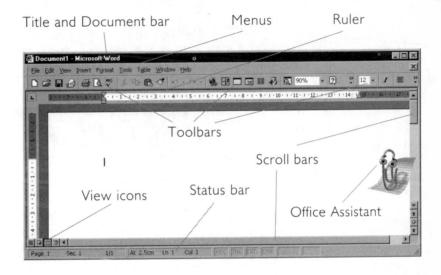

Toolbars

Scroll bars

View icons   Status bar

Office Assistant

Don't worry if the screen you see has extra items or things missing; you'll see in a moment that it's possible to configure the Word 2000 screen in different ways.

To quickly activate a toolbar, right-click the Mouse on any *currently visible* **toolbar to display a shortcut menu (see opposite). Check the toolbar of your choice.**

To deactivate a toolbar, follow the same procedure, but instead *uncheck* **the toolbar in the pop-up menu.**

Toolbars

Toolbars can appear at the top of the screen, at the bottom, or as floating palettes. They give you instant access to features without the need to search through menus and dialog boxes. There are sixteen toolbars in total, but we usually only require several at any time.

Activating/Deactivating Toolbars

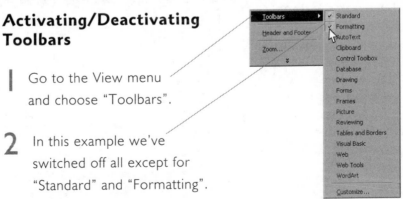

1 Go to the View menu and choose "Toolbars".

2 In this example we've switched off all except for "Standard" and "Formatting".

Page Views

There are four different ways of viewing the page, which you can select from the top section of the View menu: *Normal, Web Layout, Print Layout, and Outline.*

The quickest way to switch views is to use the icons in the bottom left corner of the screen.

Normal View

This view allows fast editing, previewing most text effects, but does not display images and other objects.

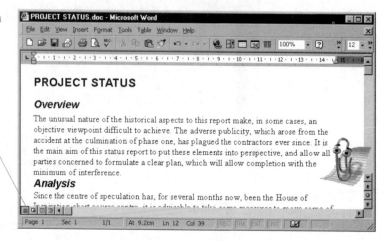

Web Layout View

This makes online reading easier by displaying text larger than it would print, and by displaying the Document Map, a tool you can use to move easily through your document.

In any of these views, paragraph symbols (markers denoting carriage returns, spaces, etc.) are by default not visible. To display them, click on the Paragraph Symbols icon normally displayed in the Standard toolbar: ¶

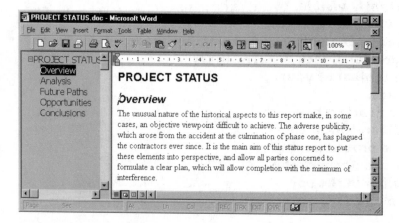

Print Layout View

This view displays your document as actual pages, previewing text and graphics effects.

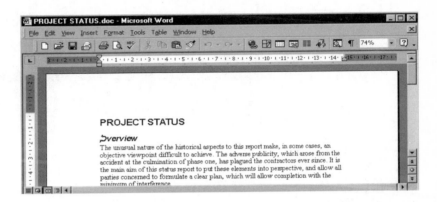

The structure of a document can be rearranged from Outline view by dragging the plus- and minus-signs to another part of the document.

Outline View

This allows you to view your text as a structured outline. Each major heading is marked with a plus-sign; subordinate headings are marked with a minus sign. To collapse a heading so that subordinate headings are not displayed, double-click on the plus-sign.

In previous versions of Word, there was an additional Master Document View. In Word 2000 this has been merged with Outline View.

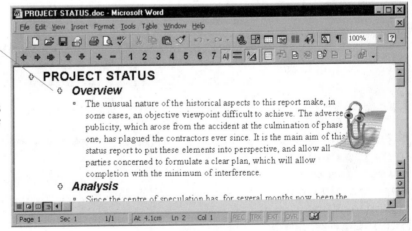

Customising the Toolbars

You can configure Word's Toolbars in a wide variety of ways.

Moving Toolbars

Move to the left edge of a toolbar. Your pointer should turn into a double arrow as shown below.

Start dragging here

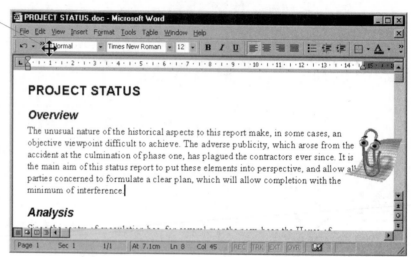

 **If you drag a floating toolbar back to the top of the screen, it will reattach itself to the toolbar area.**

2 If you drag onto the main page area, the toolbar will become "free and floating".

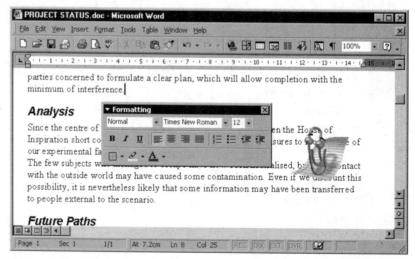

 You close down a floating toolbar by clicking on the cross in its top right corner. You can later reactivate it from the View menu or by right-clicking on any other toolbar.

Accessing extra Toolbar buttons

If a toolbar is too small to display all its icons, then you can still access them by clicking on the » icon.

Click here

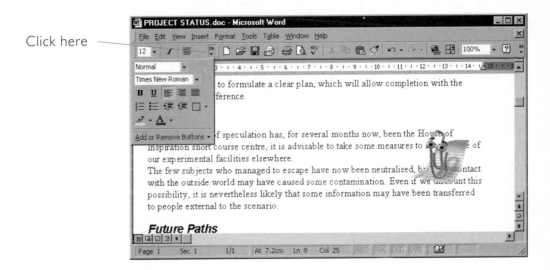

Resizing Toolbars

You can resize a toolbar by dragging on its right hand edge. Your pointer will turn into a double arrow when you are in the right place to begin dragging.

Drag from here

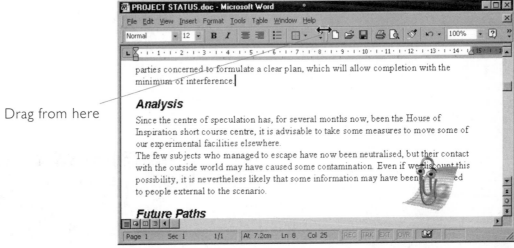

Adding or Removing Buttons

Each toolbar has a control marked "Add or Remove Buttons". If you can't see this, then click on the » symbol in the toolbar.

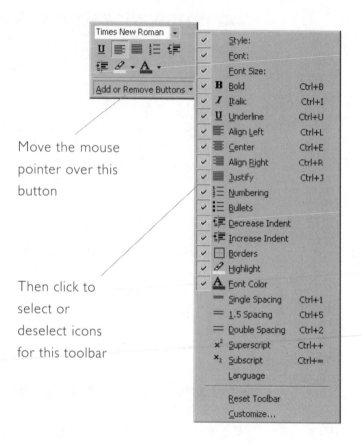

Move the mouse pointer over this button

Then click to select or deselect icons for this toolbar

You can also add and remove buttons from a floating toolbar.

Click here to access the pop-up menu

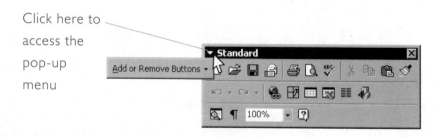

Adjusting the Page Setup

Go to the File menu and choose "Page Setup". The Page Setup dialog box appears. Like many of Word's dialog boxes, it is *tabbed*, i.e. subdivided into sections. You can select your required section by clicking on the appropriate tab at the top of the box.

1 Make sure the Margins tab is selected.

2 Type in any required changes to the margin or header/footer dimensions.

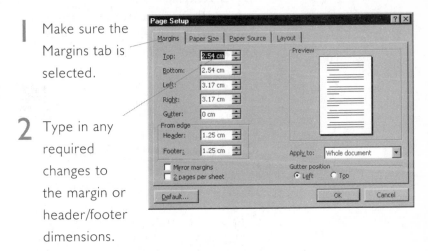

3 Click on the Paper Size tab.

4 Select a page orientation: Portrait (tall) or Landscape (wide).

You can also select tabs by pressing the Alt key together with the underlined letter in the tab name. Alternatively, pressing Control together with the Tab key itself will cycle through each tab in turn.

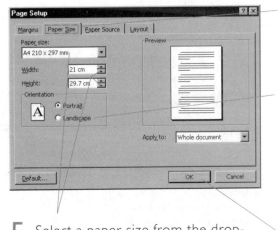

5 Select a paper size from the drop-down list, or enter custom values in the Width and Height boxes.

6 Make any necessary changes in the Paper Source and Layout tabs.

7 Click "OK" to apply your changes.

Help

Word 2000 features several basic ways of offering you help. In increasing order of sophistication, these are Help boxes, context sensitive help, and (for users of Microsoft Office 2000) the Office Assistant.

Help Boxes

If you allow your Mouse pointer to rest over an icon for a moment, a Help box will appear. This gives you a brief explanation of the icon's function.

Help box ———

Context Sensitive Help

1 Go to the Help menu and choose "What's This?".

The pointer turns into an arrow with a question mark attached until the next time you click.

2 Move your pointer to the element in which you're interested, then click. You can also open a menu to see help describing a particular option.

 The keyboard shortcut for context sensitive help is Shift + F1.

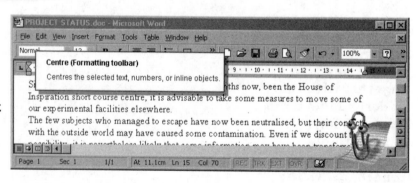

A pop-up box will appear, with a description of the item or menu option.

The Assistant

The Assistant is a "delightful" animated character who is always eager to provide you with help.

If the Assistant isn't already displayed, select Show the Office Assistant from the Help menu. When the Assistant is active, this menu option becomes Hide the Office Assistant.

1 To get help, click on the Assistant. A window appears.

2 Click one of the lightbulb icons to see suggested help information. The Assistant bases this on what you're currently doing.

3 Alternatively, enter some text relating to the information you want, then click "Search".

4 Click "Options" to set preferences for the Assistant.

 If you click on the Assistant with your right Mouse button, then a pop-up Menu appears.

Changing the Assistant

One day far into the future you may tire of your Office Assistant. Here's how to sack him/her and select another.

> Right click on the Assistant and select "Choose Assistant" from the pop-up menu.

To change the Assistant, you will probably be asked to insert your Office CD.

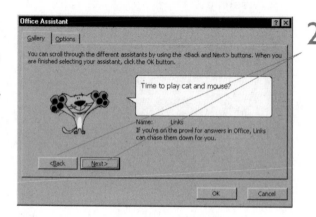

2 Click on these buttons to cycle through the different Assistants, then click "OK".

Smart Menus

When you initially open a menu, Word will show you an abbreviated list of options containing only those which are frequently used.

Any options you have used recently will automatically be added to the short menu. This way Word adapts to your working methods, so that commands you need are always within easy reach.

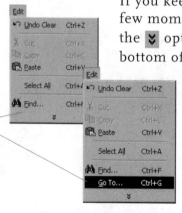

If you keep it open for a few moments, or click on the ⅋ option at the bottom of the abbreviated menu, then you'll see the full menu. (Notice that the lesser-used features are shown in a paler grey.)

Basic Text Manipulation

This chapter helps you start entering and manipulating text on the screen. It looks at different ways of editing and formatting type, as well as saving and printing your work.

Covers

Chapter Two

The Document Window

The New
Document icon

1 If there is no Document window, then create a new one by clicking on the "New" icon in the top left of the standard toolbar.

2 Enter a sentence of example text.

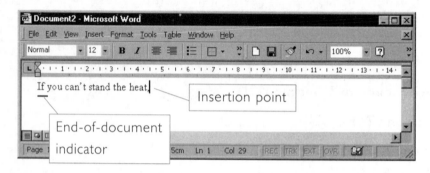

The vertical line is your *insertion point,* indicating where new text will appear. You can move the insertion point by:

Word auto-matically works out when to take a new line without breaking words. If you want to start a new paragraph, press the Return or Enter key.

- Using the cursor (arrow) keys.

- Clicking a new position with the Mouse.

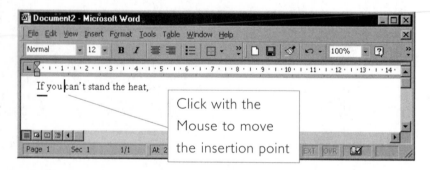

Inserting Text

1 Move the insertion point to a point where you would like to add more text.

2 Type the text. It will appear at the insertion point.

Note that the words to the right of the insertion point move along to accommodate the new text:

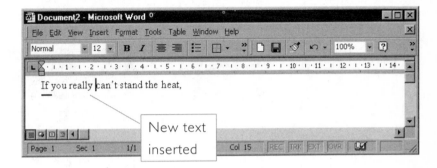

New text inserted

Deleting Text Using Backspace

Move the insertion point so that it is directly after the text you want to delete.

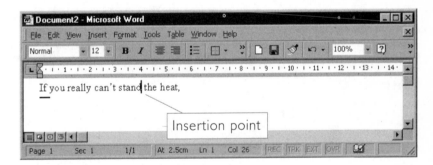

Insertion point

2 Press the Backspace key once to erase each character to the *left* of the insertion point.

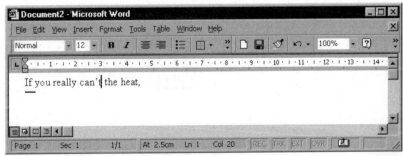

Deleting Text with the Delete Key

1 This time move the insertion point before the text to be deleted.

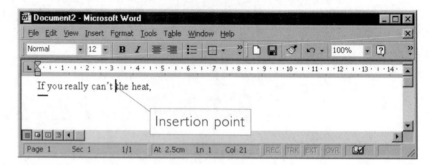

2 Press the Delete key once to erase each character to the *right* of the insertion point.

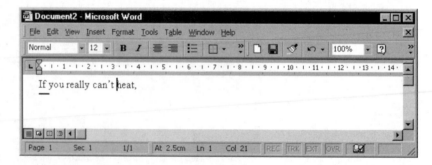

Selecting Text

You can select text by using the Mouse to drag horizontally across it, while holding down the left button:

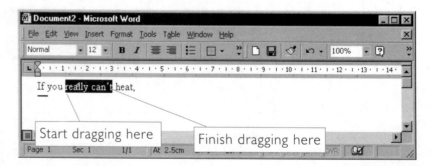

Replacing Selected Text

Anything you type will automatically replace any text which is currently selected:

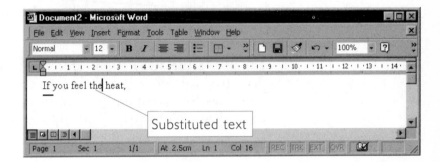

Substituted text

Adding More Text to the End of the Document

| Remember that before adding more text to the end of your document you must first reposition the insertion point:

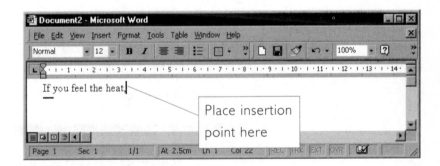

Place insertion point here

2 Add the text:

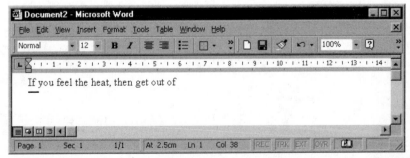

Insert versus Overtype

At the bottom of the screen, in the Status bar, the letters "OVR" should be greyed out. This indicates that you are in Insert, rather than Overtype mode.

1 Double-click the "OVR" indicator.

The text in the "OVR" indicator will turn black, showing that Overtype mode is selected. In Overtype mode, new text overtypes (replaces) any text to the right of the insertion point, instead of shifting the old text to the right.

2 Position the insertion point somewhere within your text:

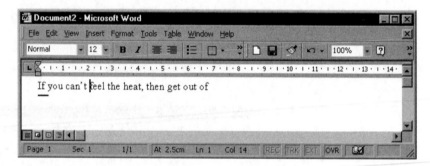

3 Type some new text.

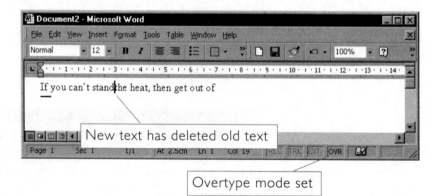

New text has deleted old text

Overtype mode set

4 Double-click once more on the "OVR" indicator to switch back to Insert mode.

Selecting All the Text in a Document

Choose the "Select All" option from the Edit Menu (or type Control+A).

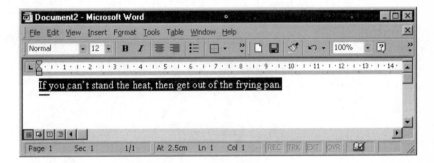

Changing the Appearance of Text

With all the text selected, open the "Size" pop-up menu from the toolbar, and increase the point size of the text to around twice the previous value.

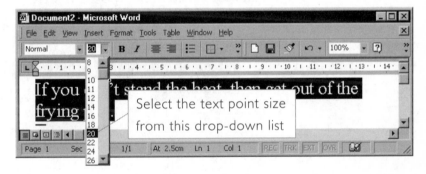

2 Select a single word. Use the toolbar to switch on the Bold effect.

The keyboard shortcut for Bold is Control+Shift+B.

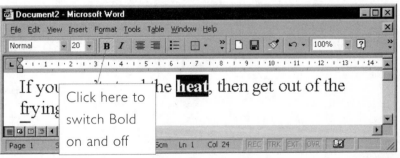

3 If you want to select text over more than one line, either drag over the area required or click at one end of the selection, then hold down Shift and click at the other end:

4 You can also select whole lines of text by dragging vertically over the area within the left margin.

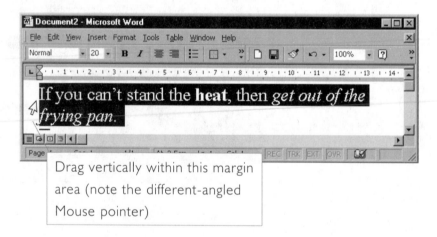

Drag vertically within this margin area (note the different-angled Mouse pointer)

5 Alternatively, you can double-click to select a single word, or triple-click to select an entire paragraph.

6 Note that if you click an insertion point and then type more text, the new text takes its attributes (appearance) from the previous character:

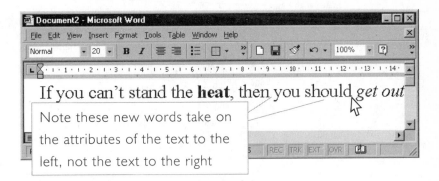

Note these new words take on the attributes of the text to the left, not the text to the right

Click and Type

This is a time saving feature, new to Word 2000. If you are in Print Layout or Web Layout view you can add text virtually anywhere on the page. Simply double-click to establish an insertion point.

If Click and Type doesn't appear to work, then first make sure that you're in Print Layout or Web Layout view. Then open the Tools menu and choose Options. Select the Edit tab and make sure that Click and Type is activated.

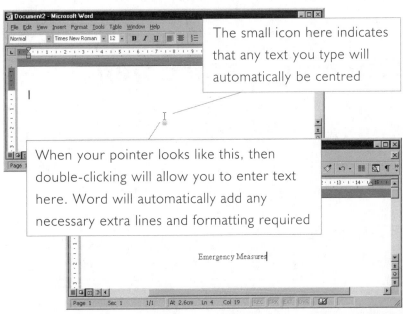

The small icon here indicates that any text you type will automatically be centred

When your pointer looks like this, then double-clicking will allow you to enter text here. Word will automatically add any necessary extra lines and formatting required

Saving a Document

The Save icon

I To Save your work either choose "Save" from the File menu, or click on the Save icon in the toolbar.

The following dialog box will appear:

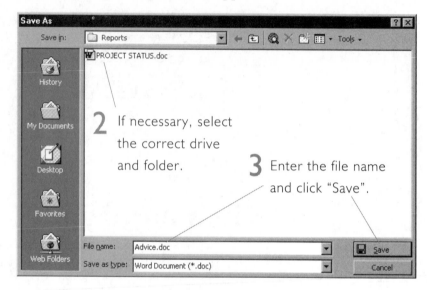

2 If necessary, select the correct drive and folder.

3 Enter the file name and click "Save".

4 If you have finished with the document, choose "Close" from the File menu.

Opening a Document

Either

- Choose "Open" from the File menu or click on the Open icon:

Or

- The last few files used are listed in the lower section of the File menu, and can be selected directly.

Print Preview

The Print Preview icon

Before you print a document, you may wish to check it on screen, in order to eliminate any errors that were not spotted at the basic text-proofing stage. Word 2000 offers a facility, Print Preview, which shows you all the pages of your document exactly as they will print, with none of the modifications made by the normal Word views. To access this special view, select "Print Preview" from the File menu, or select the corresponding icon from the Toolbar.

The following screen appears:

To edit the text in Print Preview, click here – the cursor changes back to its normal text-editing shape – then click in the text and make your changes.

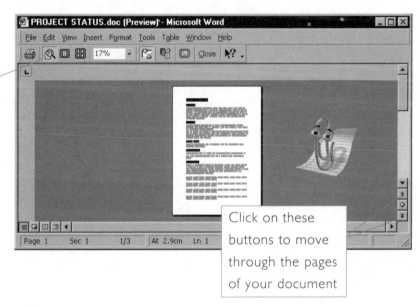

Click on these buttons to move through the pages of your document

Note that the cursor is initially in the shape of a magnifying glass. To zoom in to a particular area of the page, click over it with the left Mouse button; to zoom out, do the same.

If you are satisfied with your document, select "Print" from the File menu, or click the Print icon: ⎙ (see the following page). If you want to continue editing it, click "Close" instead.

Printing a Document

Choose "Print" from the File menu.

The following dialog box will appear:

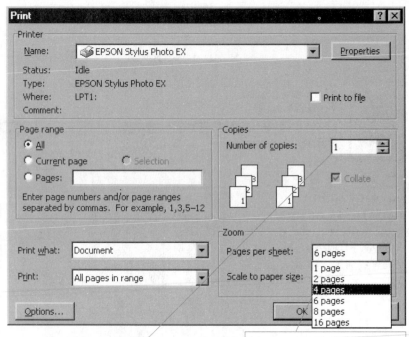

2 Enter the number of copies required.

3 Click "OK" to go ahead, or "Cancel" to abort.

You can use the Zoom facility to print out small versions of pages, up to sixteen on a single sheet

The method detailed above allows you the greatest control over how your document is printed. If, however, you do not need to make any refinements to the printing method, there is a much quicker way to print: simply click the Print icon in the Toolbar:

This begins to print immediately, bypassing the Print dialog box and using the default print settings.

Formatting Text

This chapter looks at ways in which you can change the appearance of your text. We'll start by examining what we can change on a character level. Then we'll see what we can control on a paragraph by paragraph basis.

Covers

Chapter Three

Character-level Formatting

What does "Character-level" mean?

Character-level attributes include font name, size, emboldening, underlining plus all sorts of other effects which can be applied to individual characters. If required, every single character could be given different attributes (although this would tend to make your document look a little like a ransom letter).

Using the Formatting Toolbar

1   Select the text which you want to format.

2   Choose the font required from the pop-up menu in the toolbar:

 If you highlight a portion of text, the toolbar will indicate its current formatting options.

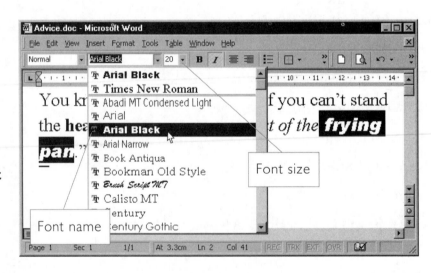

A font is a collection of characters with a particular visual style. Common fonts include:

Times or Times New Roman (useful for main text)
Arial (useful for headings)
Courier (the typewriter font)

3 Look at the font names in the pop-up list:

Printer icon

The most recently used fonts
appear above this line.

TrueType symbol

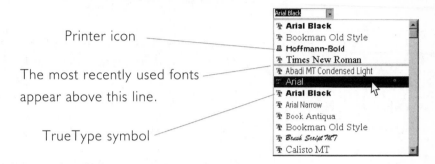

- A printer icon beside the name indicates a printer font. Your machine will use the closest available screen font (which may not match the printed output exactly).

- A double T symbol indicates a TrueType font, which is used for both screen display and printing.

- No symbol beside the font name indicates a screen font. Always check that your printer can reproduce this to a high enough quality.

4 You can use the buttons on this toolbar to add effects such as Bold, Italic, and Underline:

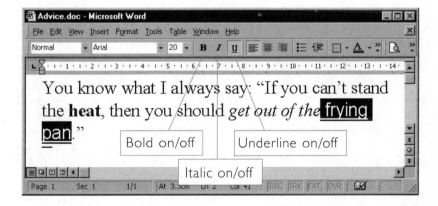

The Font Dialog Box

This controls all aspects of character-level formatting.

1 Select the text to change.

2 Either choose "Font" from the Format menu, then go to step 4, or click your right Mouse button inside the document window.

Right-clicking brings up a pop-up menu that contains options which are relevant to the task in hand. Later you will see that it changes depending on your current context.

 To change font quickly, press Control+Shift+F then type the first few letters of the Font name.

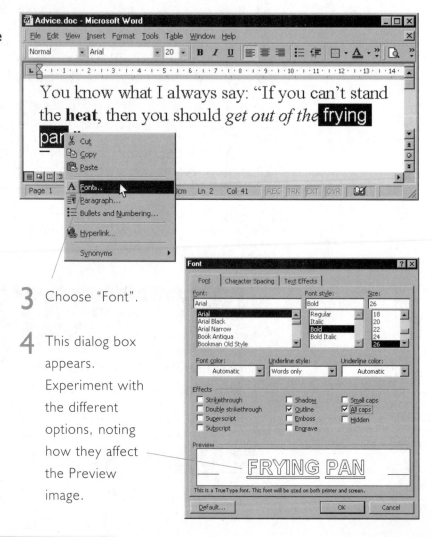

3 Choose "Font".

4 This dialog box appears. Experiment with the different options, noting how they affect the Preview image.

5 Click on the Character Spacing tab.

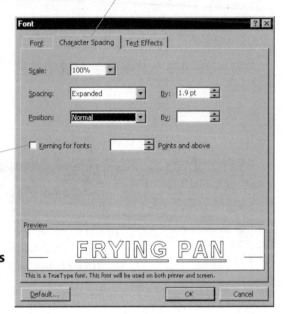

From here you can numerically control the character spacing, the position (for superscript and subscript), and kerning.

Kerning is a process used to adjust the space between certain combinations of characters. For example, when the letters "T" and "o" occur next to each other, normal spacing appears to be too wide. Kerning brings these together to create the illusion of normal spacing. Since kerning slows down the computer you can either switch it off altogether or activate it only for larger font sizes (where space is more noticable).

6 Click on the Text Effects tab.

This feature allows you to enhance text by adding animated effects to it. Until a printer manufacturer manages to develop moving ink, these effects will only be visible in on-line documents.

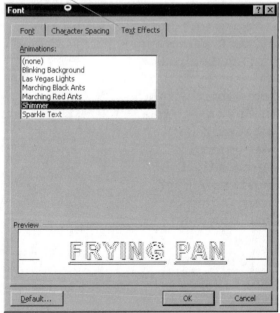

Paragraph-level Formatting

What does "Paragraph-level" mean?

Options such as alignment, left and right indents, and space above and below refer to whole paragraphs, i.e. each paragraph has only one set of these attributes.

Formatting with the Toolbar

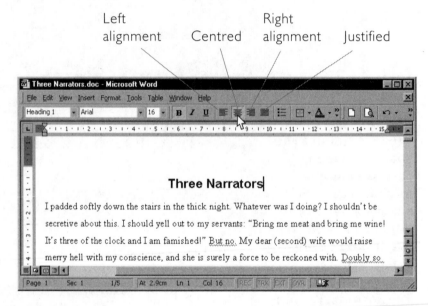

Left alignment   Centred   Right alignment   Justified

If you are changing just one paragraph you need only click an insertion point somewhere within it. Any change to a paragraph-level attribute will always affect the entire paragraph surrounding the insertion point.

1   Select the paragraph(s) to format. Remember that a heading is often a single-line paragraph.

2   Choose the form of alignment by clicking on the appropriate tool in the formatting toolbar.

Forms of Alignment

There are four forms of alignment:

Left
Text lines up along its left edge, with a ragged right edge.

Right
Here the text is moved so that the right edge is straight, and the left is ragged.

Centre
Text is centred between the left and right edges.

Justification
The text spacing is adjusted so that each line within a paragraph begins and ends in the same position (dictated by the margins and indents), giving a neat and regular appearance. Below is an example of justified text:

 The last line of every justified paragraph is only aligned left, allowing the reader to easily distinguish one paragraph from another.

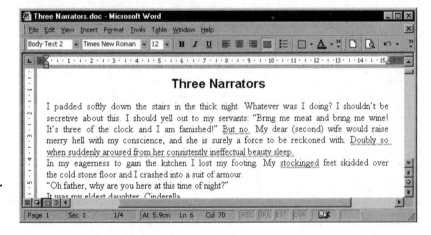

Bulleted Paragraphs

Activating Bullets

1   Select the paragraphs to be bulleted.

2   Click on the Bullet icon in the Formatting toolbar...

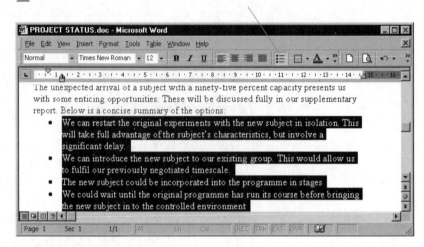

Removing Bullets

1   If necessary, re-select the bulleted paragraphs.

2   Click on the Bullet icon a second time.

Automatic Bullets

This is similar to the automatic numbering feature
discussed on page 41. If you begin a paragraph with an
asterisk, enter text in the normal way, and then press
Return – Word 2000 automatically replaces the asterisk
with a bullet, and starts the next paragraph with another.
When you reach the end of the list that you want bulleted,
erase the bullet that has just been created.

Advanced Bulleting

1 Select the text to be bulleted.

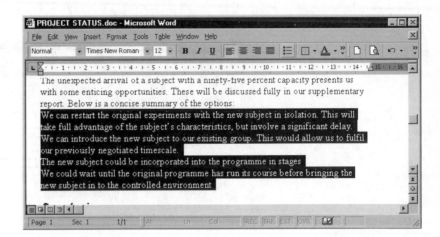

2 Choose "Bullets and Numbering" from the Format menu.

If necessary, click on the "Bulleted" tab.

You can also select "Bullets and Numbering" from the pop-up menu which appears when you click in the document window with the right Mouse button.

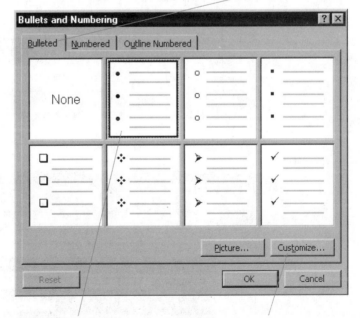

3 Choose the type of bullet text.

4 Click on "Customize" to see further options.

The following dialog box appears:

5 Choose the required settings. Click on the required bullet...

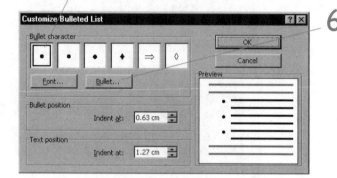

6 ...or click here to select another from the complete range of characters.

7 Select the font and character.

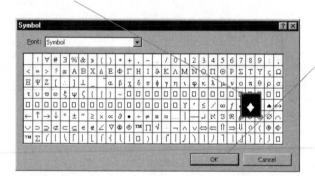

8 Click "OK" to exit all dialogs.

The selected text is now bulleted:

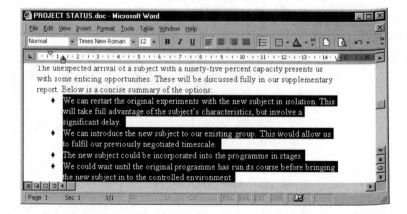

Numbered Paragraphs

1 Select the paragraphs to be numbered.

2 Click on the Numbering icon in the Formatting toolbar:

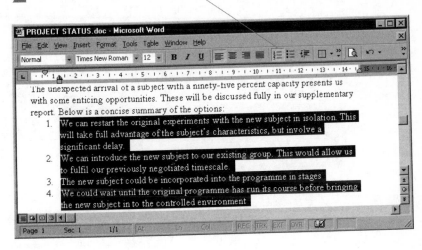

Removing Numbers

1 If necessary, re-select the numbered paragraphs.

2 Click on the Numbering icon a second time.

Automatic Numbering

If you begin a paragraph with a number, enter text in the normal way, and then press Return – Word 2000 automatically starts the next paragraph with the next number. When you reach the end of the list that you want numbered, simply erase the number that has just been created.

Advanced Numbering

1 Select the text to be numbered.

2 Right-click on the selected text, then choose "Bullets and Numbering" from the pop-up menu.

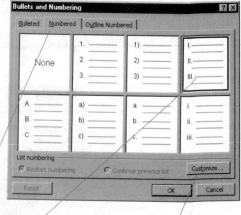

3 Select the "Numbered" tab.

4 Choose a style.

5 Click on "Customize".

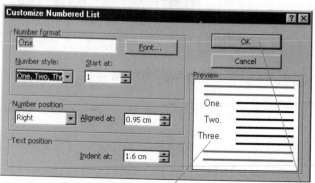

6 Experiment with different settings, referring to the Preview box.

7 Click "OK" to exit all dialog boxes.

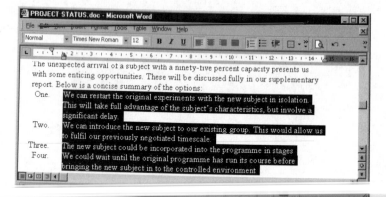

Outline Numbered Lists

Outline numbered lists contain nested sets of headings and subheadings. Because this function helps you to structure your numbered lists, you are likely to use it differently to the normal numbering function (discussed on the previous page).

With the cursor positioned at the point where you want to begin your multi-level structured list, select "Bullets and Numbering" from the Format menu, and choose the Outline Numbered tab.

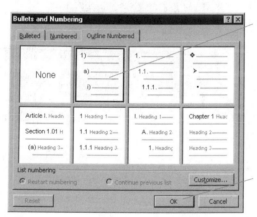

2 Select one of the numbering styles from the top row (i.e., those that don't contain any heading styles).

3 Click OK.

4 In the Word document, enter your list, pressing Return at the end of each element (now see the HOT TIP in the margin).

To place a line at a subordinate level to the one above it, right-click anywhere in the line, and select "Increase Indent". To move a line to a higher level, select "Decrease Indent".

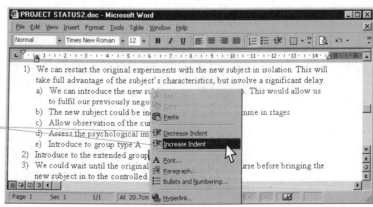

The Paragraph Dialog Box

This controls all aspects of paragraph-level formatting.

1 Select the text to be formatted.

2 Either choose "Paragraph" from the Format menu, or...

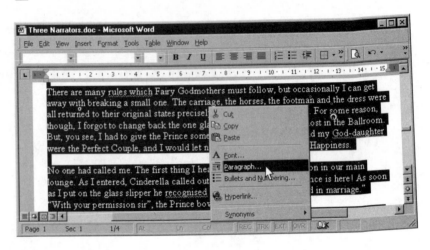

3 ...click your right Mouse button somewhere within the document window and select "Paragraph" from the pop-up menu.

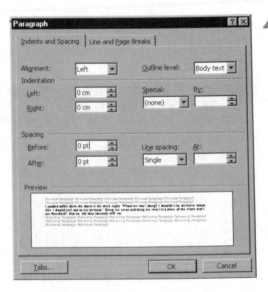

4 Experiment with the different paragraph controls, checking the results in the preview image. You can adjust the left and right indent, the space above and below a paragraph, or the line spacing within a paragraph.

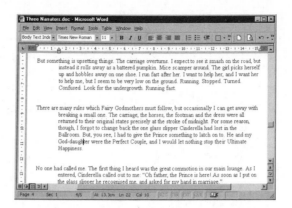

In the example shown here, a (vertical) "space before" of 6 points and a special hanging indent of 1.5cm have been set.

"Hanging indent" keeps the first line of each paragraph at the left margin, while moving all subsequent lines to the right by a fixed distance.

In the following example, the line spacing has been changed to "exactly" 16 points. This means that each line in the selected paragraphs will be given exactly 16 points of vertical space regardless of the size of font.

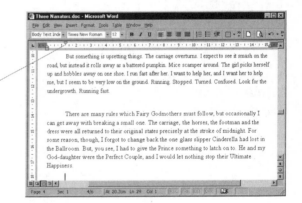

Also note that a first line indent has been set

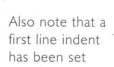

The Points System of Measurement

This system was introduced firstly in the USA in the nineteenth century, and then adopted by the UK and some European countries.

72 points is equal to 1 inch. 12 points is equal to the size of normal typewriter text.

It provides a standard way of measuring the size of type, and often refers to the vertical dimension of characters in a given font. For this reason it is often useful to adjust vertical spacing using points, so that the space between paragraphs uses the same measuring system as the paragraphs themselves.

The Line and Page Breaks Tab

1   Activate the Paragraph dialog box (either from the Format menu or by clicking in the document window with the right Mouse button).

2   Choose the Line and Page Breaks tab.

 A widow is a single line of text at the beginning of a paragraph separated from the rest by a page break. An orphan is a similar line at the end of a paragraph. Both widows and orphans look unattractive and should be avoided if possible.

Instructs Word to automatically move text onto the next page if necessary to prevent widows and orphans occurring

Makes sure that the text is kept with the following paragraph, and not broken over two pages

Word will move the text so that the paragraph is not broken over two pages

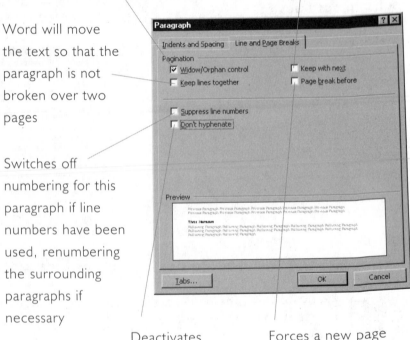

Switches off numbering for this paragraph if line numbers have been used, renumbering the surrounding paragraphs if necessary

Deactivates hyphenation

Forces a new page at the start of the paragraph

Working with a Document

This chapter helps you to find your way around a document, looking at scrolling, selecting different views and zooming in and out of the page. Additionally we'll look at Cut, Copy and Paste, the Format Painter tool and several other helpful document-formatting features.

Covers

Chapter Four

Scrolling

The scroll boxes let you know where you are in a document. For example, when the vertical scroll box is right at the top of the scroll bar, you are looking at the top (the beginning) of the document.

As you scroll down, the scroll box moves down like a lift through a lift shaft. The size of the box indicates how much of the document you are currently viewing. For example, if the box is one third the size of the scroll bar, then you're viewing a third of the document.

The Page Up and Page Down keys will scroll you up and down one screen at a time.

When your text is too large for the document window, you'll need to use one of the following navigation methods:

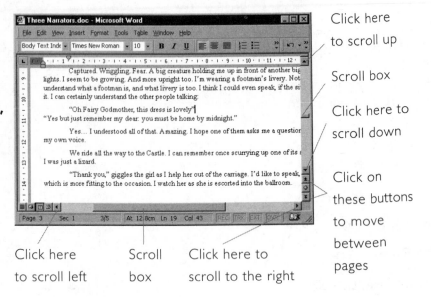

Click here to scroll up

Scroll box

Click here to scroll down

Click on these buttons to move between pages

Click here to scroll left

Scroll box

Click here to scroll to the right

Quick Ways to Scroll

- Drag the scroll box directly to a new position.

- Click in the scroll bar to either side of the scroll box. The document will scroll in that direction one screen at a time.

- As you move your insertion point, Word will scroll automatically so that it can always be seen.

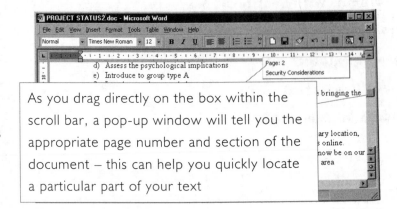

As you drag directly on the box within the scroll bar, a pop-up window will tell you the appropriate page number and section of the document – this can help you quickly locate a particular part of your text

Zooming

You can use the Zoom pop-up menu to control the level of magnification used by the document window.

Either choose an option from the pop-up menu or enter a new percentage value between 10 and 500.

If you can afford the space on screen, always maximise both the document window and the Word window itself by clicking on the Maximise button.

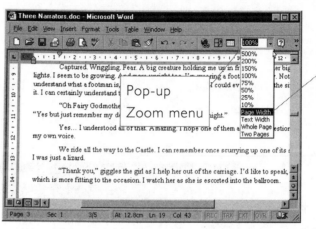

The Page Width option automatically zooms in or out so that the entire width of the page is displayed

In Print Layout view there are options to display one or more entire pages at a time.

Remember that the more you magnify the page, the more you'll need to scroll. Always try to view the entire horizontal line of text, since frequent horizontal scrolling can be tedious.

Resizing Windows

To allocate the greatest possible amount of space to a window, click on the Maximise button. To restore it to its non-maximised size, click on the Restore button.

The Restore symbol indicates that a window is already maximised. Click on this to restore the window to its normal size.

 Maximise button   Restore button

These are located in a window's top right-hand corner. To adjust the dimensions of a non-maximised window, rest the cursor over one of the window's edges (the cursor changes to a double-headed arrow), then drag the edge to where you want it.

The Ruler

The ruler gives you a visual account of the tabs and indents used for any selected text.

1 If the ruler is not visible, activate it by choosing "Ruler" from the View menu.

2 Select one or more paragraphs of text. Experiment by moving the indent markers:

General
left indent
marker

First-line
indent
marker

Default
tab stops

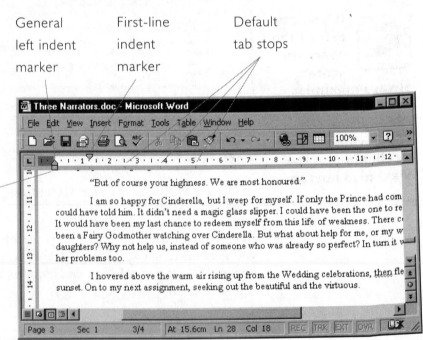

There is a small square block directly below the left indent marker. Dragging this will move both the left and first line indent markers together.

The Paragraph Dialog Box

You can also access these controls numerically from the Paragraph dialog box. See "The Paragraph Dialog Box" on page 44.

Cut and Paste

1 Select the text to be moved.

2 Right-click on the selected text, then choose "Cut".

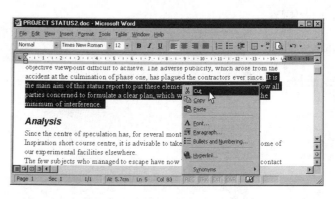

You can also Cut and Paste using the Edit menu, or the keyboard shortcuts Control+X, Control+V respectively.

The text is removed and put into the Clipboard.

3 Next position the insertion point at the destination. Click the right Mouse button, then choose "Paste".

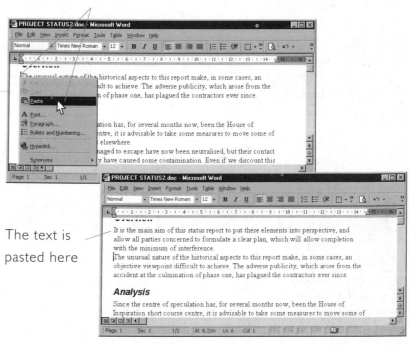

You can also make use of the Cut, Copy and Paste buttons in the Standard Toolbar:

 Cut

 Copy

Paste

The text is
pasted here

Copy and Paste

You can also Copy and Paste using the Edit menu, or the keyboard shortcuts Control +C, Control+V respectively.

| Select the text to be copied.

2 Right-click on the selected text, then choose "Copy".

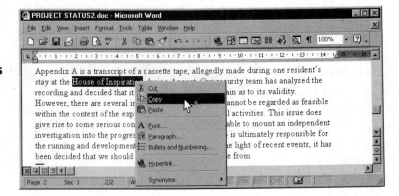

The text is copied into the Clipboard.

The quickest way to move text is to select it, then drag (from anywhere within the selected area) directly to the new position.

3 Next, position the insertion point at the destination. Click the right Mouse button, then choose "Paste".

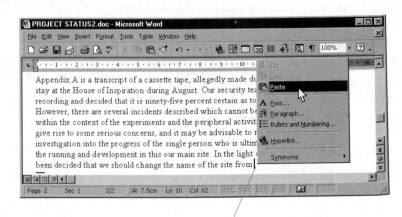

The copied text will paste here

Once something is in the Clipboard, you can paste it as many times as you like.

If you drag the selected area with the Control key held down, then the text will be copied to the new position.

Collect and Paste

Word 2000 can also make use of a special Clipboard toolbar. This allows you to store more than one item in the Clipboard.

1 Open the View menu and choose "Toolbars". Make sure that the Clipboard toolbar is active.

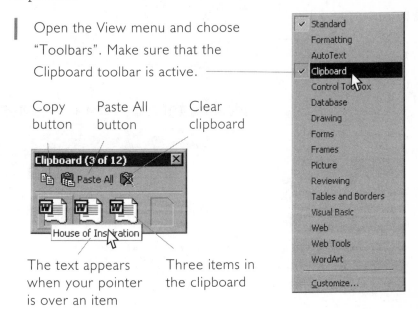

Copy button   Paste All button   Clear clipboard

The text appears when your pointer is over an item

Three items in the clipboard

2 Each time you choose Copy, an extra item appears in the Clipboard. Click where you want to paste an item in your document, then click on the icon in the Clipboard to paste in the contents. Or, click the Paste All button to paste in the whole Clipboard contents.

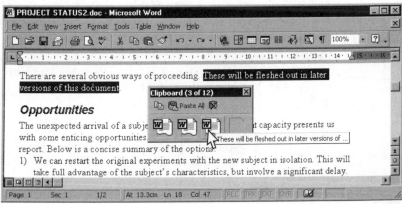

Undo and Redo

- Click the Undo button or type Control+Z to undo the last action.

- Alternatively, open the Undo pop-up menu to review and undo more than one action:

Undo button   Undo drop-down menu button

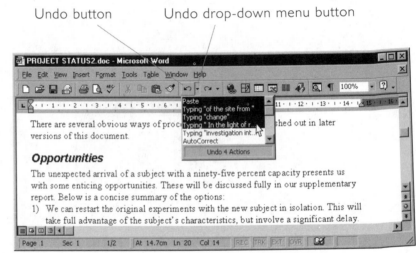

When undoing or redoing actions using the drop-down menus, drag the cursor down until the actions that you want to undo or redo are highlighted, then release the Mouse button.

- To redo the undone actions, type Control+Y or use the Redo pop-up menu.

Redo button   Redo drop-down menu button

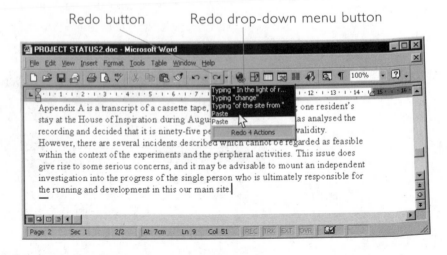

Page Breaks

Word automatically calculates the position of page breaks. These appear in the document window as a dotted horizontal line (a "soft" page break). However, you can force page breaks, as follows:

1 Choose "Break..." from the Insert menu.

2 Make sure that "Page break" is selected.

A "Hard" page break is inserted.

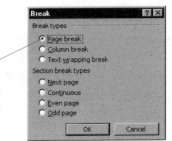

Defining Sections

Sections can be used to help organise your document. They also allow you to vary its layout, even within a single page.

1 Click an insertion point part of the way through your document (between paragraphs).

2 Choose "Break" from the Insert menu.

3 Choose the "Continuous" option, under "Section break types".

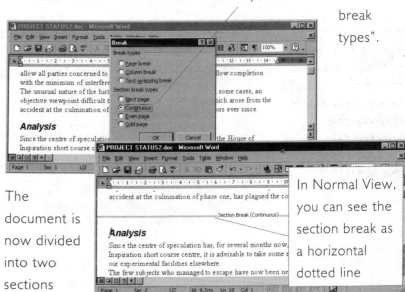

The document is now divided into two sections

In Normal View, you can see the section break as a horizontal dotted line

Using Columns with Sections

1 Make sure you are using a document which has been divided into two or more sections.

2 Click the insertion point somewhere in the second section, then choose "Columns" from the Format menu:

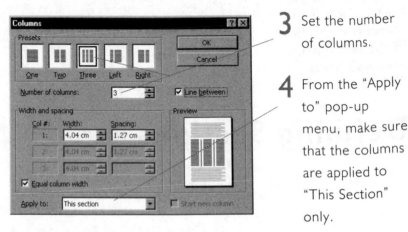

3 Set the number of columns.

4 From the "Apply to" pop-up menu, make sure that the columns are applied to "This Section" only.

5 Click "OK".

You now have a mixed column layout:

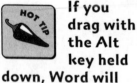

If you drag with the Alt key held down, Word will display the horizontal measurements in the ruler.

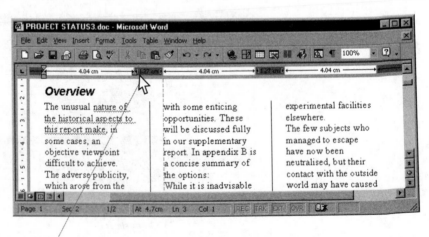

6 You can also adjust the width of columns by dragging the columns' boundary markers in the ruler.

Column Breaks

You can force text to start in a new column by inserting a hard break.

1 Place your insertion point and choose "Break" from the Insert menu.

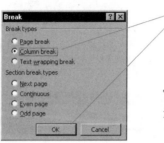

2 Select the "Column break" radio button, then click OK.

This will force the text after the insertion point into a new column.

Balancing Columns

If there is enough space on the page to accommodate all of your column text, you can balance the columns neatly:

1 Click the insertion point at the end of the last column and choose "Break" from the Insert menu.

2 Insert a "Continuous" section break.

The columns are balanced to within a line or two of each other

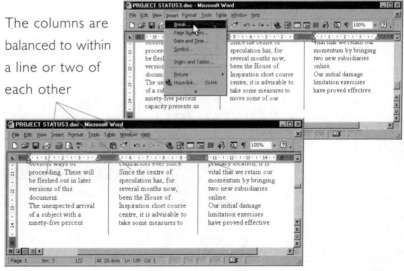

Headers and Footers

Headers normally appear at the top of every page, footers at the bottom (an example being "Word 2000 in easy steps" on this page).

Creating/Modifying a Header

1 Choose "Header and Footer" from the View menu.

Word will automatically change to Print Layout View. The main page text will be greyed out to let you concentrate on the header. The Header and Footer toolbar will also appear.

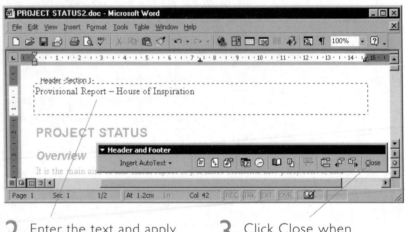

2 Enter the text and apply formatting as required.

3 Click Close when you're finished.

The Header and Footer Toolbar

Insert page number

Format page number

Insert date

Page setup

Same as previous

Switch between header and footer

Show previous

Show next

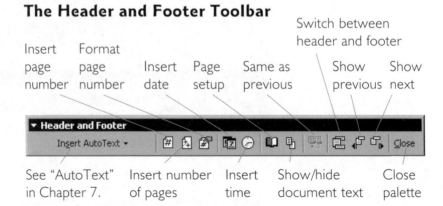

See "AutoText" in Chapter 7.

Insert number of pages

Insert time

Show/hide document text

Close palette

Creating/Modifying a Footer

1 Click on the "Switch between header and footer" button in the toolbar. This will take you to the footer text.

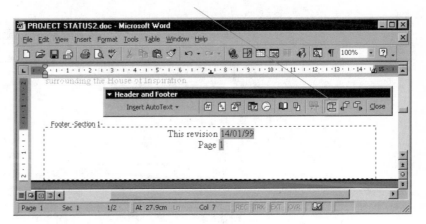

2 Enter the footer text. You can include automatic page numbers, or the current date or time by clicking on the relevant button in the toolbar.

3 Click "Close" when you've finished.

Now the header and footer text is greyed out, and you can edit the main text again. Note that the picture below shows Print Layout View. In Normal View, headers and footers do not appear at all.

By default, the header and footer on a page will apply to all remaining pages in the document. You can override this by editing the headers/footers for other pages separately.

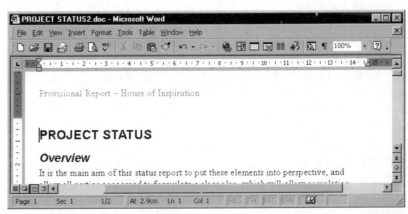

The Format Painter

This allows you to copy the formatting options from one piece of text to another:

1 Select the source text and click on the Format Painter icon.

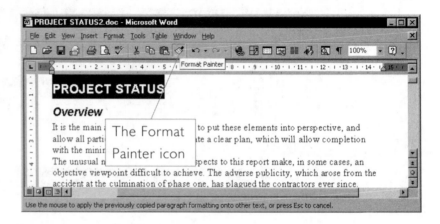

2 Now drag across the destination text. The formatting is applied to the new text.

To copy formatting to more than one destination, simply double-click the Format Painter icon. You can then apply the new formatting to as many pieces of text as you wish. When you've finished, either click back on the icon or press the Escape key.

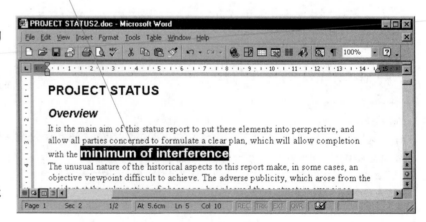

Document Properties

Windows 95/98 (and later versions) allow you to enter file names which are longer (and so more descriptive) than the Spartan eight characters allowed by MS-DOS. Even so, it is useful to record additional information as part of each Word document to help you organise your work, and remember your document's purpose.

1 Go to the File menu and choose "Properties".

2 Enter the relevant details. These will be saved along with your document.

3 Click OK when you're done.

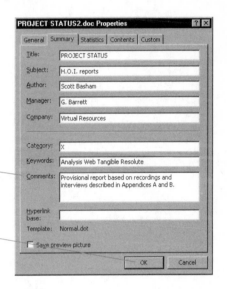

 The Statistics tab in the Properties dialog will show you useful information about your document.

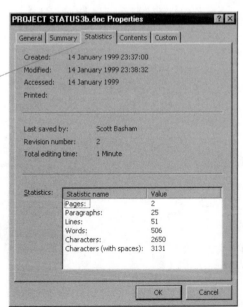

4 When you use the Open document dialog, you can click on the "Advanced" button to tell Word to search on the basis of the information entered in a document's properties.

The Document Map

The Document Map is a feature new to Word 2000, which uses the headings in your document to create an outline of the document's structure. It appears in a separate pane to the left of the main editing area, and can be used to navigate easily through the document. To display the Document Map, do the following:

1 Click on the Document Map button.

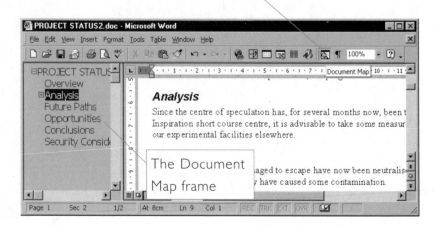

The Document Map frame

2 To jump to a heading listed in the Document Map, simply click on its entry.

Note that, in the illustration above, the heading "Analysis" has a small plus-sign next to it. This indicates that there are subheadings beneath it. To display these headings, click on the plus sign:

To collapse the structure to show only the main headings, click on the minus-sign

The subheadings are now displayed

Styles and Themes

Styles help you to easily apply a consistent set of formatting commands to main text, headings and other elements of your document.

Once you start using styles, you'll be able to control your document's presentation with the minimum of tedious manual editing.

Themes allow you to give a collection of your documents the same consistent look and feel.

Covers

Chapter Five

Using the Default Styles

A style is a complete collection of type attributes saved under a single name. There are two main benefits to this:

- Your document will have a visual consistency if, for example, all your subheadings look the same.

- You can quickly make drastic but coherent changes to the format of your document by redefining the styles already used by the text.

Applying a Style

1 Select the text.

2 Select a style from the Style drop-down menu:

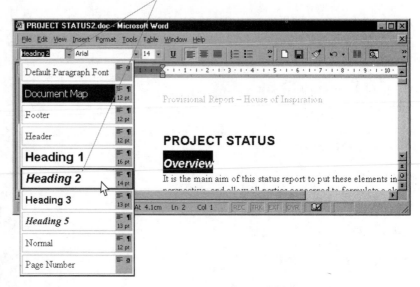

You can also use the keyboard shortcut Control+ Shift+S to open the Style drop-down menu. Then type the first few letters of the style, press the down arrow key, and press Return to apply the style.

The text has now been set to this style. Whenever you select text on the page, the Style menu will indicate which style is currently being used.

By default all text starts off using the style "Normal".

Editing an Existing Style

1 Select some text in the document which already uses the style to be changed.

2 Use the toolbar and menus as normal to experiment with changes in formatting (see Chapter Three).

3 When you are happy with the changes, reselect the style from the pop-up list:

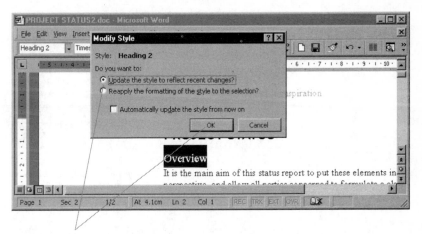

4 In the dialog which appears, make sure the "Update the style..." option is selected and click "OK".

All text in the document using this style will now change automatically...

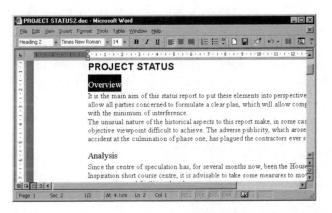

Creating a New Style

You can easily create a new text style in Word 2000, simply by altering existing text, and then entering a name for the new style, which will take these properties.

1 Format the text as normal in the document (see Chapter Three), then select it.

2 When you are happy with its appearance, click on the Style menu box, enter the new style's name, and press Enter:

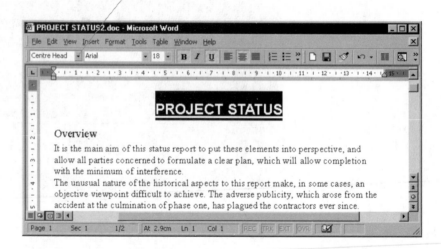

The new style is automatically created, and can now be applied to other text.

Automatic Style Creation

When you alter the formatting of text, Word 2000 can create a new style for you. For example, if you enter a small number of words without punctuation on a single line, apply some changes to the font, size or font effects, and then press Enter, Word will usually assume that this is a new heading style, and create a new style automatically. Thus, if you already have three heading styles, named "Heading 1", "Heading 2", etc., the new style will be named "Heading 4".

The Style Dialog Box

Word 2000 allows you to make most of the style changes you should need from the Formatting toolbar; but the Style dialog allows you to preview potential style changes on a large portion of text, and then to cancel out of the dialog without actually making any of the changes. To open the dialog, do the following:

Select "Style" from the Format menu. The dialog appears:

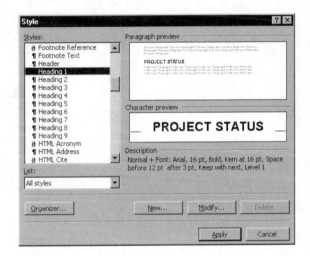

Creating a New Style Using the Style Dialog Box

1 Click on the "New" button in the Style dialog box (see above).

2 Enter the new style's name.

3 See the "Setting the Format" topic on the following page to see how to change the new style's properties.

Setting the Format

Click on the Format button in the New Style dialog box:

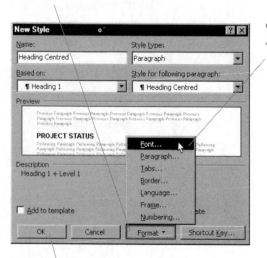

2 This menu appears, from which you can select the dialogs that control the various properties of the style. Make the appropriate changes, referring to the formatting topics in Chapters Two, Three and Four.

3 When you have made your changes, click "OK". The new style is added to the list.

Modifying a Style

From the Styles dialog box, click on "Modify".

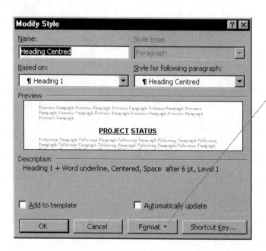

2 Use the Format button to make the desired changes (see Setting the Format, step 2, above), then click "OK".

...cont'd

Setting a Keyboard Shortcut for a Style

1 Click the "Shortcut Key" button in the Modify Style or New Style dialog box.

Word tells you if your proposed shortcut key is currently being used for something else. If you go ahead, then your style shortcut will override the previous setting.

The Customize Keyboard dialog appears:

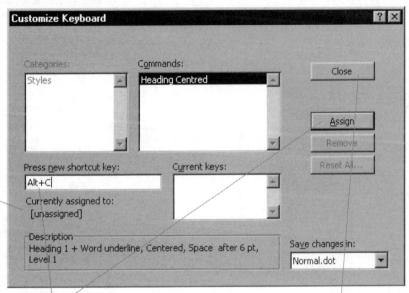

Most single keystrokes will already be assigned a function, so you will probably need to use a combination of keys, using the Ctrl and/or Alt keys. When you enter the shortcut key combination, all you have to do is press the keys that you want to use: you don't have to type out "Ctrl" or "Alt" in full.

2 Enter the shortcut key combination for the style and click the "Assign" button. You can repeat this process to add more than one keyboard shortcut for the same style.

3 When you have finished, click the "Close" button to return to the previous dialog box.

5 **Styles and Themes** **69**

Character-level Styles

Normally styles operate on a paragraph level, i.e. they only apply to whole paragraphs.

To create a character-level style:

1 Choose "New" from the Style dialog.

2 Select "Character" from the "Style type" pop-up menu.

3 Enter a name for the new style here.

4 Use the "Format" pop-up to set the character-level attributes.

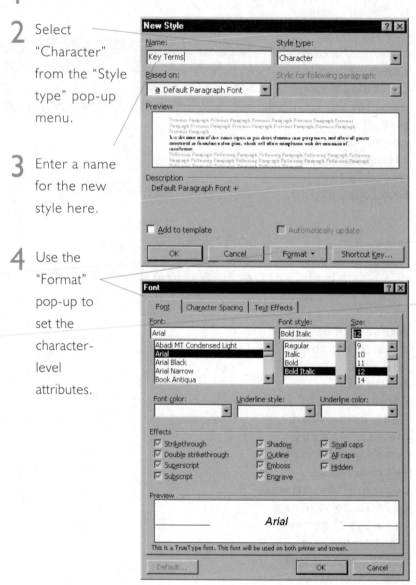

You can now apply your character style to individual words or phrases without affecting the entire surrounding paragraph.

If text already uses a paragraph style, then the character style will override these settings:

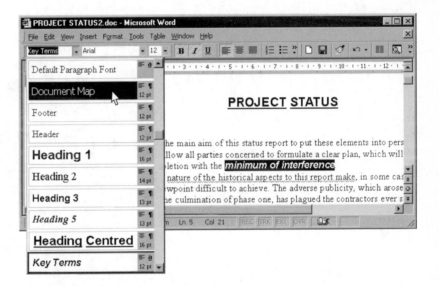

Identifying Character and Paragraph Style Names

Character-level style names are labelled in the pop-up list with **a**. Paragraph styles are labelled with ¶.

Once a style has been created, it cannot be changed from a character to a paragraph style, or vice versa. However, you can always create a new copy of the style by choosing "Styles" from the Format menu, then selecting the style you want to copy and then clicking on "New". Since this is a new style you can now select the style type.

AutoFormat

Word uses a feature called AutoFormat to apply suitable styles automatically to the different parts of your document, without you having to select them. For example, it analyses whether a paragraph seems to be functioning as body text, as a heading, or as part of a list. AutoFormat is turned on by default, but you can change this as follows:

1 Choose "AutoCorrect" from the Tools menu, then select the "AutoFormat As You Type" tab.

2 Select which formatting changes AutoFormat should make automatically as you enter your text.

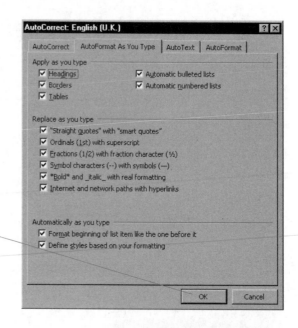

3 Click "OK".

If you click the Options button, you will be presented with the AutoFormat options tab, which will allow you to control the types of changes that Word will make.

If AutoFormat has been deactivated while you have typed in a document, and you subsequently want to have the document formatted automatically, do the following:

1 Select "AutoFormat" from the Format menu.

2 Tell Word what sort of document this is, then click "OK".

Themes

Themes allow you to give a unified look and feel to a document. They contain settings for styles, bullets, colour and graphics.

Applying a Theme to a Document

1 Choose "Theme" from the Format menu. The following dialog box appears:

If you have Microsoft FrontPage version 4 (or later) installed, you can use its Themes as well as those supplied with Word.

You can also download additional Themes by choosing "Microsoft on the Web" from the Help menu.

2 Select a Theme from the list.

3 Check the sample of the theme. If you are happy with its look, then click "OK".

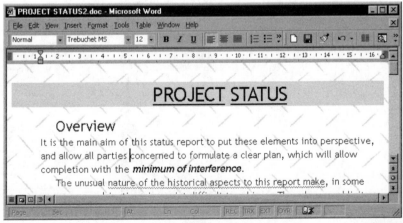

Your document will now reflect the new Theme.

You can still change your mind at this point by using the Undo button.

Alternatively, select a different Theme from the Theme dialog box.

The Style Gallery

When you work on a document, a template is used to tell Word which formatting properties to use for the different character and paragraph styles. You can use the Style Gallery to apply the properties of different templates, to produce an instant overall change to the appearance of your document.

A **Template differs from a Theme in that it only contains style definitions, and no colour schemes or graphics. However, a Template will generally contain far more style definitions than a Theme.**

1 Go to the Format menu, and choose "Theme".

2 Click on the Style Gallery button.

3 Choose a template design, then a preview option.

"Document" shows you how your document would look with the proposed style definitions. "Example" shows you an example document, demonstrating the different styles.

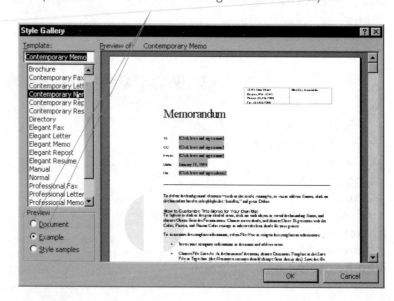

"Style samples" lists each style name using its own attributes

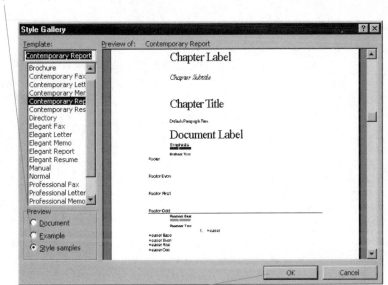

4 Click "OK" if you want your document to adopt these new style definitions.

Your document will now use the styles from the template.

If your document currently doesn't use any of the style names defined in the Template, then applying the Template will have no initial visible effect. However, you can now use these new styles by applying them manually to your text.

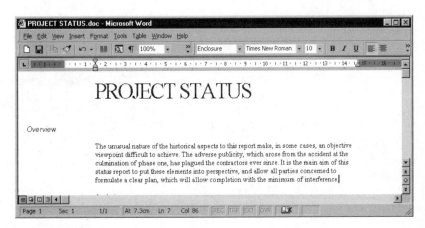

Displaying Style Names

Sometimes it is useful to see instantly which styles are being used by the paragraphs in your document.

1 Make sure that Normal View is active (you can set this using the View menu or the icon at the bottom left of the screen).

2 Choose "Options" from the Tools menu.

3 Click on the View tab.

4 Set the "Style area width" to a figure greater than zero.

5 Click "OK".

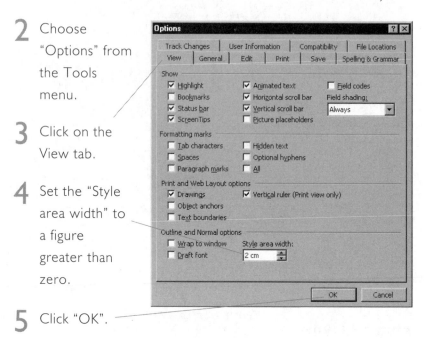

In this example we've used a 2cm margin area in which to list the styles used.

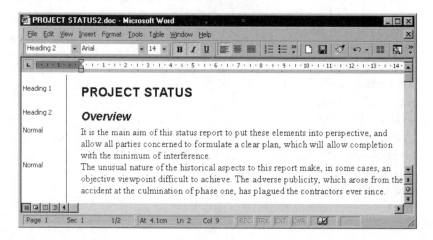

Tabulation

Text which is laid out with correct and accurate horizontal alignment greatly helps to give a document a professional look.

Effective use of white space, including tabulation, is one of the most important considerations when using a word-processor. This chapter deals with a range of tabulation features and examples.

Covers

Chapter Six

Default Tabulation

Do not feel tempted to space out text by pressing the space bar lots of times. This will not produce consistent results – use tabulation instead.

The default tab stops are set every half inch. When you press the Tab key, Word automatically moves across the page, stopping when it reaches the next tab stop position.

To see how this works:

1 Make sure that the ¶ button is active.

2 Enter items of text separated by a single tab character.

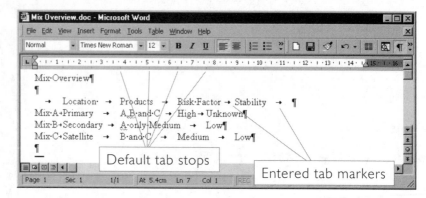

Creating Your Own Tabulation

1 Select the text.

To make the ruler display the distances between tab stops when dragging a new tab, hold down the Alt key.

2 Click in the lower half of the ruler (or the grey bar beneath it) to create a new tab (shaped like an "L") and drag to adjust its position.

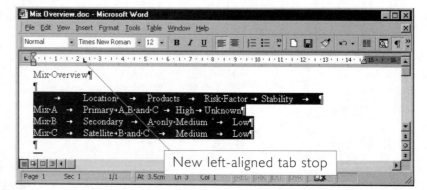

...cont'd

Any new tab stops you create will automatically override the default tabs.

3 Repeat this process to create more tab stops.

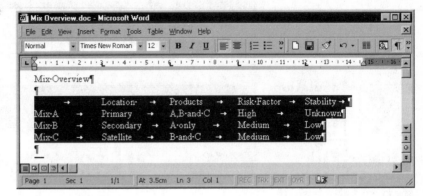

Deleting Tabs

You can delete your tab stops simply by dragging them downwards out of the ruler.

Different Types of Tab

You can move your own tab stops at any time by dragging them within the ruler - but be sure to select the main text first.

So far you've created left-aligned tabs, which cause text to align along its left edge under the tab stop.

1 Click the Tab Alignment button once to change to centre tabs.

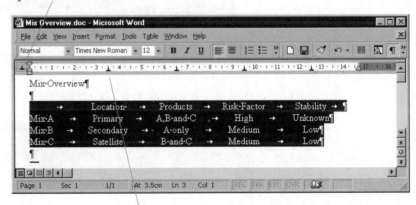

2 You can now create centred tabs by clicking in the ruler.

As you click on the Tab Alignment button, it cycles between Left, Centre, Right and Decimal alignment.

Here is an example of right-aligned tabs:

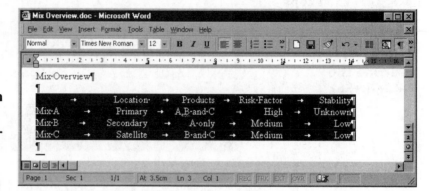

Tabulation is a paragraph-level attribute. Each paragraph can have its own tab stops if necessary.

Decimal tabs are used to line up numbers along the decimal point:

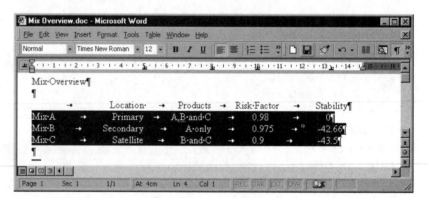

Usually a mixture of different tabs is required:

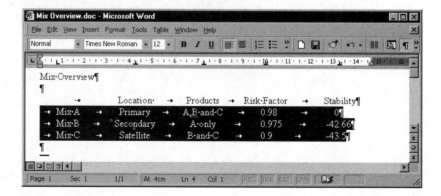

The Tabs Dialog Box

More options can be found in the Tabs dialog box.

You can also access the Tabs dialog box by double-clicking directly on a Tab marker in the Ruler.

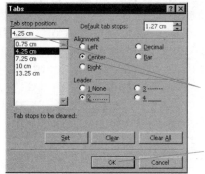

I Choose "Tabs" from the Format menu.

2 Set the position and alignment of the tab.

3 Click "OK".

This example also uses a leader consisting of a row of dots

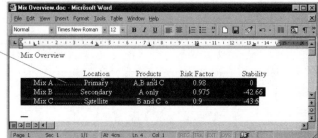

Bar Tabs

These can only be accessed from the Tabs dialog box (follow the steps above). Setting a bar tab causes a vertical line to appear in the text at the specified position.

You can also access the Tabs dialog via the Paragraph dialog (see page 44).

Bar tab

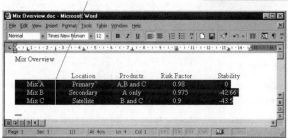

Using Tabs to Create Tables

The examples used on the preceding pages of this chapter have demonstrated the properties of tabs by using them to create a simple table. However, although this table presents a small amount of information clearly, it contains none of the additional effects that are often used to enhance the presentation of tables: e.g., borders, shaded cells. Word 2000 does allow you to create tables that can use such effects, using a very simple click-and-drag method (see Chapter 10, "Tables and Charts", for how to do this); but if you have already entered your table data as we have in this chapter, you won't want to type it in all over again. Fortunately, Word allows you to convert such data into true tables very easily:

1 Highlight the data you want to convert.

2 Go to the Table menu, open the Convert submenu and choose "Text to Table".

3 If you have separated your columns using tabs, make sure this option is selected.

4 Click "OK". The table is created automatically:

If the width of a column needs adjusting, rest your cursor over the table column icon to its right, then click and drag it to where you want it.

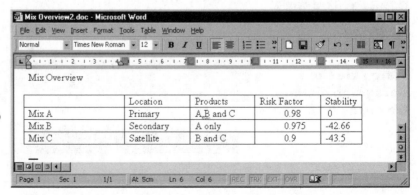

Automatic Features

Word has many automatic features which will operate on selected text or a complete document. This chapter looks at many of these, including search and replace tools and facilities for correction of spelling and grammar.

Covers

Chapter Seven

Find and Replace

Finding Text

Word can be instructed to search through your document for particular words, groups of characters, or formatting attributes.

┃ Choose "Find" from the Edit menu, or type Control+F.

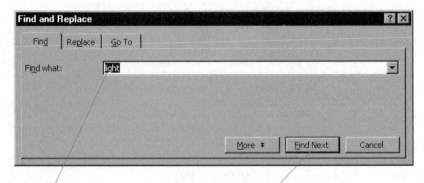

2 Enter your search text here.

3 Click on the Find Next button.

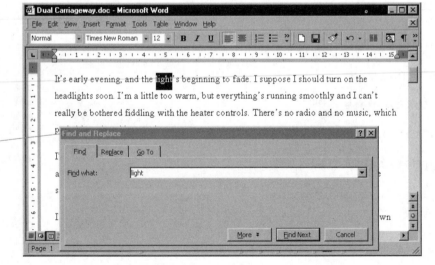

Word keeps this dialog box open in case you want to search on to the next occurrence of your text.

Word will highlight the next instance of the search text within your document. The Office Assistant will let you know if the end of the document was reached without Word finding any occurrences.

Even if you close the Find and Replace dialog, you can still continue your search by using the two blue buttons in the vertical scrollbar.

More or Less

1 If the Find and Replace dialog is not currently being displayed, then choose "Find" from the Edit menu, or type Control+F.

Using the checkboxes in the centre of the dialog, you can set the Find dialog to look for text in a particular case, for whole words (rather than groups of letters), to use wildcard searching, or phonetic matching.

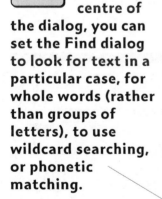

2 Click the More button to display more options, or the Less button to see the abbreviated version of this dialog box.

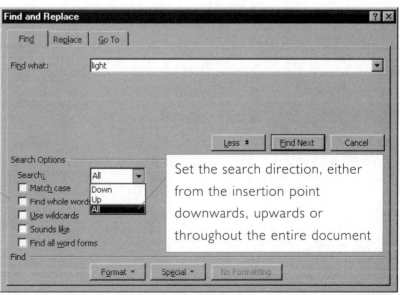

Searches based on Attributes

Your search can be based on attributes as well as specific text. You can even search for particular text and attributes simultaneously.

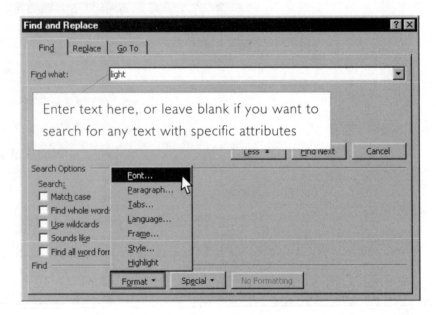

Enter text here, or leave blank if you want to search for any text with specific attributes

| In the Find and Replace dialog box, open the Format pop-up menu and choose the relevant option(s).

In this example we're searching for Arial Italic 11 point text.

2 Click "OK" to return to the Find dialog, then click on the Find button to start the search.

Word will now look through your document to find any text which matches *both* what you typed for "Find what" *and* the attributes you specified:

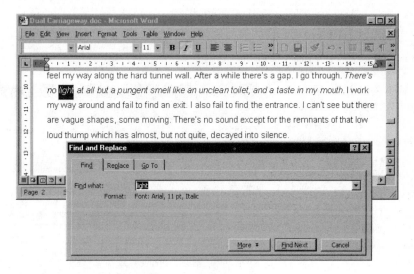

Cancelling Attribute Searches

If you have previously specified attributes for your search, then you can clear these quickly by clicking on the No Formatting button.

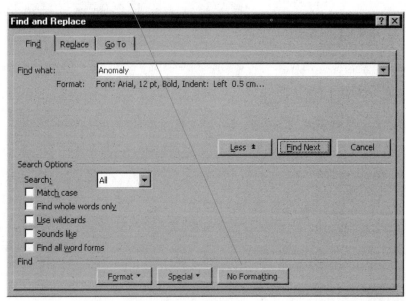

Replacing Text

Once you have found an instance of the text you are searching for, you can choose to replace it with some different text.

 Before clicking on the Format button, be sure to click in either the "Find what" or "Replace with" parts of the dialog. This determines whether you want to specify a Format to search for, or to replace with.

1 Click on the Replace tab.

2 Enter the "Replace with" text.

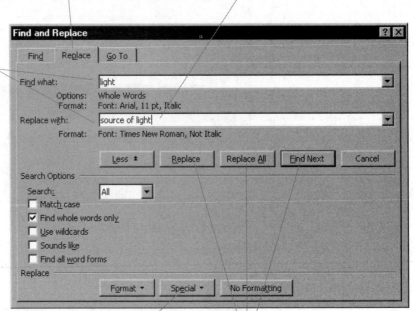

 To open the Find and Replace dialog with the Replace tab active, you can choose Replace from the Edit menu, or type Control+H. You can then enter the "Find what" text here before continuing with step 2. However, if you want to search for text with a particular format, you'll have to use the Find tab.

3 If you wish to replace the search text with text that has different format attributes, click here and choose the relevant options.

4 Click "Replace" to change just this instance of the target text, "Replace All" to change every instance in the document, or "Find Next" to skip to the next instance.

5 When you're done, click "Cancel".

Special Characters

You can use the "Special" pop-up menu in the Find and Replace tabs to easily insert the keyboard codes for special characters.

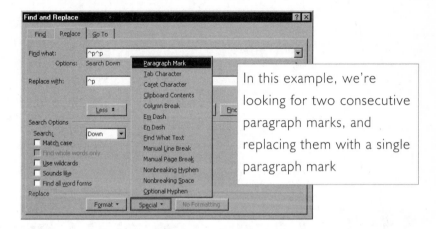

In this example, we're looking for two consecutive paragraph marks, and replacing them with a single paragraph mark

Wildcards

If you want to search not for a specific piece of text, but for text that follows a certain pattern, select the "Use wildcards" checkbox before clicking the "Special" button. You will then find that "Special" pop-up menu contains some extra entries – e.g. to search for words that follow the pattern "g?ve" (where "?" represents any single character), you would do the following:

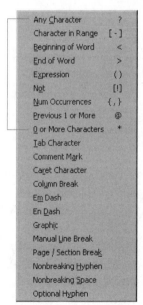

1 Enter the letter "g" in the "Find what" box.

2 Click the "Special" button and select "Any Character" from the menu.

3 Enter the letters "ve".

This search will highlight all words like "give", "gave", and (if you don't have the "Find whole words only" checkbox selected) words like "given", too.

Another very useful wildcard feature available from the "Special" menu is the "Character in Range" function. This allows you to search for numbers or letters in any range you specify. For example, to search for references to years between 1961 and 1967, make sure that the "Use wildcards" checkbox is selected, then do the following:

1 In the "Find what" box, enter "196".

2 Click on the "Special" button and select "Character in Range" from the menu. The text "[-]" will be inserted.

3 Edit the contents of the "Find what" box so that it now reads "196[1-7]".

Spelling and Grammar Checking

Word allows you to check your spelling and grammar in two ways: either from a special dialog, or "on the fly". The dialog is used as follows.

The shortcut key for Spelling and Grammar Checking is F7.

1 If you don't want to spell check your entire document, then select only the text you require.

2 Choose "Spelling and Grammar" from the Tools menu, or click on the corresponding icon:

Click on Ignore All to skip over all other instances of the current word. Similarly, Change All will apply the current suggestion to all other instances as well.

Word 2000 highlights spelling mistakes in red, and possible grammatical problems in green.

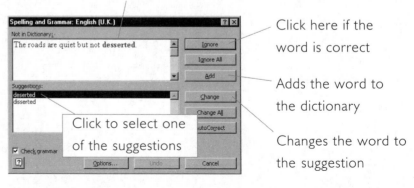

Click here if the word is correct

Adds the word to the dictionary

Changes the word to the suggestion

Click to select one of the suggestions

...cont'd

Here's an example of Word questioning some grammar. The rule being tested is explained by the Office Assistant.

If you disagree with Word's grammar advice, then either click Ignore to skip the current phrase or Ignore Rule to stop Word applying the rule altogether.

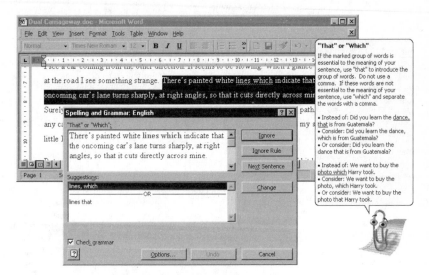

3 Clicking the "Options" button takes you to the "Spelling & Grammar" options dialog box:

You can also access the Spelling & Grammar options as a tab of the main options dialog: select Options from the Tools menu.

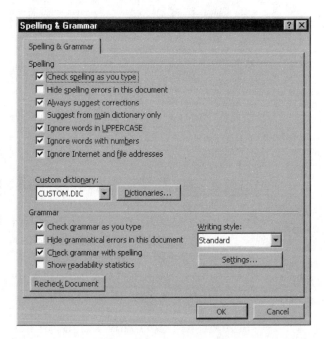

Readability Statistics

It is possible to make Word 2000 display readability statistics for your document, after it has finished performing a Spelling and Grammar check.

1. Select Options from the Tools menu, and choose the Spelling and Grammar tab (illustrated on page 91).

2. Make sure that the "Show readability statistics" checkbox is checked, then click "OK".

After you have performed a Spelling and Grammar check, this dialog is displayed:

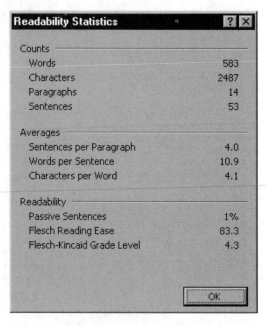

Unfortunately no one has, as yet, figured out a way of automatically analysing the boredom level of a document. This is one job still left to us lucky humans.

A United States Grade Level of 3 roughly equates to an age of 8.

The Flesch Reading Ease value is in the range 0...100, increasing with ease of reading. Standard text rates between 60 and 70. The Grade Level values give an indication as to the school grade appropriate for your text. For example, a level of 3 means that it would be understandable by someone in the third grade or below. Standard text normally weighs in between 7 and 8.

Checking on-the-fly

While the dialog-box method of checking your spelling and grammar offers you the greatest amount of control over exactly how the checking is done, Word 2000 can check your grammar and spelling automatically as you type, highlighting any problems it finds on the page. Consider the following example:

Both the Spelling and the Grammar pop-up menus offer a quick route to the full Spelling and Grammar dialog box: simply select the bottom entry, marked with 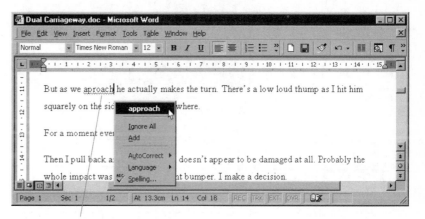.

This spelling mistake is underlined in red. To correct, right-click on it then select the correct suggested word from the pop-up menu. If the suggestion is not suitable, attempt to correct it yourself, then see if it is still flagged.

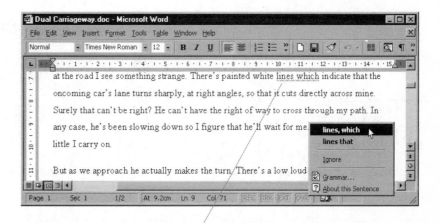

This grammar mistake is underlined in green. Right-click on it, then select the correct suggestion from the menu.

Word Count

Word provides a quick and easy way of counting the number of words in your document:

1 To count the words in one area only, select it in the normal way – otherwise the entire document will be scanned.

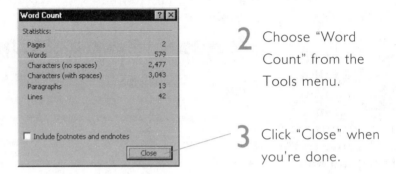

2 Choose "Word Count" from the Tools menu.

3 Click "Close" when you're done.

Thesaurus

If you need to search for a word's synonyms (i.e., words closely related in meaning), you can use the built-in Thesaurus.

1 Select the word to be used.

2 Choose Language > Thesaurus from the Tools menu.

The shortcut to the Thesaurus feature is Shift+F7.

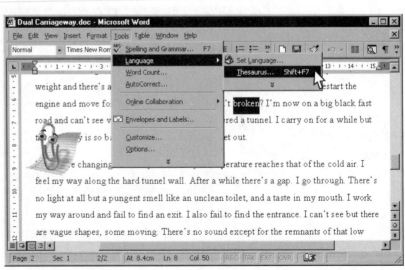

...cont'd

The Thesaurus dialog box appears:

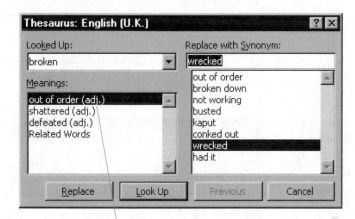

3 Double-click here to search for the related words.

If none of the words you see listed in the Synonyms pane at step 5 are suitable, try clicking on another entry in the Meanings section. Alternatively, double-click on one of the words in the Synonyms area to see the synonyms stored for *that* word. You can continue in this manner indefinitely.

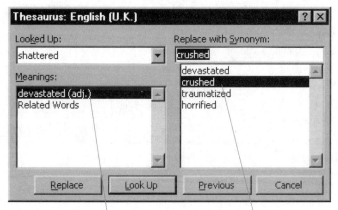

4 The different possible categories of meanings related to your word are listed in this area. Click on whichever best summarises the meaning you are aiming for...

5 ...to see the relevant synonyms listed here. If one of these is suitable, click on it, then click the "Replace" button to change the word in your document.

AutoCorrect

Often, the same spelling or typing mistakes are made again and again. You can instruct Word to substitute the correction automatically :

| Choose "AutoCorrect" from the Tools menu, and make sure that this tab is selected.

 You don't have to enter all the AutoCorrect data yourself: Word 2000 contains a large number of corrections, including common mistakes for "necessary", "occasion", and transposition errors such as "knwo" instead of "know". You can browse through these from the AutoCorrect dialog.

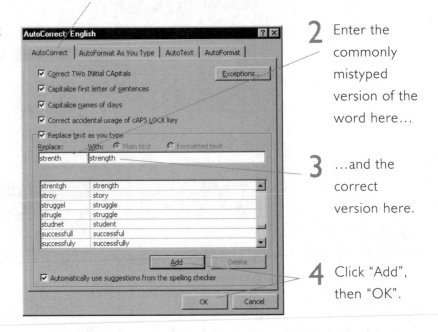

2 Enter the commonly mistyped version of the word here...

3 ...and the correct version here.

4 Click "Add", then "OK".

If you type the error now, Word spots it and substitutes the correct word automatically, instead of merely flagging it as a possible spelling mistake:

original text typed   *corrected by Word*

You can now continue through the rest of your life completely unaware that you are consistently failing to spell correctly.

AutoText

This is a less automatic version of AutoCorrect, and is useful for setting up your own abbreviations.

If you find that you often need to type the same text, then it would be worth setting up an AutoText entry:

Creating an AutoText Entry

1 Type the text and select it.

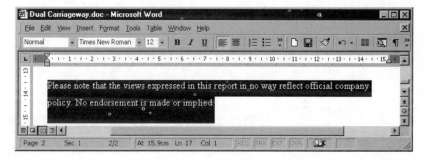

2 Choose "AutoCorrect" from the Tools menu and select the AutoText tab.

3 Edit the entry in this box to the abbreviation you require.

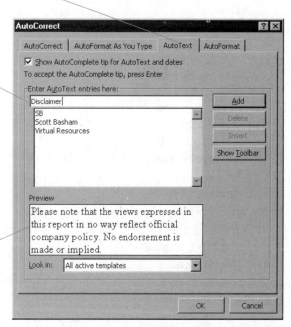

4 Click "OK".

The selected text is automatically inserted into the this area of the AutoText dialog box.

Using AutoText

You can also insert AutoText by selecting it from the AutoText tab of the Tools> AutoCorrect dialog box.

1 Simply type the abbreviation:

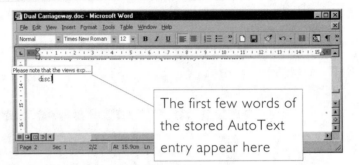

The first few words of the stored AutoText entry appear here

2 Press Enter or F3 to replace the abbreviation with the full text.

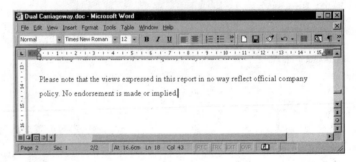

The Spike

You can repeat this more times if necessary. Each time you press Control+F3, any selected text is put onto the Spike.

The Spike is a temporary piece of AutoText which can be added to with a single key command.

Creating a Spike

1 Select some text and type Control+F3 (the text disappears: it has been impaled on the Spike).

2 Repeat the process with a second piece of text.

3 Finally, place the insertion point at the destination for the text and press Control+Shift+F3.

The text is pulled off the Spike and placed back into the document.

AutoComplete

AutoComplete is somewhat akin to AutoText, in that it offers suggestions for the completion of words or phrases that you only need to begin typing. However, while AutoText uses a list of commonly used phrases which have first to be recorded, AutoComplete offers to fill in other sorts of text which can be worked out from the context. For example, AutoComplete can enter:

- the current date

- your name

- your company's name

- any day of the week

- any month

Begin to type in one of the words or phrases listed above (here we're entering today's date).

If Auto-Complete doesn't appear to be functioning, choose "AutoCorrect" from the Tools menu, select the AutoText tab, and make sure there is a tick in the checkbox labelled "Show AutoComplete tip for AutoText and dates".

AutoComplete offers to fill in the whole of today's date

To fill in the whole date, simply press Enter or F3.

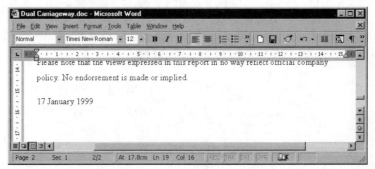

AutoSummarise

This feature uses complex procedures to analyse a document and determine which sentences are likely to carry the document's most significant, salient points. It does this by calculating which words and phrases in the document are used most often. The resulting analysis can then be presented in several different ways.

To use AutoSummarise, do the following:

Open the document you want to summarize, then choose "AutoSummarize" from the Tools menu. The following dialog box appears:

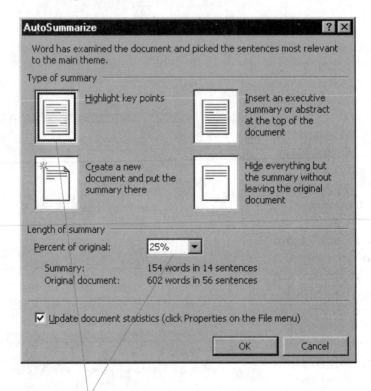

2 Select the way you want to present the summary, and the summary's level of detail, then click "OK".

If the "Highlight key points" option is selected, the whole document is displayed, with the most significant points highlighted. Perform any of the following steps, as appropriate:

3 Click here to toggle between displaying the whole text with the summary highlighted, or the summary only.

4 Click here to increase or decrease the summary's level of detail – i.e. the percentage of the document that is highlighted.

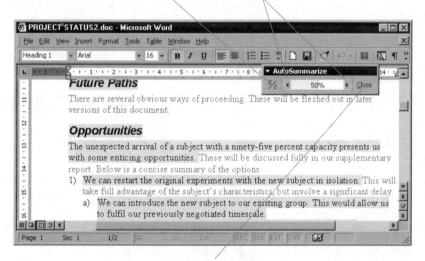

5 Click "Close" to shut down the AutoSummarize control palette and return to the normal document view.

In this example, Word appears to have determined that the headings and initial items in lists have a greater importance.

Hyphenation

You can change the hyphenation options for your document by choosing Tools>Language>Hyphenation:

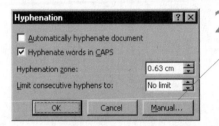

2 If you click on the "Manual" button you can review hyphenation manually throughout your document...

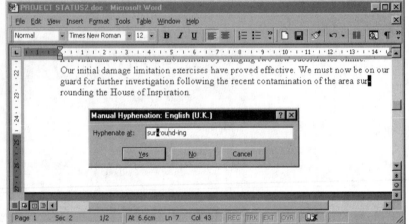

To take even greater control of hyphenation in your text, you may want to use the following keyboard shortcuts: Control+Hyphen will insert an optional hyphen in a word as you type. Control+Shift+ Hyphen will insert a non-breaking hyphen into your text (this is a hyphen where Word is not allowed to break the word over successive lines).

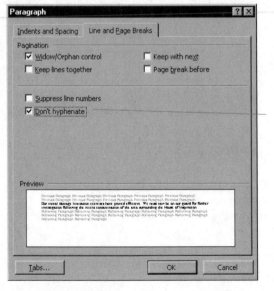

You can also override hyphen- ation for individual paragraphs by selecting the "Don't hyphenate" checkbox in the Line and Page Breaks tab of the Paragraph dialog box (choose "Paragraph" from the "Format" menu).

Templates and Wizards

Templates act as blueprints for standard types of document which you would need to use again and again. Examples may be standard memos, reports, letters or faxes. A Wizard is a "live" document which guides you through its own design.

This chapter shows you how to use templates and Wizards, customise a template for your own purposes, or create a new template.

Covers

Chapter Eight

Using Templates

A template contains a range of settings to be used as a starting point for a new document.

 If you select the "New" icon 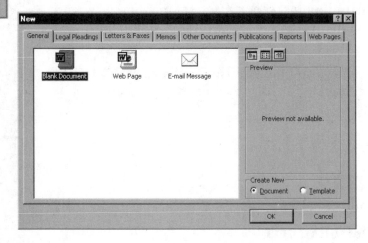 **instead of the File menu, Word uses the "Blank Document" or "Normal" template.**

The Normal Template

1 Choose "New" from the File menu:

Word lists the templates available. Often you'll use the simple "Blank Document" template.

2 Click on the other tabs to see more available templates.

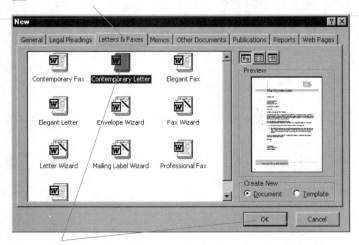

3 Select the template you want to use and click "OK".

Template Defaults

Defaults are settings which are used initially when you create a new document or add new text. To change the defaults for a template, do the following with a template open:

1 Open the Font dialog box from the Format menu.

2 Choose your required settings and then click on the "Default" button.

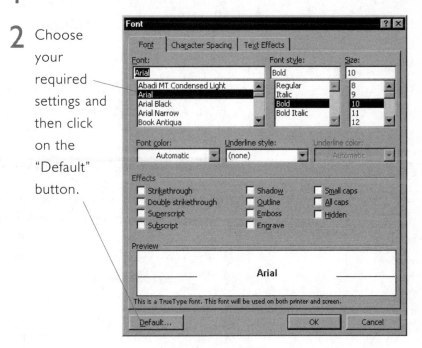

The Office Assistant will ask you whether you're certain that you want to change the Template itself.

3 If you click "Yes", the font information will be saved into the currently used template document.

Form Templates

By designing a Form Template, you can create a document which is very easy to use, even for people who have minimal experience of Word 2000.

You simply create a document in the normal way, apart from adding some special "form fields". These can be text containers, checkboxes or drop-down selection fields.

Creating Text Form Fields

1 Make sure the Forms palette is active (if necessary, go to the View menu and choose Toolbars).

2 Place your insertion point where you'd like the field, then click on the Text Form Field button in the Forms palette.

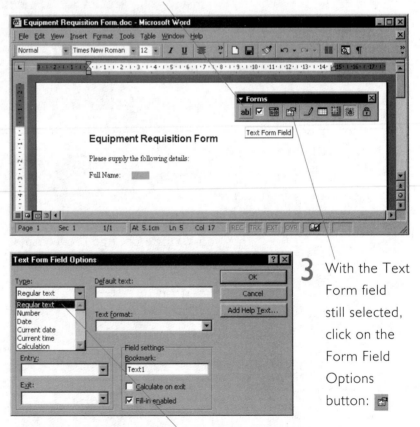

3 With the Text Form field still selected, click on the Form Field Options button:

From here you can select options such as the content type.

Creating Drop-Down Form Fields

Drop-down lists allow users to select from a pop-up restricted list of options. This way they can fill out values within a form without typing anything.

1 Decide where you want the field and position your insertion point accordingly.

2 Click on the Drop-Down Form Field icon in the Forms palette.

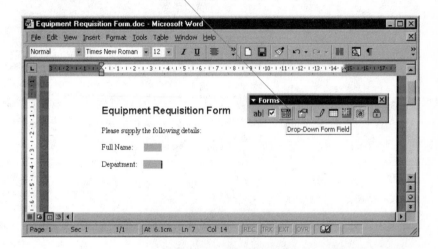

3 With the field still selected, click on the Form Field Options button:

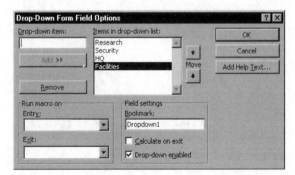

From here you can build the list of options for the drop-down list. Simply enter an item and click the Add button. You can also use the move buttons to reorder the items in the list, or Remove items altogether. When the list is complete, click "OK".

Check Box Form Fields

These act as simple on/off switches for your user. A single-click will toggle a checkmark on and off within the box.

1 Decide where you want the field and position your insertion point accordingly.

2 Click the Check Box Form Field icon in the Forms palette.

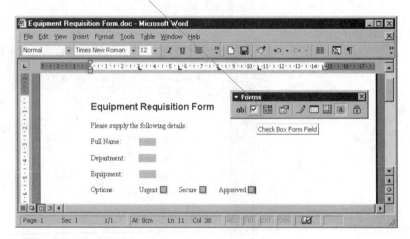

Protecting the Form

1 Click on the Protect Form icon 🔒 to stop users from editing your document. From now onwards the only items which can be edited are the Form Fields themselves.

Close down the Forms Toolbar when you've completed your form. This will discourage users from attempting to edit the document itself.

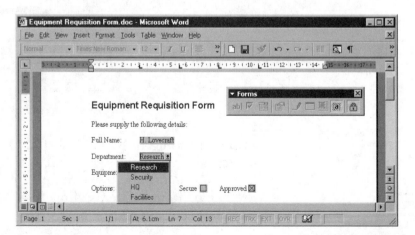

Setting Up a New Template

Any document can be saved as a template, but in this example we'll use the form we've created. With the document open, do the following:

You can also switch protection on and off using the Forms Toolbar. However, from the dialog box, you can additionally set a password. This would prevent others from unprotecting your document.

1 Select "Protect Document" from the Tools menu.

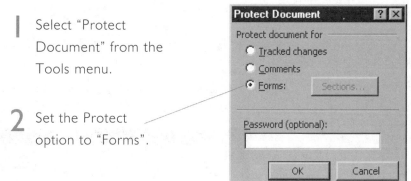

2 Set the Protect option to "Forms".

Note that you only need to do this if the template is to be used as a form.

3 Choose "Save As" from the File menu:

If you're using a normal document, rather than a form, you need only follow steps 3 and 4.

4 Choose "Document Template" as the file type.

5 Enter a suitable name for the file and click on Save

The document will automatically be saved with a .DOT extension within Word's Templates folder.

Changing Styles in a Template

When you open a document, Word uses the styles built into the template selected.

As we saw earlier, you can alter these styles for individual documents using the "Style" dialog:

1 Select "Style" from the Format menu.

2 Click on the Modify button to display the following dialog:

If you record a style change to the "Blank Document" or "Normal" template, this will affect most new documents.

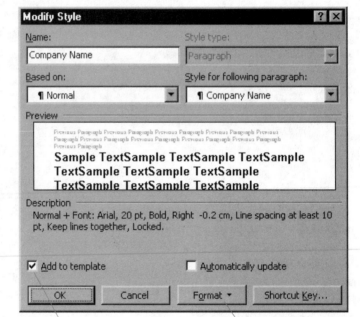

3 To copy a style change back into the template itself, make sure the "Add to Template" box is checked.

4 Make any appropriate changes using the dialogs that can be selected from the Format button pop-up menu.

5 Click "OK".

The Templates and Add-Ins Dialog

Word always keeps track of the template used to create a document. It is possible to change this even after you've started work:

1 If necessary, unprotect your document (Tools menu).

2 Choose "Templates and Add-Ins" from the Tools menu.

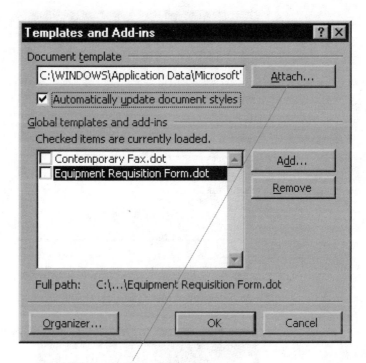

 You can use the "Add" button to make available styles stored in other templates. Any templates listed in the "Global" box are always available.

3 Use the "Attach" button to attach a new template. If you select "Automatically update document styles" then the Styles from the new template will be reapplied to the document text.

4 Click "OK" when you're done.

Wizards

A Wizard is a kind of "intelligent" template: it helps you design and build a document by asking you a series of questions. You answer these either by selecting from a choice of radio buttons, or by entering text in a box.

An Example

1 Choose "New" from the File menu, then select this tab.

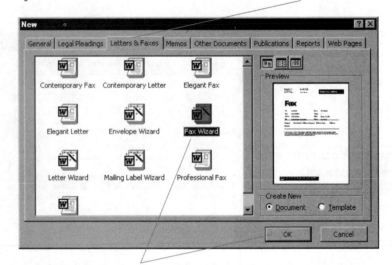

2 Select the "Fax Wizard" icon, then click "OK".

3 Start working through the Wizard by clicking the Next button.

...cont'd

 The Fax Wizard is actually capable of sending out faxes directly, provided you have a fax capable modem properly installed in your system. In this example, however, we're instructing the Wizard to create a document which we would firstly print, then send manually using a Fax machine.

4   Each page of the Wizard will ask you more questions. As you work through the pages, the flowchart on the left side will indicate your progress.

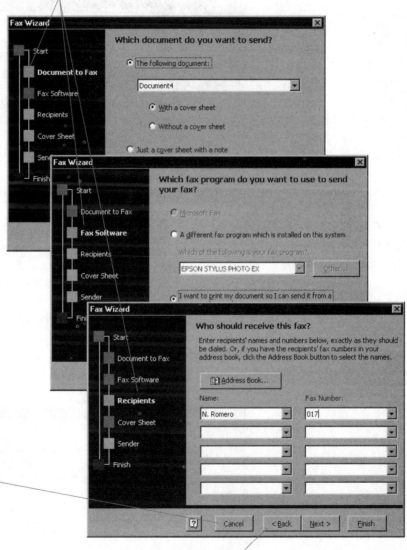

 If you decide that this isn't the Wizard for you after all, then click on the Cancel button.

5   At any point you can go back to a previous page simply by clicking the Back button. This way you can fill out the settings in any order you choose.

6 When you have finished making the settings, click on the Finish button.

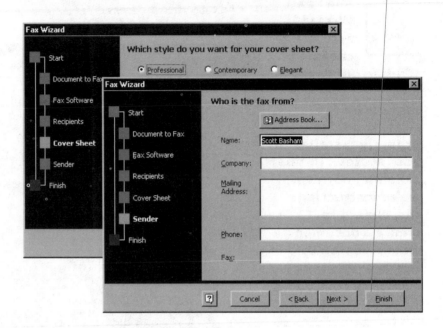

The document is now automatically generated using the settings we supplied. We can continue to edit this manually, if appropriate, then save or print in the normal way.

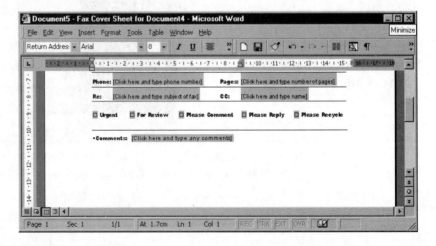

Graphical Features

Although not a full-blown graphics package, Word contains a comprehensive collection of clip art as well as a respectable range of graphical editing features. This chapter takes you through the processes involved with incorporating pictures and illustrations into your document.

Covers

Chapter Nine

Inserting Pictures from Disk

Word 2000 has its own folder of clip art illustrations, but you can also import from a wide range of graphic file formats.

 If you installed the Microsoft ClipArt Gallery with Word, you can alternatively select Insert>Picture> ClipArt. You may need to insert your Word CD to access all available pictures.

1 Click the insertion point at the destination for the graphic.

2 Go to the Insert menu, choose "Picture" and "From File".

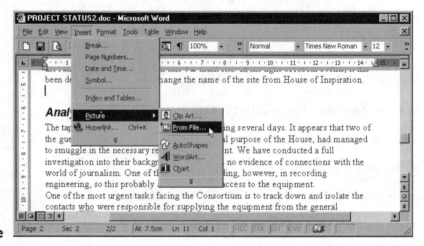

 By default Word will embed a copy of the graphic in your file. This will allow you to make changes to the graphic within Word, but tends to make your files larger.

If you choose the Link to File option, then Word doesn't store its own local copy. This keeps your Word files smaller, but make sure that you keep the original graphic file where Word can find it.

3 Locate the file you require and click "Insert".

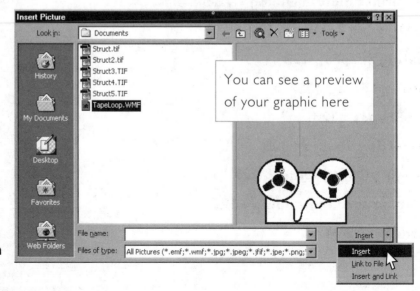

You can see a preview of your graphic here

...cont'd

The picture is inserted into the document:

Don't worry if the picture appears in the wrong size. It is easy to resize, as you will see on the next page.

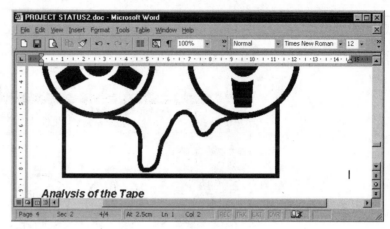

Types of Graphic File

Word can import many types of graphic file format. WMF, CGM, WPG, DRW, EPS and PCT files normally contain Draw-type objects which can be scaled up or down with no loss in quality, because they are stored as vectors (mathematical objects).

On the other hand BMP, PCX, TIF, JPG and GIF files are bitmapped: the image is stored as a structure of tiny dots or blocks. Be careful not to enlarge these pictures too much, or the dots will become very noticeable, causing a marked deterioration in quality.

If you have a scanner or a digital camera installed in your system then you can scan directly into Word. Choose "Insert" then "Picture" and "From Scanner or Camera".

Manipulating Graphics

When you click on a graphic you will see eight blocks appear around it: one at each corner, and one at the middle of each side. These are the graphic's control handles, which can be used to change its dimensions.

Click on the graphic to make its handles appear.

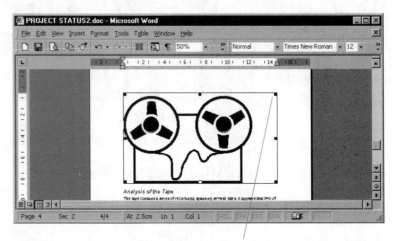

2 Drag on a handle to resize the picture.

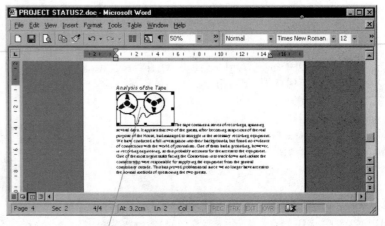

3 To move, drag anywhere within the object.

Note that the graphic is treated like a text item, so when you drag it to a new position, the surrounding text moves to make room.

The Picture Toolbar

The Picture toolbar appears when you insert a picture into a Word document, and provides an easy way of making a wide range of changes to your pictures. It can be used for the following functions:

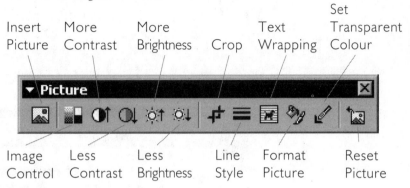

Insert Picture — More Contrast — More Brightness — Crop — Text Wrapping — Set Transparent Colour

Image Control — Less Contrast — Less Brightness — Line Style — Format Picture — Reset Picture

Cropping a Picture

If you want to display only part of an image in your Word document, you should crop it. This cuts away a part of the picture from any of its four sides.

1 Select the image.

2 Click on the Crop icon in the Picture toolbar.

![DON'T FORGET elephant icon] **Cropping is non-destructive. This means that you can restore the rest of the picture by dragging the edges back with the Crop tool, or by clicking on the Reset Picture icon.**

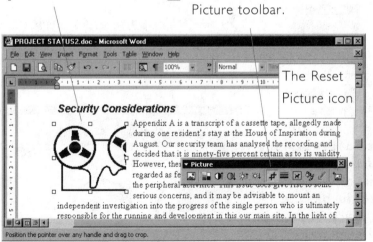

3 Rest your cursor over any of the picture's control handles, then drag the edges to where you want them.

Editing an Imported Picture

Most normal clip art pictures that you import will be in vector format (they'll usually have the .WMF extension), which means that they can be broken down into simple, individual elements which can be edited separately. To edit a vector clip art image, simply do the following:

1 Right-click on the image in your Word document and choose "Edit Picture".

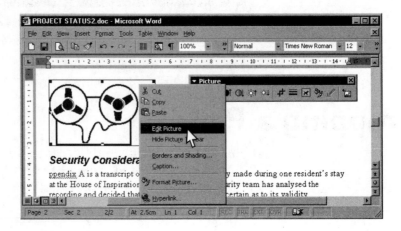

2 You will now find that the clip art object is in fact composed of several different objects, which can be selected individually. Click on one, then try stretching or deleting it.

If you extend the picture beyond its normal bounding rectangle, click this button to reset the picture boundary. This also applies if you reduce it in size.

3 Click here when you've finished editing.

Wrapping Text Around Graphics

When a graphic is inserted into a Word document, it is placed into the text by default as a simple object, on a new line. However, you can very easily change this, so that text wraps around the image in any of a number of ways:

1. Select the picture.

2. Click on the Text Wrapping icon in the Picture toolbar, and select how you want the text to wrap around the image.

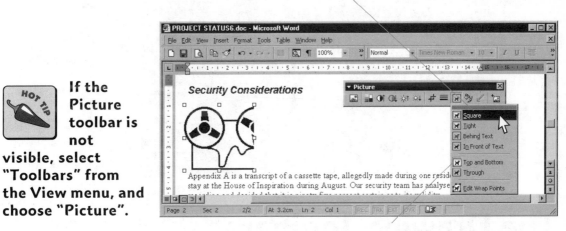

This is the default text wrap.

If the Picture toolbar is not visible, select "Toolbars" from the View menu, and choose "Picture".

The text now wraps around the image. This is "Square" wrap: the text wraps around a rectangular area that borders the graphic.

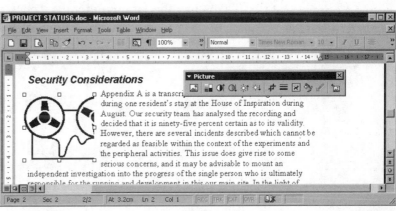

The Format Picture Dialog

From here you can numerically change all the properties of a graphic, including its size, position, text-wrap properties and crop parameters.

| Select the picture.

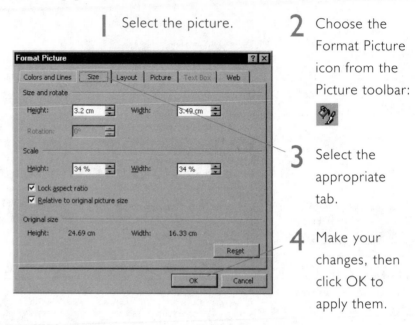

2 Choose the Format Picture icon from the Picture toolbar:

3 Select the appropriate tab.

4 Make your changes, then click OK to apply them.

The Drawing Toolbar

Click here to see other drawing-related commands, as shown below:

When working with graphics in Word 2000, you are not limited to using ready-made clip art; you can create your own drawings using Word's Drawing toolbar.

To display the Drawing toolbar, click on the Drawing icon in the Standard toolbar, or select View>Toolbars>Drawing:

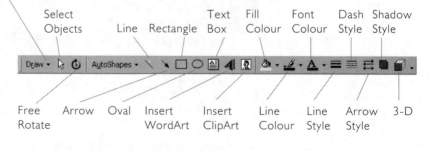

Select Objects · Line · Rectangle · Text Box · Fill Colour · Font Colour · Dash Style · Shadow Style

Free Rotate · Arrow · Oval · Insert WordArt · Insert ClipArt · Line Colour · Line Style · Arrow Style · 3-D

Creating Shapes

1 Select the appropriate shape tool.

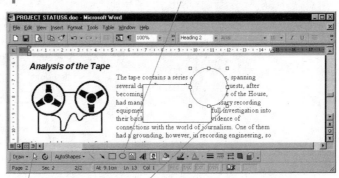

2 Click and drag within the document to create the shape. For lines, drag from one end-point to the other; for boxes and ovals drag diagonally from one corner to the other.

3 Click on a shape with the pointer to select it. Then you can drag it to another location, or resize it by dragging directly on one of its handles.

Lines and Fills

Click on a shape then use the Fill and Line pop-up menus to select colour, shading and line patterns.

Click on the arrow to the right of the icon to produce the pop-up menu

Click here to add special effects to the object's fill

These properties can also be changed using the Format AutoShape dialog box: right-click on a shape, then select Format AutoShape from the pop-up menu.

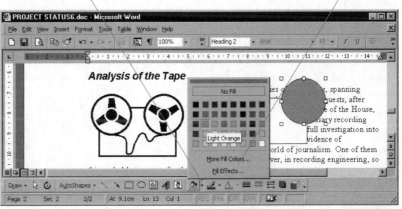

AutoShapes

AutoShapes allow you to insert commonly used shapes, many of which otherwise might take you some time to draw. To insert an AutoShape, do the following:

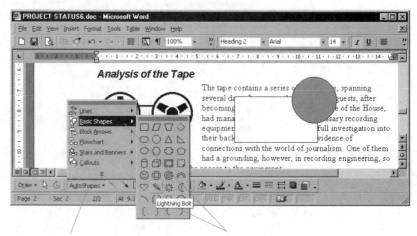

1 Click on the AutoShapes button.

2 Select an AutoShapes category, then click on a specific shape.

If you plan to use several AutoShapes in one session, you can simply drag one of the submenu palettes away from the main menu, to create a floating palette. It will then stay on-screen when the AutoShapes menu disappears.

3 Click in the area of your document where you want the AutoShape to appear.

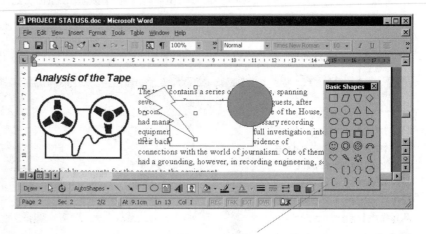

Free-floating Shapes palette

Formatting Shapes

Many objects' properties can be amended by accessing the pop-up menus in the Drawing toolbar. However, by right-clicking on a shape you can summon a dialog box that allows you to change many of these properties straight away. Right-click on the AutoShape whose format you want to change, choose "Format AutoShape" from the pop-up menu, then select the appropriate tab...

HOT TIP

To set the properties for more than one shape, you should first select all the shapes you want to change. To do this, you have two options:

1) Click successively on each object while holding down the Shift button; or

2) Click in the document area and drag a selection box around all of the objects.

Once all the objects are selected, change the properties as you would for a single object (e.g., right-click on any object, then select "Format AutoShape" from the pop-up menu).

The Colors and Lines Tab

Use this to set the shape's fill and line attributes.

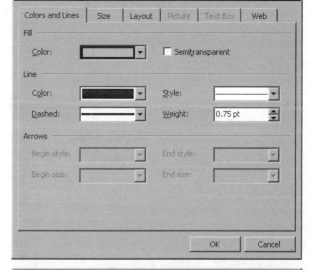

The Size Tab

Use this to set the shape's dimensions, scale properties and rotation value.

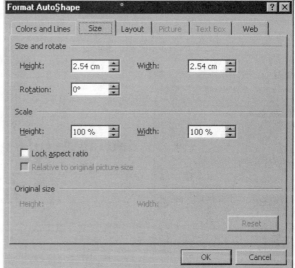

The Layout Tab

From here you can control the way text wraps around the AutoShape.

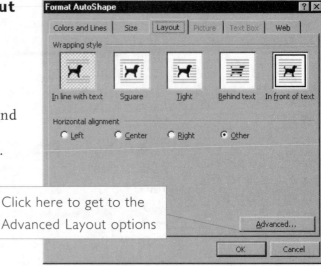

Click here to get to the Advanced Layout options

Advanced Layout

Here you can set the coordinates used to determine the object's precise position on the page.

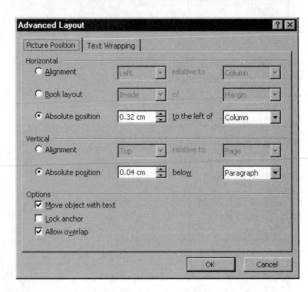

Setting AutoShape Defaults

To set the properties that all AutoShapes will have when they are created, do the following:

1 Format an existing AutoShape using the Drawing toolbar or the Format AutoShape dialog.

2 Right-click on the shape, then select Set AutoShape Defaults.

Changing Object Order

When you place a new image or shape in a document, it appears in front of all the other objects that were inserted before it. To change the relative order of objects subsequently, select the object(s) to move, then...

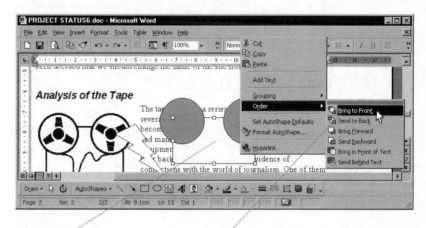

1 Right-click on one of the shapes and choose "Order" from the pop-up menu.

2 Choose whether to send the object in front of or behind all other objects, or whether to move it just one step.

Sending Objects Behind the Text Layer

By default, all graphic objects appear in front of the text in your document. However, you can send objects behind the text by selecting "Bring in Front of Text" or "Send Behind Text" from the "Order" sub-menu:

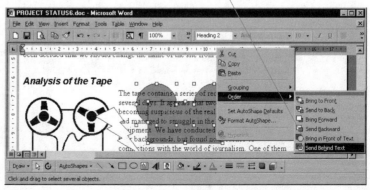

Grouping and Ungrouping

There are two basic ways of selecting a group of objects:

1) Click successively on each object while holding down the Shift button; or

2) Click in a vacant part of the document area and drag a selection box around all of the objects.

Once you have placed several objects in your Word document, you may no longer need to treat them separately, but might benefit from treating them as a single object which can be moved and modified easily. To make this possible, you should group the objects, as follows:

1 Select all of the objects that you want to be grouped together.

2 Choose "Group" from the pop-up Draw menu in the Drawing toolbar.

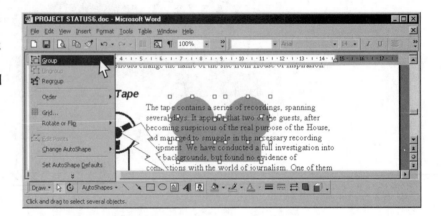

Subsequently, any changes made to the group are applied to all of the grouped objects:

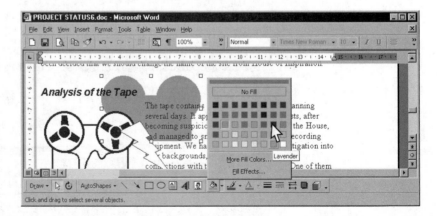

WordArt

WordArt is a tool you can use to apply a wide range of special graphical effects to type that you use in your Word documents. The objects created by WordArt are treated not as plain text but as drawing objects, so they can be manipulated further with the tools from the Drawing toolbar. To use WordArt, do the following:

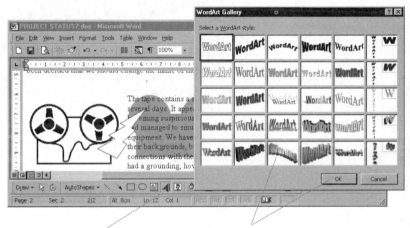

1 Click on the WordArt button in the Drawing toolbar.

2 Select a style (you can change it later), then click "OK".

3 Enter your text here, then click "OK".

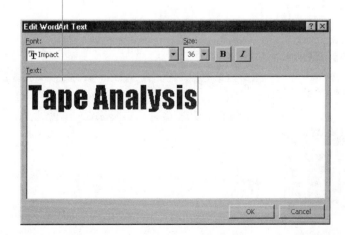

The WordArt is placed, and can now be edited:

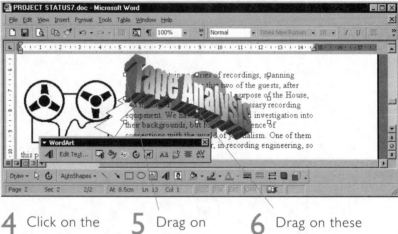

4 Click on the text with the cursor, and drag it to the desired position.

5 Drag on the text's control handles to change its size.

6 Drag on these special yellow handles to alter the characteristics of this particular WordArt effect.

When you select the "Change WordArt shape" icon, you are presented with a palette containing 40 different text shapes. This offers a wider range of shapes than the Gallery:

The floating WordArt toolbar appears whenever you select a WordArt object. You can use it for the following functions:

Return to the text-editing box encountered in step 3

Open the Format dialog to alter colour, size, position, text wrap

Allow text to be rotated freely

Edit text wrapping

Toggle between horizontal and vertical text

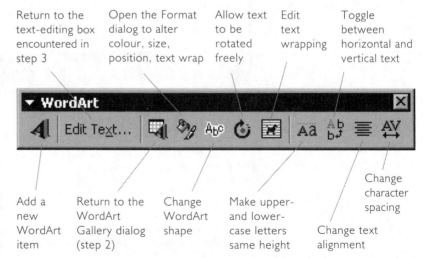

Add a new WordArt item

Return to the WordArt Gallery dialog (step 2)

Change WordArt shape

Make upper- and lower-case letters same height

Change character spacing

Change text alignment

Tables and Charts

Tables allow you to organise and manage text in rows and columns. Charts provide a valuable way of presenting numeric table information in pictorial form, making statistical information much easier to understand.

Covers

Chapter Ten

Inserting a Table

If you want to insert a simple table with more than five columns or four rows, select "Insert Table" from the Table menu. This will summon a dialog box, where you can specify the table's dimensions.

You can resize a column by moving your Mouse pointer to the border between the columns: it will turn into a black double headed arrow ←|→. You can resize rows in the same way.

Hold down the Alt key while dragging a column or row to see the measurements in the ruler.

If you want to insert a simple table of no more than five columns and four rows, you can use the Table icon in the Standard toolbar:

1 Place the insertion point on a blank line in the document.

2 Click on the Table icon in the Standard toolbar and, in the pop-up table box, drag downwards and to the right.

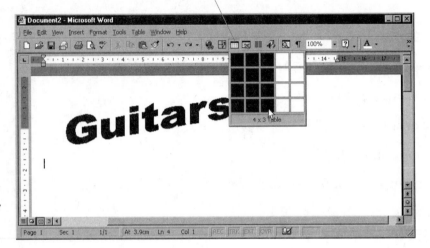

The further you drag, the larger the table. In this case a table of 4 rows and 3 columns is being created.

The table is inserted into your document:

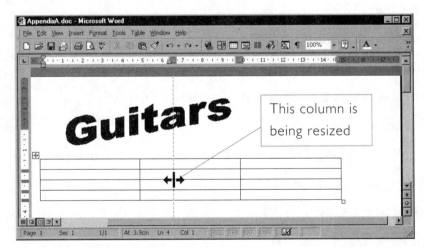

Drawing a Table

Word 2000 offers you an alternative method to create tables. The Draw Table tool lets you draw a table directly into your document without using dialogs or pop-up boxes.

There is an alternative way to begin drawing a table and specify the width of its columns visually: in normal text-entry mode, enter a line using plus and minus symbols, like this...

+---+------+------+

When you press Return, Word will automatically convert this into the first line of a table, the plus signs becoming column boundaries. If this doesn't work, select Tools>AutoCorrect, choose the "AutoFormat As You Type" tab, and check the "Tables" box.

| Select "Draw Table" from the Table menu.
The Tables and Borders toolbar appears:

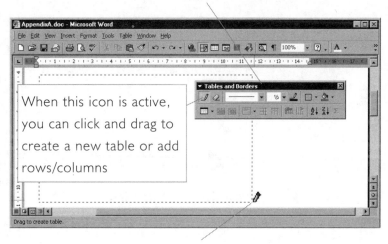

When this icon is active, you can click and drag to create a new table or add rows/columns

2 Your pointer will turn into a pencil shape (if not then make sure that the Draw Table tool is active). Drag an initial shape for the table within your document.

3 Click and drag anywhere in your table to draw a column or row boundary.

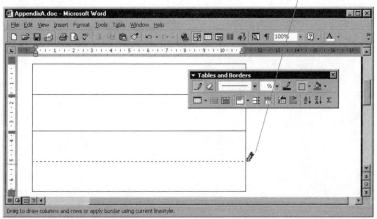

Drawing Diagonal Table Lines

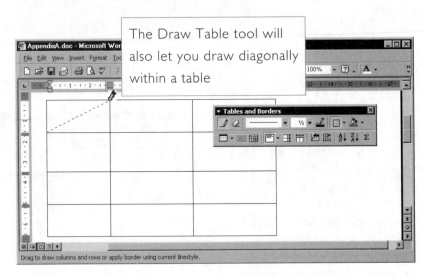

The Draw Table tool will also let you draw diagonally within a table

Erasing Table Lines

| Click on the Eraser tool in the Tables and Borders palette.

Your cursor turns into an eraser shape.

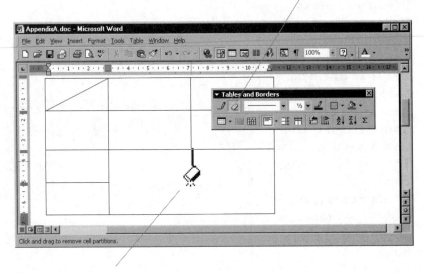

2 Click directly on a line within the table to make it disappear.

Creating Irregular Tables

The table drawing tools make it easy for you to create irregularly structured tables.

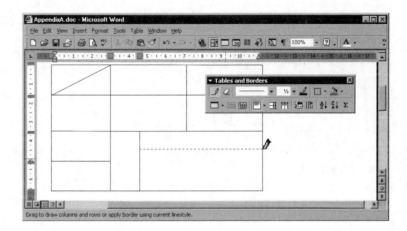

Entering Text

You can add text to your table by clicking in each cell in turn. All the normal formatting commands still apply. A quick way to get to the next cell is to press Tab. Shift+Tab takes you back to the previous cell.

If you actually need to enter a Tab character within a cell, press Control+Tab.

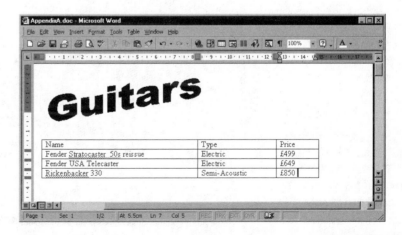

You can have more than one line within each cell. The Table row will expand to accommodate any extra text.

Formatting

You can format the contents of a whole row or column – or several rows or columns – at once. To select a row, drag across it, or click in the space just to its left.

The same applies to columns. To select, click slightly above the top cell of the column.

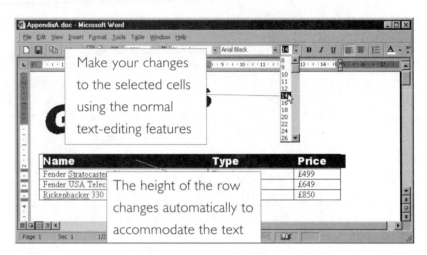

Make your changes to the selected cells using the normal text-editing features

The height of the row changes automatically to accommodate the text

Inserting a Row/Column

To insert a row into an existing table, do the following:

To add a column, first select the column to the right of where you want to insert.

1 Select the line below where you want the new row.

2 Click the right Mouse button on the selected row, and choose "Insert Rows" from the pop-up menu.

To insert multiple columns or rows, select the amount of columns/rows you want inserted before right-clicking.

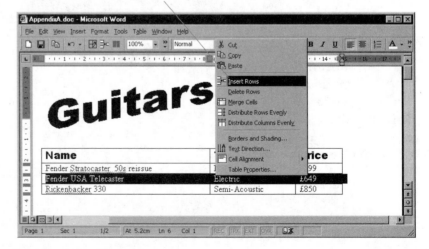

Cutting and Pasting

1 Select the row/column or cells.

2 Right-click on the selected cells and choose "Cut" from the pop-up menu.

3 Select the destination row/column or cells.

4 Right click on the selected cells and choose "Paste..." from the pop-up menu.

The text is pasted back into the table, immediately above the selected row, or to the left of the selected column.

Merging Cells

Any number of adjacent cells can be merged to create a single cell, by selecting the cells and then choosing "Merge Cells" from the Table menu.

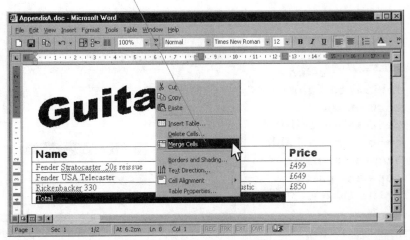

Controlling Height and Width

To select an entire table, choose "Select", then "Table" from the Table menu, or type Alt + Numeric keypad "5" with the Num Lock turned off.

1 Select the cell(s) to change, or the entire table.

2 Choose "Table Properties" from the Table menu, or by right clicking.

3 Click on the Row tab, then the Column tab to see all the options available.

4 The Table Tab will let you set properties such as overall size, alignment and text wrap behaviour.

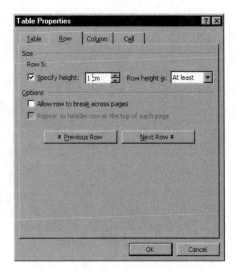

Nested Tables

This feature is new to Word 2000. You can now insert a table within another table. You can draw the inner table in the normal way with the Draw Table tool:

Another way to create a nested table is to right click on the destination cell and choose Insert Table. You can also cut, copy and paste entire tables.

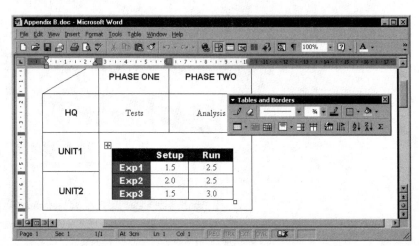

Formulae

If you want one cell of a table to display a number derived from a calculation (based on the numeric contents of other cells), Word can insert a code to perform this task automatically. In this example, we want to total the price of the three guitars in the table.

For the Sum function to work properly, all rows above the current cell must have the same number of columns. If you merged the cells for the last example, you will need to split them again (choose "Split Cells" from the Table menu).

1 Click in the cell which is the destination for the calculation, and choose "Formula" from the Table menu.

2 Enter the formula or select from the list of "Paste functions". Word correctly suggests the "=SUM(ABOVE)" function, which adds up the contents of the cells above the destination cell.

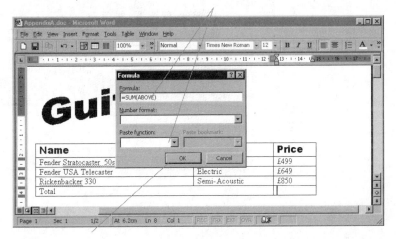

Unlike a spreadsheet (such as Excel), Word does not automatically update the contents of cells containing a formula when the values of cells used in the equation are changed. To update a formula, right-click on the cell and choose "Update Field" from the pop-up menu.

3 Click "OK". The total is displayed in the destination cell:

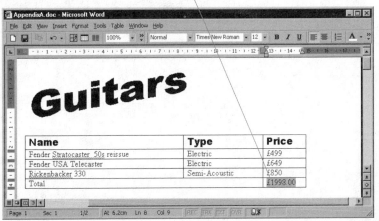

Borders and Shading

Word 2000 allows you to enhance your tables very easily using the Borders and Shading dialog. To use it, do the following:

1 Select either the entire table or just a range of cells.

2 Right-click on the selected cells and choose "Borders and Shading" from the pop-up menu.

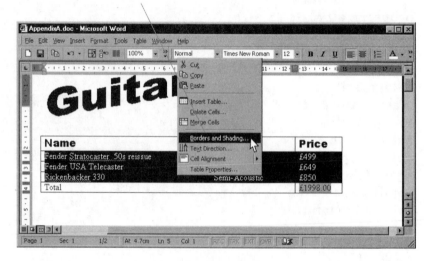

3 If necessary, activate the Borders tab and choose your borders options.

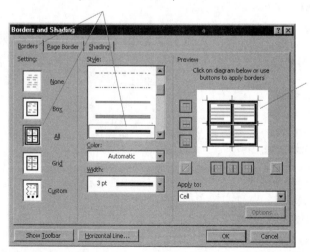

You can click on various parts of this diagram to activate different perimeter and internal lines

4 Now click on the Shading tab and set your shading preferences.

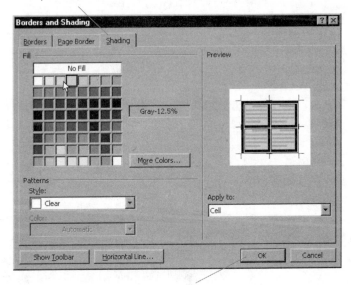

5 Click "OK". Your selected cells now have a border and shading applied:

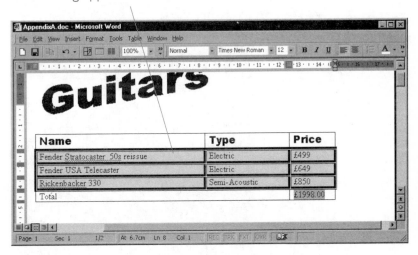

In the example above, the Borders and Shading dialog box has been used to alter the style of all the lines in the selected area, and to give those cells a fill of 12.5% grey.

Table AutoFormat

As an alternative to defining the format piece by piece (i.e., specifying the font, borders, shading, etc.), Word 2000 allows you to apply many different pre-defined formats to existing tables. To use AutoFormat, do the following:

1 Select the table.

2 Choose "Table AutoFormat" from the Table menu, or click on this button.

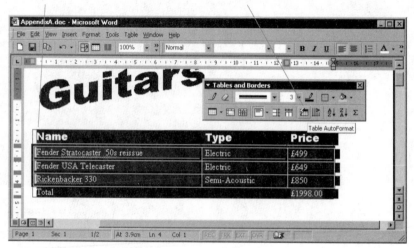

The following dialog appears:

3 Choose a Format style.

The AutoFormat preview reflects the changes you are about to make

4 Select which elements of the table you want the AutoFormat to apply to.

5 Click "OK" to apply your changes.

The changes that you have just specified are applied automatically to your table:

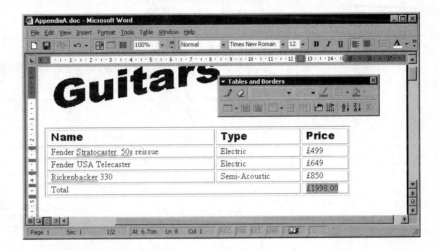

Using the Tables and Borders Toolbar

You can use the Tables and Borders toolbar to make many of the formatting changes that we have discussed earlier in this chapter. If it is not already activated, select View>Toolbars>Tables and Borders, or click on the appropriate icon in the Standard toolbar:

The Tables and Borders toolbar offers the following functions:

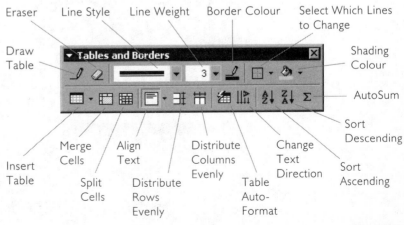

Graphics within Tables

With Word 2000 you can paste or insert graphics directly into cells. Once there you can right-click on the graphic and choose Format Picture to control properties such as text wrap. In the example below, text and graphics coexist within the same cell.

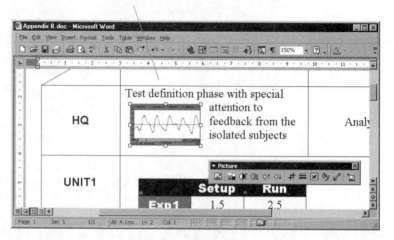

Text Wrap around Tables

If you right-click on a table and choose Table Properties, you can control how text wraps around the table itself. In the example below, a text wrap setting of "Around" allows the table to be included within the main text area.

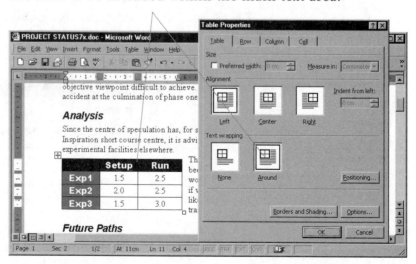

Creating a Chart from a Table

You can use the Microsoft Graph 2000 feature to convert a table you have created into an attractive chart.

I   Select the data in the table.

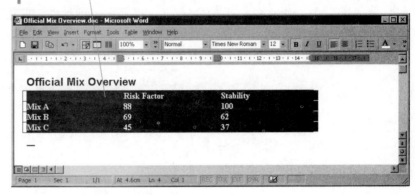

2   Choose "Object" from the Insert Menu.

3   Choose "Microsoft Graph 2000 Chart" from the Create New tab of the Object dialog, then click "OK".

You can also activate the Chart application by clicking on the Chart tool: If this is not visible, then right-click on a toolbar and choose "Customise". The Chart icon is available under the "Insert" category. From here you can drag it onto any toolbar.

Microsoft Graph 2000 automatically generates a suitable graph based on your data, and places it in your document:

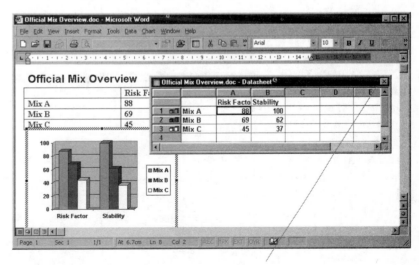

4   If you don't want to amend your data yet, close this window.

Formatting a Chart

Once your chart is placed in your document, you can very easily edit it to amend the format that Microsoft Graph applied by default.

1 Double-click on the chart to open it for editing. A striped border appears around it, and special Microsoft Graph icons appear in the toolbar.

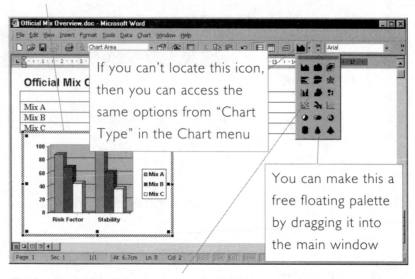

If you can't locate this icon, then you can access the same options from "Chart Type" in the Chart menu

You can make this a free floating palette by dragging it into the main window

Microsoft Graph 2000 uses two main windows, one for the data and one for the chart itself. You can turn the Datasheet on and off using the View menu, or the Datasheet icon on the toolbar:

2 To change the type of chart, click on the arrow to the right of the Chart type icon and select an option from the palette.

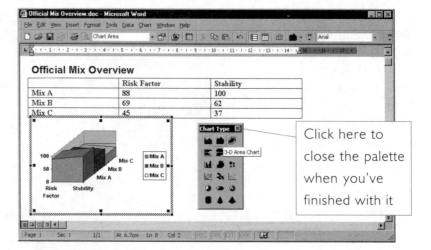

Click here to close the palette when you've finished with it

...cont'd

You can change the number format of any of the data used in your chart. Simply select the relevant cells then choose "Number" from the Format menu. In the "Format number" dialog, select the number type from the "Category:" options, then make any amendments in the context-specific boxes and click OK.

3 To change the properties of a 3D graph, rest your cursor over the chart area until the "Chart Area" bubble appears, then right-click.

4 In the pop-up menu that appears, select "3-D View".

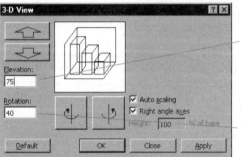

Clicking here would produce a dialog that offers an alternative way of selecting the chart type from the method in step 2

5 Click here to change the elevation of the view.

6 Click here to change the degree of rotation.

When changing the format of a chart, always use the bubbles that appear when you rest your cursor over a chart area. You can then be sure that you are about to format the area that you mean to, before you double-click or right-click on it.

7 To change the properties of an individual chart element, double-click on it. Here, the font properties of the axis legends are being changed.

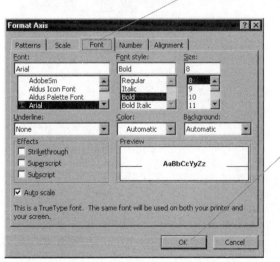

8 Click "OK" to apply your changes.

Importing Data into a Chart

To import data from an external source into a chart, make sure that it is open for editing (it will have a striped border around it, and the Microsoft Graph toolbar will appear), then do the following:

If there is no striped border around the chart, then double-click directly on it. This will open the chart for editing.

| Select "Import File" from the Edit menu.

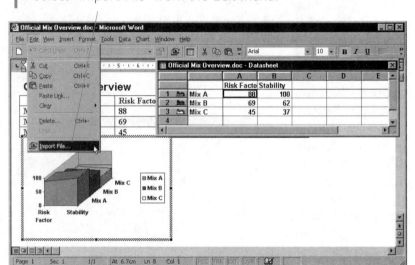

When you are working on a chart, you are effectively using the Microsoft Graph application. This means that the menu options and toolbar icons that you see are relevant only to Microsoft Graph.

To exit this mode and return to the normal Word 2000 environment, simply click your cursor anywhere outside the chart area; the Word toolbars and menu options will then return.

2 In the Import File dialog, select the file you want to import, then click Open.

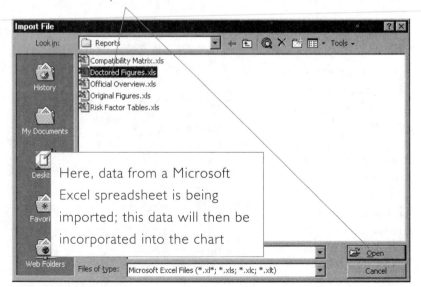

Here, data from a Microsoft Excel spreadsheet is being imported; this data will then be incorporated into the chart

On-line and Internet Documents

Word 2000 contains many new features relating to the Internet and documents intended for viewing on-line. Items normally incorporated into web pages, such as hyperlinks, can be incorporated into standard Word documents allowing instant access to files stored locally or anywhere on the Internet. Also, HTML is now a native file format to Word 2000, allowing editing of HTML Web pages using Word. The Web Page Wizard will even automatically set up a structure and basic functionality for your pages.

Covers

Chapter Eleven

Introduction

In the past, word-processors were used as tools for producing pure text documents and little else. Recent years have seen popular word-processors become embellished with new graphically-oriented features, which previously would have been found only in high-end Desktop Publishing packages.

Until recently, the aim of most people using a word-processor was to produce something that would ultimately be output on paper. However, the growing importance of the Internet and Intranet environments has seen a change in this situation. Communication which was once conducted on paper is increasingly being carried out in a purely electronic medium.

This electronic communication is carried out in a variety of forms. The World-Wide Web is a vast resource containing endless linked pages, with text and pictures on virtually any topic imaginable. Until recently e-mail had been restricted to text, and remained essentially a means of communicating with a more restricted set of people.

However, these boundaries are beginning to be blurred. Word, for example, allows you to create an electronic document which is not simply text but which may contain animations, pictures, sounds, videos, and links to other documents or Web pages. In fact, any document which you create in Word 2000 (or in any element of Office 2000) may be placed on the Internet. You can even use Word as your primary means of composing and editing e-mail messages.

Word also allows you to create Web pages in the Web's native format, HTML (HyperText Mark-up Language), without having to learn the many HTML codes. You can either use the Web Page Wizard to create a new set of HTML documents quickly and easily, or you can convert an existing Word document.

Using the Web Page Wizard

The Web Page Wizard is the most effective way of using Word to create an HTML document, and allows you more control over the finished product than you would have if you converted an existing Word document. To launch it, do the following:

1   Select New from the File menu.

2   Select the Web Pages tab.

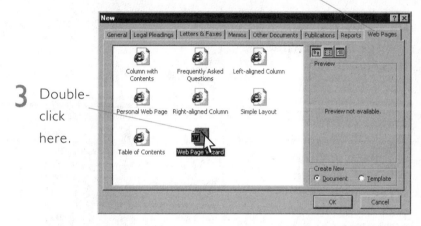

3   Double-click here.

The Web Page Wizard dialog appears. This will guide you through five steps, asking questions about your planned document.

You can go directly to any Wizard page by clicking on one of the icons in this progress chart. The green box tells you where you are currently.

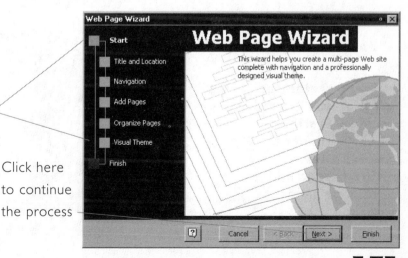

Click here to continue the process

By default this title will be used as the directory for your Web files, within "my documents". However, you can change it by editing this field.

4 Enter a title for your Web site.

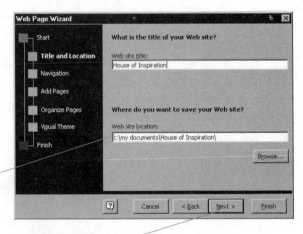

Click "Next" when you're ready

The "frame" options split the screen into two sections: one for navigation and one for content.

5 Next, choose a navigation model, then click "Next".

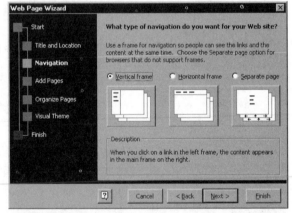

As long as the Wizard is still running, you can always return here to add or remove pages from the list.

6 By default, the Wizard will create three pages. Click here to add more.

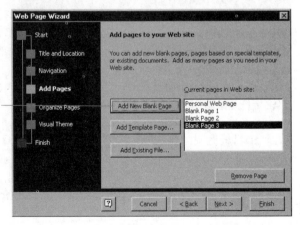

7 From here you can rename your pages, and change their order.

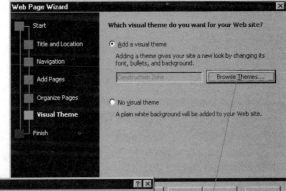

Click here or double-click on the page name to edit

8 Finally, you can select a Theme to give your Web pages a consistent look and feel.

See Chapter 5, "Styles and Themes", for more information about Themes.

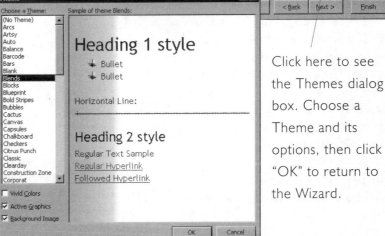

Click here to see the Themes dialog box. Choose a Theme and its options, then click "OK" to return to the Wizard.

9 You are now ready to generate your Web site. Click the Finish button.

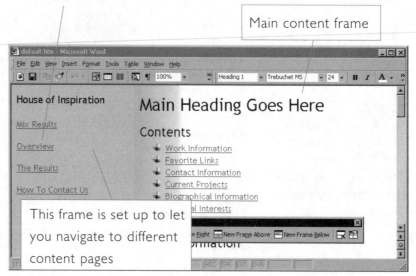

The Wizard now generates the necessary Web pages, saved as .HTM files in the directory specified in step 4. You can view these directly in your Web browser by choosing its Open file option. However, Word's Web layout view will let you view and edit .HTM files.

The Web pages are automatically connected using hyperlinks created by the Wizard. For example, clicking on the Overview hyperlink will cause the main content frame to load up the Overview.htm file.

Now that the Wizard has set up the initial Web document, it is up to you to edit the actual text to your own needs. Word has put placeholder information in each significant area of each page. You simply change and add to this sample text.

Frames

Frames allow you to divide your screen into rectangular areas, each of which can be used to view a different Web page (or a different part of the same Web page). In our example the Wizard has set up two frames: the left frame is used for navigation while the right shows the main content.

The Frames toolbar appears automatically when the Web Page Wizard completes. However, you can summon or dismiss it at any time using the View menu or by right clicking on an existing toolbar.

The Frames Toolbar

Create a new frame to the left of the currently selected frame

New frame to the right

New frame immediately above the current frame

New frame below

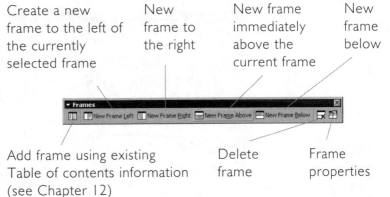

Add frame using existing Table of contents information (see Chapter 12)

Delete frame

Frame properties

Adding a New Frame

Here we've clicked on the New Frame Above button to add a new frame along the top of the document. We'll use this to display a constant header for our pages.

The use of Frames is not limited to Web documents. Another useful tool for normal documents is the Text box (see chapter 12).

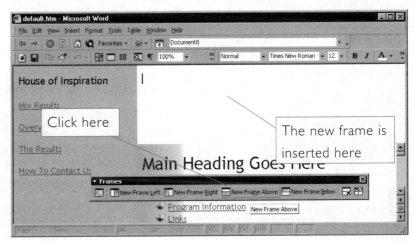

Adding Text and Graphics to a Frame

Once you've added a frame, it behaves like an independent document, so you can add and edit text or other objects in the normal way.

In the example below we've inserted a picture from a file and also incorporated some WordArt.

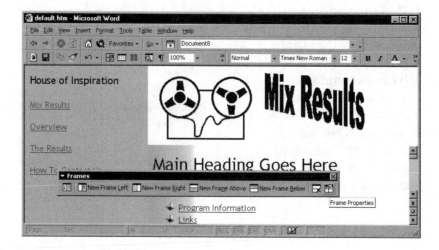

The Frame Properties Dialog

1 Make sure your insertion point is somewhere inside the relevant Frame.

2 Click on the Frame Properties button in the Frames toolbar.

3 From the Frames Tab you can set the name, size and Web page. From the Borders tab you can switch on the Frames border, allowing users to resize the Frame.

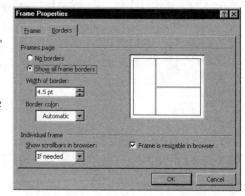

You can also access this dialog box by right-clicking inside a Frame and choosing "Frame Properties".

4 Click OK. In this example the user can now resize the frame by dragging directly on the border.

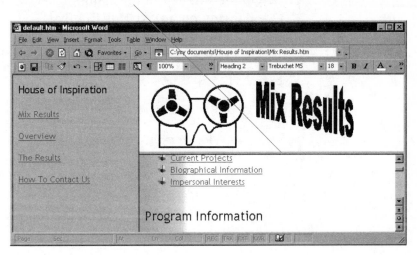

Alternative Text

It is important to remember that some Web Browsers do not display graphics. Furthermore, because graphics take much longer to download from the Web, a user may decide to switch off a graphic display preference. In these cases, you can set text to be displayed as an alternative.

Alternative text also displays while a picture is loading. You may want to include the graphic's file size to give your users an idea of how long the loading process will take.

1 Right-click on the graphic and choose "Format Picture" from the pop-up menu.

2 Click on the Web tab and enter the text.

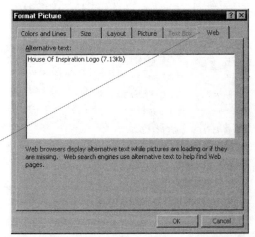

The Web Tools Palette

Word 2000 provides you with a powerful set of tools to enhance your Web pages. This can be activated just like any other palette, either using the View menu or by right-clicking on an existing Toolbar.

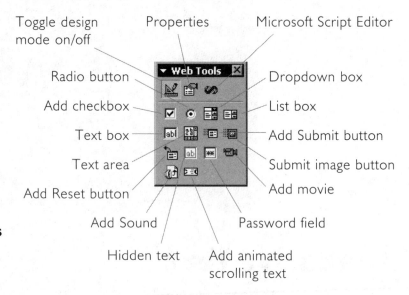

Toggle design mode on/off — Properties — Microsoft Script Editor

Radio button

Add checkbox

Text box

Text area

Add Reset button

Add Sound

Hidden text

Dropdown box

List box

Add Submit button

Submit image button

Add movie

Password field

Add animated scrolling text

As soon as you select one of the tools for adding objects to your Web page, Word 2000 automatically activates design mode.

Design Mode

When design mode is active you can add, edit or delete objects such as radio buttons or text boxes.

When design mode is inactive you can test out your objects. Clicking on a check box, for example, will switch its checkmark on and off.

Microsoft Script Editor

This allows you to add functionality to your Web page by adding scripts written in Microsoft Visual Basic® (scripting edition) or JScript® (Java Script).

For more details about how to write and edit Scripts, refer to the Microsoft Development Environment online Help.

Adding Video Clips

Most Web pages are a collection of text, images and links to other pages. However, as the multimedia capabilities of PCs increase, other types of media are becoming ever more common on the Web. For example, you can place video clips on your Web pages.

1 Place the cursor where you want to insert your video.

2 Click on the Add movie button in the Web toolbar.

You can add a movie to a normal document by choosing Object from the Insert menu.

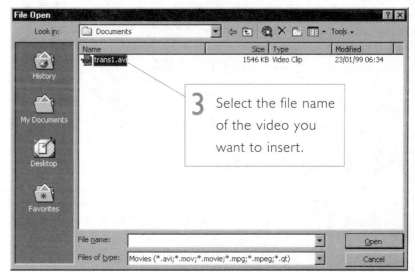

3 Select the file name of the video you want to insert.

4 You can set an alternate image to be displayed if the browser doesn't support video playback, or if it is disabled by the user.

5 Set the Start and Loop options, then click OK.

The video clip appears at your insertion point.

6 You can alter the size of the video in the normal way by dragging on its control handles.

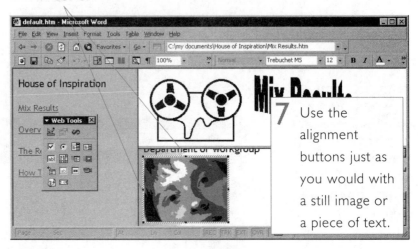

7 Use the alignment buttons just as you would with a still image or a piece of text.

Adding Sound

You can add background music or sound recordings to your web page just as easily as adding the video. Word 2000 allows you to use files in a number of formats including WAV and MIDI files. Whenever someone accesses your page, this file is played providing the browser allows background music, and also if a suitable driver for the type of sound file has been installed.

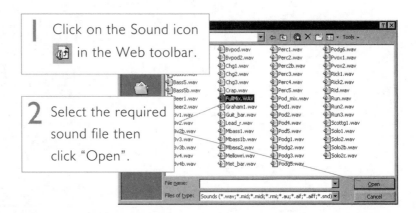

1 Click on the Sound icon in the Web toolbar.

2 Select the required sound file then click "Open".

...cont'd

3 Set the looping option then click "OK".

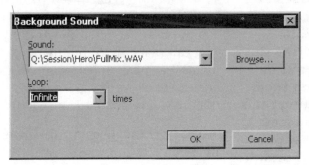

In this example the file FullMix.WAV will play and repeat indefinitely as longs as the user is working with the current Web page.

Measuring Using Pixels

When working with Web pages, the computer screen is the primary output device. It is therefore much more convenient to measure objects in pixels rather than units like centimetres or inches.

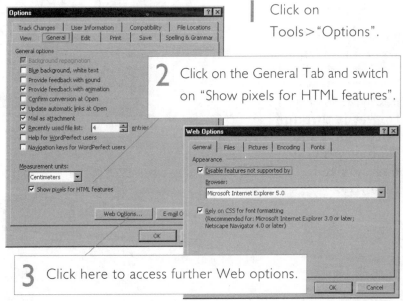

1 Click on Tools>"Options".

2 Click on the General Tab and switch on "Show pixels for HTML features".

3 Click here to access further Web options.

Hyperlinks

In the earlier topic "Using the Web Page Wizard" (page 151), hyperlinks were used to provide a method of moving between one HTML document and another. In Word 2000 you are not restricted to using hyperlinks in HTML pages. You can place them in any normal Word document to link to another place in the same document, to another Word document on your hard drive/local network, or even to a file anywhere on the Internet/Intranet.

AutoFormatting Hyperlinks As You Type

By default, Word 2000's AutoFormat feature will automatically convert any piece of text that looks like an Internet address or other file location to a hyperlink. These addresses must be in the standard URL format, with which you will be familiar if you have any experience of using a Web browser:

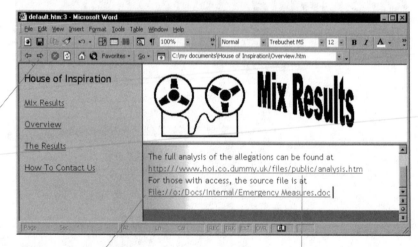

This is a link to a Word file on the same hard drive as the current document. Note the prefix "File://" is needed for Word to recognise this as a file location.

This is an Internet URL, linking to a web site. You must be connected to the Internet for this link to work.

Inserting Hyperlinks Manually

The AutoFormat method is fine for converting actual Internet addresses and file locations to hyperlinks, but most hyperlink markers do not take this format; instead the hyperlink is represented by some more meaningful text, or even an image. You can use Word to make either of these into a hyperlink.

1 Select the text or image that the user will click on to jump to your linked file or Web site.

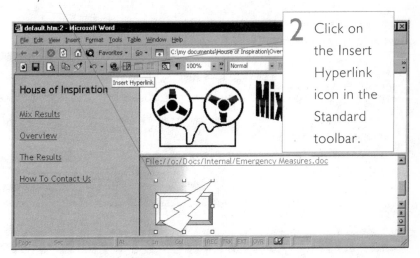

2 Click on the Insert Hyperlink icon in the Standard toolbar.

3 Type or select the name of the file you wish to link to. This can be a file or a Web page. Use the Browse buttons to search in a particular location.

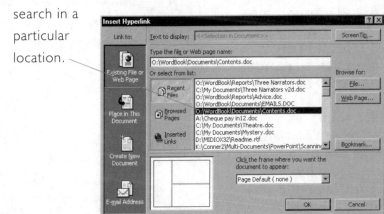

Saving HTML Files

HTML is a native file format for Word 2000. This means that you can open, edit and save in .HTM format just as easily as the .DOC files more traditionally associated with Word.

If you have just created some Web pages from scratch, you will need to choose "Save as Web Page" from the File menu.

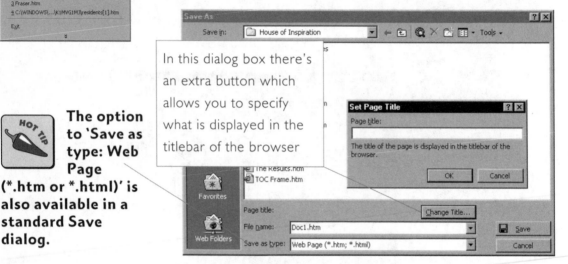

In this dialog box there's an extra button which allows you to specify what is displayed in the titlebar of the browser

HOT TIP

The option to 'Save as type: Web Page (*.htm or *.html)' is also available in a standard Save dialog.

Editing Existing HTML Files

Some specialist programs, such as Microsoft FrontPage, allow you to design Web pages using advanced effects like animated buttons. You can still take the files produced by FrontPage and edit them using Word.

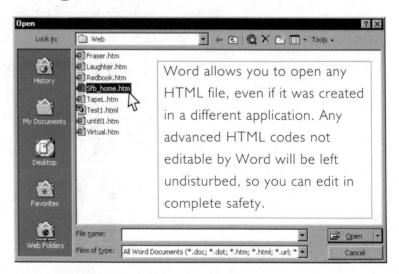

Word allows you to open any HTML file, even if it was created in a different application. Any advanced HTML codes not editable by Word will be left undisturbed, so you can edit in complete safety.

...cont'd

If you have been editing a file which has already been saved in .HTM format, you don't necessarily need to use the "Save as Web Page" option. A simple "Save" will suffice.

In this example we've opened a file created by a separate Web design package. Word will now let us edit its text, graphics and even the hyperlinks.

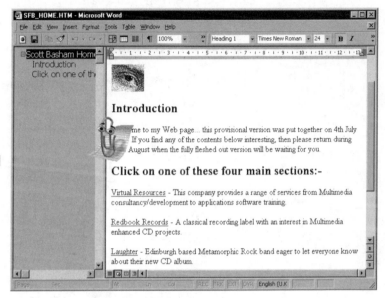

View HTML Source

This tool scores over a straight text editor in a number of ways. It allows you to see an organised view of your Web pages, and also uses a colour coding system to help you distinguish the syntax.

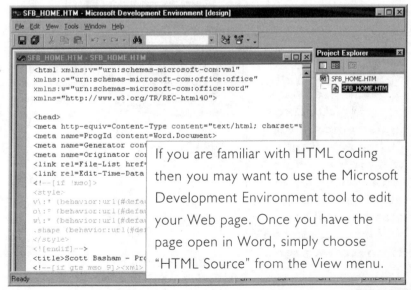

If you are familiar with HTML coding then you may want to use the Microsoft Development Environment tool to edit your Web page. Once you have the page open in Word, simply choose "HTML Source" from the View menu.

Using Word 2000 for E-mail

Using Word as Your E-mail Editor

If you use Microsoft Outlook or Exchange, your e-mail composition can be enhanced by many Word 2000 features such as spelling and grammar checking, version tracking and the use of tables.

To set up Word as E-mail Editor from Outlook

1 From Microsoft Outlook, open the Tools menu and choose Options.

2 Select the Mail Format tab and click on "Use Microsoft Word to edit e-mail messages".

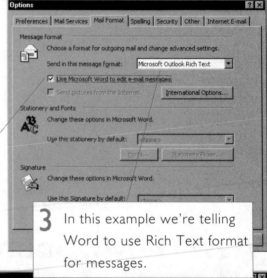

3 In this example we're telling Word to use Rich Text format for messages.

 The first time you use Word 2000 for e-mail editing, the Office Assistant will offer you help with setting up an autosignature or stationery. These will be discussed on the next few pages.

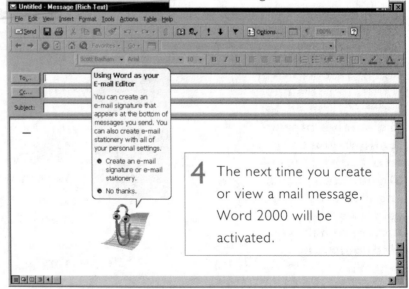

Using Word as your E-mail Editor

You can create an e-mail signature that appears at the bottom of messages you send. You can also create e-mail stationery with all of your personal settings.

● Create an e-mail signature or e-mail stationery.

● No thanks.

4 The next time you create or view a mail message, Word 2000 will be activated.

Choosing Rich Text or HTML Format

Rich Text format allows many text formatting features (such as font, size, style and colour) to be used in e-mail messages. This is compatible with a wide range of e-mail applications.

Alternatively, you can choose HTML format, which will provide many more features including tables and graphics.

To use HTML as the Message Format

1 From Microsoft Outlook, open the Tools menu and choose "Options".

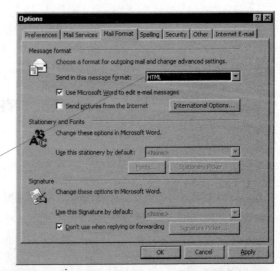

2 Choose HTML from the "Send in this message format" option.

Look in the title bar if you want to check to see if the e-mail format is set to use Rich Text or HTML.

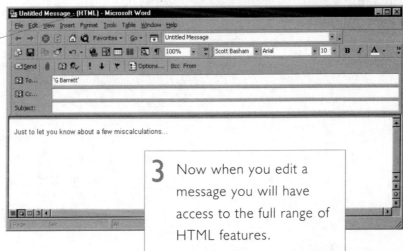

3 Now when you edit a message you will have access to the full range of HTML features.

E-mail Signatures

A special signature can be automatically added to the end of any e-mail message. This can contain text (including hyperlinks) or graphics.

Ⅰ Go to the Tools menu and choose "Options". Select the General tab and click on the E-mail Options button.

2 Enter a name for your signature.

HOT TIP

From the Personal Stationery tab you can choose a Theme for your messages. You can also set a specific font for new messages, and a separate font for replies or forwarded messages.

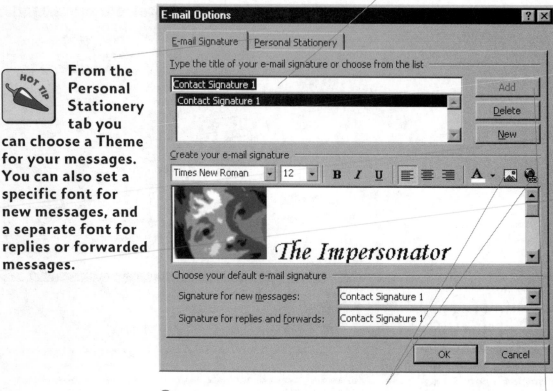

3 Type in its text. You can click on the Insert Picture or Insert Hyperlink buttons to add graphics or references to other pages.

4 Click on "Add".

The signature will now be available for any new messages you may send.

Advanced Topics

Word 2000 has many advanced features. Some are designed to generally make life easier while others allow you to enhance your documents with comments, tables of contents or even by compiling an index.

Covers

Chapter Twelve

The Reviewing Toolbar

Animated text is another feature you can use in on-line documents: refer to the topic "The Font Dialog Box" in Chapter 3.

Word 2000 incorporates several sophisticated features that allow you to review documents clearly, and track the various stages of these reviews. The Reviewing toolbar contains icons that allow you to access these features easily. It can be displayed in the normal way from the View menu.

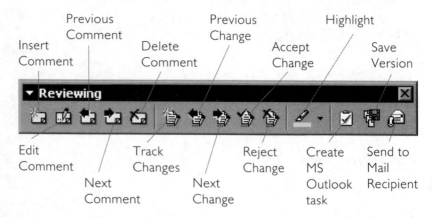

Insert Comment
Previous Comment
Delete Comment
Previous Change
Accept Change
Highlight
Save Version

Edit Comment
Next Comment
Track Changes
Next Change
Reject Change
Create MS Outlook task
Send to Mail Recipient

Inserting Comments

To insert a comment on a section of your document, do the following:

1 Highlight the text on which you wish to comment.

2 Click the Insert Comment icon.

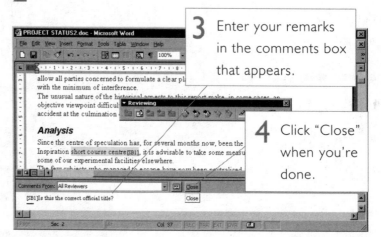

3 Enter your remarks in the comments box that appears.

4 Click "Close" when you're done.

Highlighting Text

If you want to mark a piece of text without appending any additional notes, you can highlight it, just as if you were using a real highlighter pen on paper. To do this, follow either of the steps below:

If you use the highlighter icon's pop-up menu, then you can choose from a range of colours. Selecting "none" will remove the highlight altogether.

1 Select your text with the cursor tool, then click on the Highlighter icon.

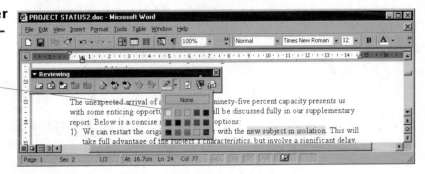

2 Alternatively click on the Highlighter icon first, to enter Highlighter mode, then highlight as many different pieces of text as you want. To return to normal text-editing mode, click on the Highlighter icon again.

Versioning

This is the facility to save the various stages of the evolution of a document, allowing you to see how its content has developed, and (if appropriate) which of the different authors of a document have made which changes. To save a new version of a document, do the following:

1 Click on the Save Version icon in the Reviewing toolbar.

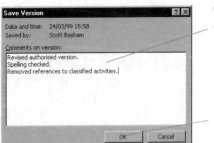

2 Enter your description of this version, and/or your comments on it, in this box.

3 Click "OK" to save the version.

To review the different versions of a document, follow these steps:

Select "Versions" from the File menu.

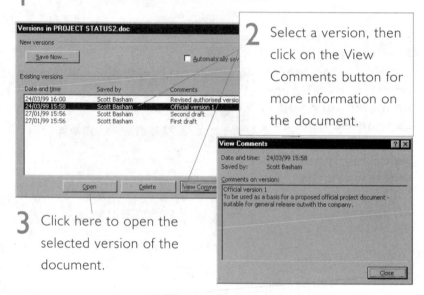

2 Select a version, then click on the View Comments button for more information on the document.

3 Click here to open the selected version of the document.

Macros

Macros are recordings of common activities. You can record your own Macros, and play them back whenever necessary.

Recording a Macro

Go to the View menu, choose "Toolbars" and make sure that the Visual Basic Toolbar is active.

This gives you access to two buttons for recording and replaying Macros.

 You can also access Macro recording and playback by opening the Tools menu and choosing Macros.

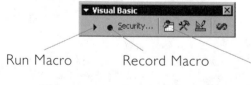

Run Macro   Record Macro

Visual Basic Editor (can be used for editing Macros on a command by command basis)

...cont'd

2 The Record Macro dialog box appears. Enter a name for
your Macro. This must begin with a letter and can contain up
to 80 letters and numbers. Spaces or special characters are
not allowed.

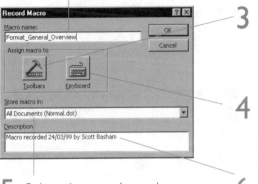

3 Click here to assign
your new Macro to a
toolbar.

4 Click here to assign
your new Macro to a
keyboard shortcut.

5 Select the template where you
want to store the Macro.

6 Enter a description
for your Macro.

**You can
also stop
Macro
recording
by opening the
Tools menu and
choosing "Macros".**

7 When you click OK, recording becomes active. You can now
"walk through" the commands you wish to be included in
the Macro. During this time your cursor takes the form of a
pointer with a cassette tape attached. There is also a small
toolbar which allows you to pause or stop recording:

8 When you have finished recording, click the Stop icon.

Running a Macro

**You can
run a
Macro
from a
toolbar icon or
keyboard shortcut
if you chose either
of these options
when creating the
Macro.**

1 To play back a
Macro, click the Play
button and choose
your Macro from the
dialog box.

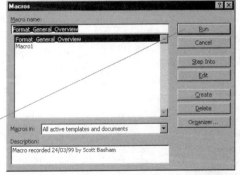

2 Click "Run".

Collaborating on Documents

If each of the different reviewers of a document works from a different computer, which is used by them alone, then there should be no need to alter the reviewer information as this should have been established when Word 2000 was installed. However, if a computer is shared by a number of people to review Word documents, then the user information should be changed whenever a reviewer begins, so that it is clear who made which comments.

1 Select "Options" from the Tools menu.

2 Choose the User Information tab.

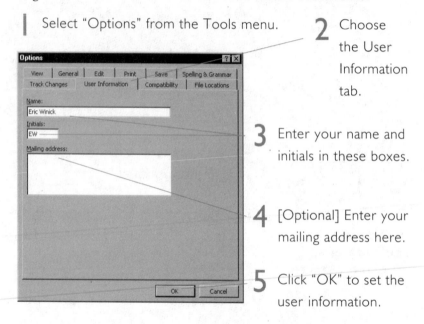

3 Enter your name and initials in these boxes.

4 [Optional] Enter your mailing address here.

5 Click "OK" to set the user information.

Merging Documents

If a number of reviewers have been working together on the same document by updating the same Word file, then the sum of all their efforts is collected in the most up-to-date version of the document. However, if different reviewers have made changes to a document and saved the results as a different file (e.g., to take the document away to work on at home), it is possible to merge the files back into one document

1 With one of the files open, select Tools>Merge Documents.

2 In the file dialog that appears, double-click on the file to merge.

Text Boxes

Text boxes give you independent control over text flow and positioning as well as other attributes.

Inserting a new Text Box

1 Go to the Insert menu and choose "Text Box". You cursor will turn into a cross symbol.

2 Click and drag diagonally to create the Text Box.

The first thing you'll probably want to do is apply Text wrap to the new Text box. To do this, right-click on one of its edges and choose Format Text box. Activate the Layout tab.

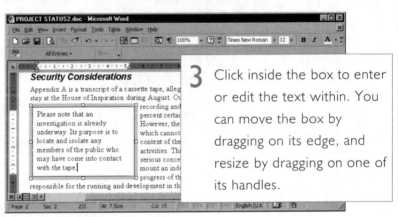

3 Click inside the box to enter or edit the text within. You can move the box by dragging on its edge, and resize by dragging on one of its handles.

The Text Box Toolbar

This gives you access to additional Text box options.

Break link   Previous text box   Next text box

Link text boxes   Change text direction

To link text boxes, click on the first box, then the Link button in the toolbar, then on the second box. Any text which doesn't fit in the first box will now flow automatically into the second.

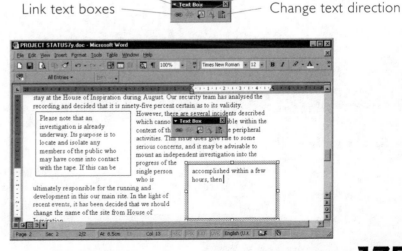

Footnotes and Endnotes

Word 2000 allows you to add footnotes (which appear at the bottom of a page), or endnotes (which appear at the end of your document). These reference text on the main page, usually using a superscript number.

1 Select the text which will reference the footnote or endnote, then choose "Footnote" from the Insert menu.

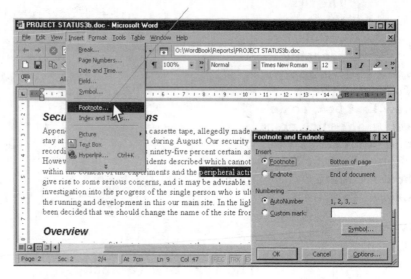

2 Choose Footnote/Endnote, a Numbering option, then click "OK".

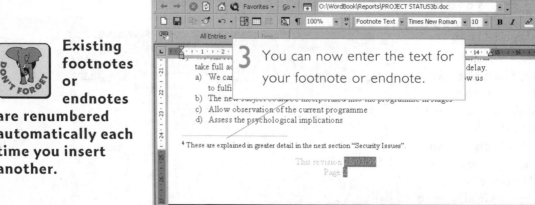

Existing footnotes or endnotes are renumbered automatically each time you insert another.

Tables of Contents

You can automatically create a Table of Contents for your document by asking Word 2000 to look for instances of particular styles, or entries that you create manually. Word will take care of tracking the page numbers of each entry.

Creating a new Table of Contents

1 Place your insertion point at a suitable location for your Table of Contents.

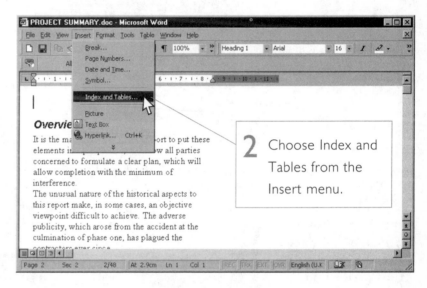

2 Choose Index and Tables from the Insert menu.

3 Make sure the Table of Contents tab is active.

By default, Word will use instances of the styles Heading 1, 2 and 3 to build the Table of Contents. You can change this by clicking on the Options button.

4 Set the page and tab options.

5 Choose a style for your table from the Formats pop-up list then click "OK".

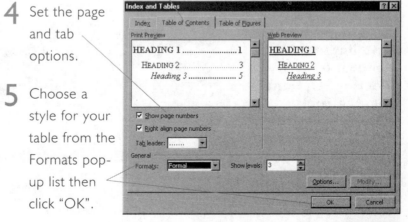

Word scans through your document for instances of different heading styles, and creates the Table of Contents.

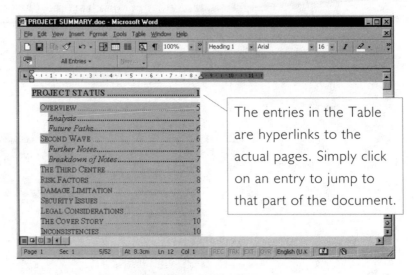

The entries in the Table are hyperlinks to the actual pages. Simply click on an entry to jump to that part of the document.

The grey background on the Table of Contents indicates that you're looking at a Word Field. Fields contain text which Word automatically generates. The background doesn't print, but you can change it by selecting "Options" from the Tools menu. Click on the View tab and choose a different option under Field shading.

Updating a Table of Contents

If you have added new headings, or edited your document so that the page numbers are different, then you'll probably want to update the Table of Contents to reflect the changes.

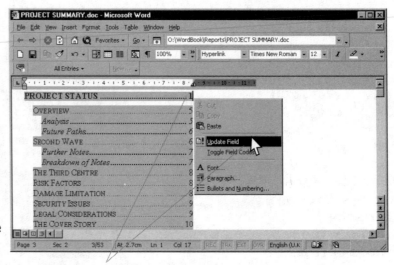

Right-click on the Table of Contents and choose Update Field from the pop-up menu.

...cont'd

If you have added or removed headings or Table of Contents entries, then you will need to choose Update entire table.

2 In the dialog box which appears, decide whether to update just the page numbers or to rebuild the whole table.

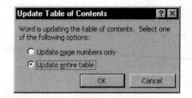

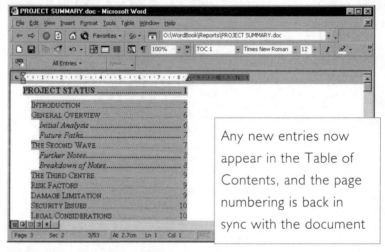

Any new entries now appear in the Table of Contents, and the page numbering is back in sync with the document

Entries in the Contents Table use special styles which have been set up automatically (they are named "TOC" plus a level number).

   Any formatting changes you make normally affect these styles. This means that the new formatting will be retained even if you rebuild the Table of Contents.

Changing the Appearance of the Table of Contents

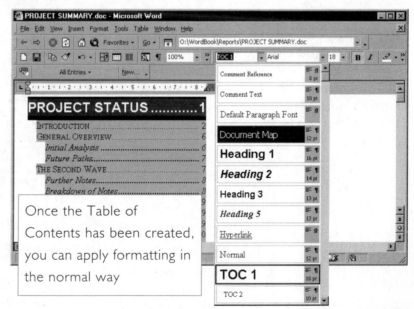

Once the Table of Contents has been created, you can apply formatting in the normal way

Adding a Manual Entry to the Table of Contents

Sometimes you may want to add an entry which does not use one of the Heading styles.

1   Click an Insertion Point in the relevant part of the document.

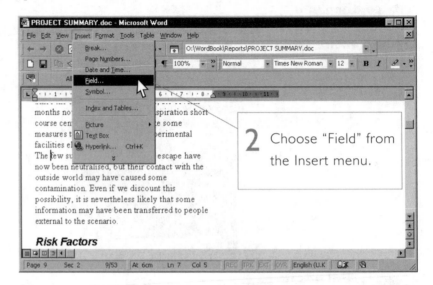

2   Choose "Field" from the Insert menu.

3   The Field dialog box appears. Under Categories, choose "Index and Tables".

 You can get Word to add the \l parameter for you by clicking on the Options button.

4   For field names choose "TC".

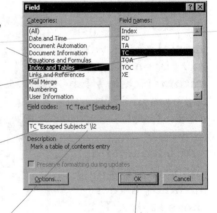

5   "TC" will appear here. Add the text for the entry enclosed inside double quotes.

6   To set the entry at a particular level in the table, add a backslash followed by a lower case letter "l" then the level number.

7   Click "OK".

...cont'd

The field for the TOC entry is added to your document.

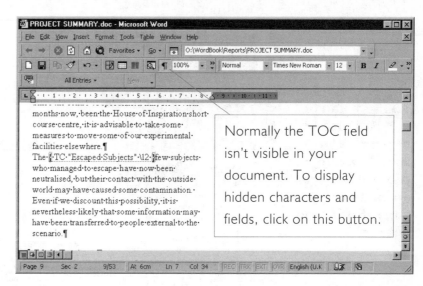

Normally the TOC field isn't visible in your document. To display hidden characters and fields, click on this button.

8 Now you need to rebuild the Table of Contents. Click to select your existing table, then choose "Index and Tables" from the Insert menu.

When you click to select your Table of Contents, Word will probably decide that you want to follow the hyperlink and jump elsewhere in your document. To prevent this happening, click instead just to the right of an entry in the Table of Contents.

9 In the Index and Tables dialog, click the Options button.

10 Make sure that "Table entry fields" is selected.

11 Click "OK" when asked if you want to replace the current Table of Contents.

Bookmarks

A Bookmark can help you keep track of a location in your document.

Bookmarks can be used to let you specify a range of pages when creating an index entry. See page 184 for more details.

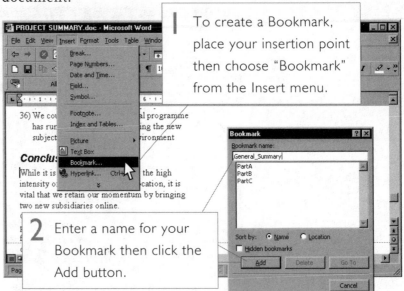

To create a Bookmark, place your insertion point then choose "Bookmark" from the Insert menu.

2 Enter a name for your Bookmark then click the Add button.

Indexing

Word 2000 makes the process of creating an index relatively straightforward.

Adding an Index entry

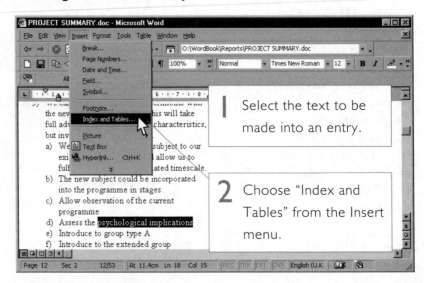

Select the text to be made into an entry.

2 Choose "Index and Tables" from the Insert menu.

The Index and Tables dialog box appears:

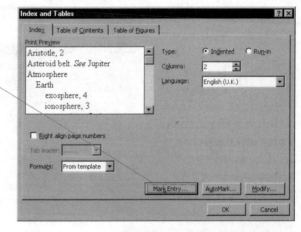

3 Click on the Mark Entry button.

4 The Mark Index Entry dialog appears. If necessary, edit the text inserted in Main entry.

5 For a simple entry, leave the options set at Current Page and click on "Mark".

Topics and Subtopics

Most entries will probably only need to have text in the Main entry part of this dialog box.

However, if you want an index which includes topics and subtopics, then fill in the main topic under Main entry, then the subtopic under Subentry.

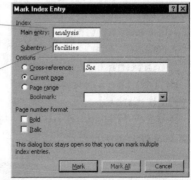

Specifying Ranges of Pages

For most index entries you'll want just a single page number to appear. If you want a range of pages:

You can also create cross-reference entries. Click on the Cross-reference option and type in the relevant text for the entry.

1 Move to the end of the topic and create a bookmark (see page 182).

2 Locate the start of the topic and mark the index entry. Set the Options to Page range, and select your bookmark from the pop-up list.

Generating the Index

1 When you are ready, click an Insertion point where you'd like the Index to appear.

2 Go to the Insert menu and choose "Index and Tables".

3 Make sure the Index tab is active.

As with the Table of Contents, you can rebuild the Index at any time, or change its formatting by editing the styles (each named "Index" followed by a level number).

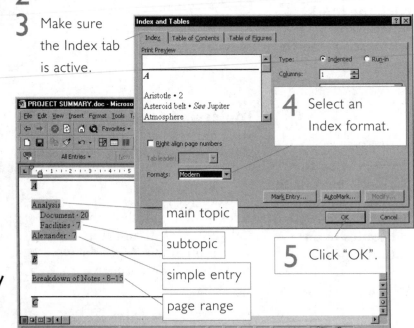

4 Select an Index format.

main topic

subtopic

simple entry

page range

5 Click "OK".

Language Autodetect

If you have multiple languages installed, Word 2000 can automatically select the correct language based on what you're currently typing.

Installing Multiple Languages

 If you only have one language currently installed, you will need to install at least one more for the Language Autodetect feature to work.

1 Click on the Windows Start button, choose Programs>Office Tools>Microsoft Office Language Settings.

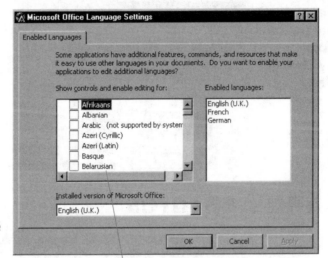

 When you change the Microsoft Office Language Settings, Windows needs to shut down any Office Applications (such as Word). A dialog box will appear, offering to do this for you automatically.

2 To add a language, select it from the list on the left. Continue to select all the languages you require then click "OK" or apply.

3 Back in Word choose Tools> Language>Set Language. Make sure that "Detect language automatically" is switched on.

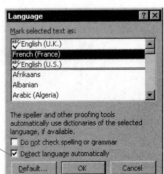

Compatibility Options

You can customise how Word displays documents which have been saved in another format.

These settings only affect how Word displays a document which has been saved in a particular format. It does not permanently change its formatting.

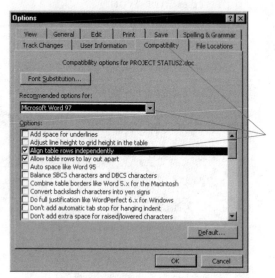

| Go to the Tools menu and choose "Options".

2 Click on the Compatibility tab, select the file format and view or change its options.

Installing Features

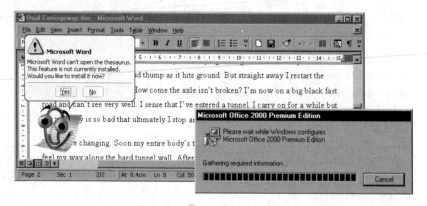

In order to conserve hard disk space, you can choose to include only the commonly used features when you first install Word. Later on, if you try to use a feature which isn't installed, Word will ask you if you want to load it there and then. If you answer "Yes", you'll need to insert your original CD. This feature is commonly known as "install on demand".

Index